365 Great Soups & Stews

Georgia Chan Downard and Jean Galton

A JOHN BOSWELL ASSOCIATES BOOK

HarperCollins*Publishers*

23185$$fm4   12-11-95 15:46:23   ② Ⓜ

1x—365 Soups & Stews Recipes—11/11.5 Palatino   x28.6   BOS (1231)

HarperCollins books may be purchased for educational, business, or sales promotional use. For information please write: Special Markets Department, HarperCollins Publishers, Inc., 10 East 53rd Street, New York, NY 10022.

FIRST EDITION

Series Editor: Susan Wyler
Design: Nigel Rollings
Index: Maro Riofrancos

Library of Congress Cataloging-in-Publication Data

Downard, Georgia.
   365 great soups & stews / Georgia Chen Downard and Jean Galton. — 1st ed.
     p. cm.
   "A John Boswell Associates book."
   Includes index.
   ISBN 0-06-016960-5
   1. Soups. 2. Stews. I. Galton, Jean.
TX757.D68   1996
641.8'13—dc20   95-45403

96 97 98 99 00 DT/HC 10 9 8 7 6 5 4 3 2 1

Contents

Introduction

There is nothing more appealing and comforting than the smell of a wonderful soup or stew gently simmering away on the back burner of the kitchen stove. Most of us have memories of savory aromas wafting through the house while our mothers or grandmothers stood over the pot, stirring patiently, throwing in a pinch of this, a dash of that, to make it taste just right. Perhaps it's this heirloom quality, which clings to these warming one-pot meals, that makes them so appealing, whether they are, in fact, traditional recipes or not. Even modern recipes, zipped up in flavor, containing more contemporary ingredients, and streamlined in technique, yield a satisfaction that's hard to beat.

Besides the pleasures of flavor and association, there's a convenience associated with soups and stews that makes them perennial favorites. They cook largely in one pot. Both can be ladled up into bowls. And while some soups are light and more appropriate as starters, just add a salad and good bread to either, and have a complete light lunch or hearty supper.

One of the joys of soups and stews is the variety of ingredients they employ. Just look in your refrigerator, and you probably have the fixings for one or the other. With 365 ways to choose, you'll never find yourself short of ideas.

Because of the way so many of us are eating, striving for less fat and more nutrition, many of the soups in this book feature vegetables as the main ingredient. Ideally, vegetables should be purchased when they are in season and at their peak of flavor, texture, and color. An added bonus in buying seasonal vegetables is that they are usually a best buy. In most cases, vegetable soups are prepared quickly and do not need long cooking times. Several recipes for roasted vegetable soups may require a little more time, but they are well worth the effort. The intensified flavor of roasted vegetables lends itself beautifully to soups.

In addition to the vegetable soups, there are tasty chicken- and meat-based soups; soups loaded with pasta, beans, and grains; seafood chowders; and short-cut soups, which take less than 30 minutes to prepare. You will find soups prepared with foods that cook quickly, ingenious ways for using leftovers, and an array of combination soups featuring pastas, grains, and beans.

We have drawn the recipes from many different cultures. There are time-honored classics, such as Chinese Hot and Sour Soup and Beefy Borscht, as well as soups reflecting the assimilation of cuisines as in Quick Three-Bean Soup with Fresh Tomato Salsa and Garlic Soup with Orzo and Green Beans.

Finally, a selection of soup recipes would not be complete without the inclusion of cold vegetable and fruit soups, for those hot and humid days when you just want to spoon up something light and chilled right from the fridge. Certainly not a trend or a fad, fruit soups have been eaten in Eastern Europe and Scandinavia for generations. And it is not uncommon to find the inclusion of fresh fruit soups on restaurant menus during the warmer months of the year. They are light and refreshing and may be eaten as a first course or dessert.

Homemade soups are much easier to prepare than many people imagine. To make them even simpler, many of these recipes call for either a basic homemade stock— which you can make ahead and freeze—or a canned substitute. The relatively new reduced-sodium chicken broth is perfectly acceptable in most instances, and makes scratch soups a snap to prepare. For cooks with the least time, we've even included an entire chapter of "Short-Cut Soups," which you can put on the table in half an hour or less.

In between soups and stews, we've devoted a separate section to "Chilis, Gumbos, and Curries." It seems we Americans cannot get enough spicy or highly seasoned flavors. For festive, zesty food, this is the place to turn. You'll find a lively assortment of dishes, from Southwestern Beef Chili and White Chicken Chili to Chicken Curry with Broccoli and Scallop Gumbo.

Stews are more robust than soups and generally call for less liquid. Because stews are simmered on top of the stove or slowly braised in the oven, foods are specified to be cut into larger pieces than for a soup, thus requiring the addition of fork and knife to the spoon.

The most memorable meat stews are prepared with inexpensive cuts of meat. Meat from the shoulder, shank, and leg have far more flavor than their more expensive cousins. In order for the stew to achieve a perfect blend of flavors and for the meat to become meltingly tender, it must simmer slowly for at least 1 to 2 hours. However, it cooks virtually unattended except for an occasional stir or two. Ask anyone who has tasted Beef Stew with Onions and Mushrooms in Red Wine if it warranted the wait, and we're sure the answer would be a resounding "yes." In these chapters, you will find old favorites alongside new entries.

In addition to meat stews, there is a wonderful selection of chicken, seafood, and vegetable stews. In general, these stews take less time to cook but are as flavorful and satisfying as the meat stews.

Stews only improve with age. Therefore, they are ideal for advance preparation. If planned wisely, a stew can be assembled and cooked when time permits and reheated 1 to 2 days later. Simply let cool to room temperature and refrigerate. Before reheating, remove any solidified fat from the surface. Or they can be frozen for up to 3 months. Thaw in the refrigerator and reheat. Since they can be prepared in advance, they are perfect for entertaining.

One of the most important characteristics of both soups and stews is that they both require a liquid—usually stock, wine, water, or a combination. A good stock is the foundation upon which all fine soups and stews rest.

The chapter on "Basic Stocks" includes recipes for traditional stocks, as well as their browned variations, and a vegetable stock. Although time consuming, stocks are relatively easy to prepare. An added bonus is that most of the stocks use meat, poultry, and meat bones and trimmings that would otherwise be discarded. These trimmings can be accumulated in the freezer until a good supply is on hand for making the stock. All that is then needed is water, some vegetables, and herbs.

Stocks can be stored in the refrigerator in covered containers for several days or frozen for up to three months. To freeze stock, cool it, chill it overnight, and remove the layer of fat next day. Freeze the stock in ice cube trays or plastic containers. When frozen, transfer the cubes to plastic bags to be used in small amounts as needed. Frozen cubes of stock are especially useful when small amounts are needed.

In an ideal world, we would all have homemade stocks on hand. Since life isn't always perfect, we have given quick alternatives to the classic stocks. These can be prepared in a fraction of the time required for the traditional versions.

The quick stocks offer a homemade taste that is far superior to the plain canned broths one buys at supermarkets. These canned broths tend to be very salty—the reason we have called for reduced-sodium canned broth whenever listed as an alternative to a stock.

Being mindful of the demands and pressures of everyday life, we have also tried to provide recipes that can be prepared quickly with a minimum of fuss. As mentioned above, it is always best to buy seasonal fresh vegetables. But if these vegetables are not available or time doesn't permit their use, then by all means use frozen alternatives. The frozen vegetable alternatives we have called for are those that retain their flavor, texture, and taste well even after freezing. We have also included some convenience foods in our recipes, including tomato sauces, packaged biscuits, and refrigerated pastas —again in an effort to minimize cooking preparation and time.

We would be remiss if we did not include flavorings and accompaniments for our soups and stews. Easily recognizable are traditional flavorings like Aioli and Pistou as well as variations on classic themes, such as Cilantro Pesto.

During the past several years flavored oils have

become popular for soups and stews. They are easy to make and, if stored properly, may be prepared in advance. The ones we have chosen to include, such as Garlic-Chive Oil and Basil Oil, may be used not only in the soups they accompany, but in many of the other recipes as well.

Croutons, garlic toasts, cheese toasts, herb toasts, biscuits, and corn sticks are delicious accompaniments to soups and stews and add new dimension to their flavors. In addition, where appropriate, we have included recipes for accompaniments, such as Saffron Rice in the chapter that includes curries.

In terms of cooking equipment, the most essential tools you'll need for making these soups and stews are a good sharp knife and a soup pot or heavy-bottomed flameproof casserole, or Dutch oven. This should be heavy enough to allow even heat distribution and be made of a nonreactive material, such as stainless steel or enamel-coated cast iron, which won't affect the taste or color of dishes containing wine, spinach, tomatoes, or other acidic foods. Be sure the pot is large enough to avoid spillage. A 4-quart ovenproof pot with lid is generally ideal. Helpful additional equipment would include a food mill, processor or blender for pureeing, and a large strainer.

Armed thus, you can begin to create a legacy of memories for your own family and friends, evoking a feeling of well-being and the expectation of comforting wholesome food to be enjoyed and shared by all.

Chapter 1

Hot and Hearty Vegetable Soups

From childhood on we have been told that vegetables are good for us. As it turns out, modern research in health and nutrition has proven this to be true. Most vegetables are rich in vitamins, minerals, and dietary fiber, and some have been found to contain natural components that appear to help prevent certain diseases. Best of all, practically all vegetables are free of saturated fat.

Aside from their health benefits, vegetables are colorful and subtly tasty, and they lend themselves to all kinds of preparations and pairings. Indeed, we are very lucky to have such a wide variety of vegetables available to us year-round—either in fresh or frozen form. Supermarket produce sections have burgeoned in recent years, and farmers' markets have proliferated. Many Americans now have easy access not only to the traditional standbys—broccoli, green beans, and cabbage—but to a whole new world of international vegetables and herbs—snow peas, broccoli rabe, and fresh ginger, for example.

The recipes that follow feature a wide range of vegetables in all their glory—from Orange-Ginger Carrot Soup to Kale and Mustard Green Soup with Potatoes and White Beans. There are starter soups and main-course soups, smooth bisques and chunky chowders, traditional recipes and plenty of new ideas.

1   GINGERED ACORN SQUASH SOUP
Prep: 10 minutes   Cook: 38 minutes   Serves: 6

2 tablespoons butter
1 cup chopped leek (white part only)
1 tablespoon minced fresh ginger
2 pounds acorn squash, peeled, seeded, and chopped
6 cups Chicken Stock (page 262) or reduced-sodium canned broth

1 teaspoon grated orange zest
½ teaspoon cinnamon
¼ teaspoon ground cloves
1 cup light cream or half-and-half
⅛ teaspoon grated nutmeg
½ teaspoon salt
¼ teaspoon pepper

1. In a large saucepan, melt butter over medium heat. Add leek and ginger and cook, stirring frequently, until the leek is tender, 3 minutes. Add squash, chicken stock, orange zest, cinnamon, and cloves. Bring to a boil, reduce heat to medium-low, partially cover, and simmer 30 minutes.

2. In a food processor or blender, puree soup in batches until smooth. Return to pan and add cream, nutmeg, salt, and pepper. Bring to a boil, reduce heat to low, and simmer 5 minutes. Serve hot.

2   CREAM OF BROCCOLI SOUP
Prep: 10 minutes   Cook: 18 to 25 minutes   Serves: 4 to 6

Serve this soup for lunch with biscuits or muffins and a salad on the side. Or, pack it in an insulated container and send the kids to school with a deliciously nourishing hot lunch.

2 tablespoons vegetable oil
2 medium onions, chopped
2 garlic cloves, chopped
4½ cups chopped broccoli (about 1 pound)
1 large red potato, peeled and diced

5½ cups Chicken Stock (page 262) or reduced-sodium canned broth
¾ cup milk
¼ cup heavy or light cream
Salt and pepper

1. In a large saucepan, heat oil over medium heat. Add onions and garlic and cook, stirring frequently, until softened but not browned, 3 to 5 minutes. Add broccoli, potato, and chicken stock. Bring to a boil. Reduce heat to medium-low, partially cover, and cook until vegetables are soft, 15 to 20 minutes.

2. In a food processor or blender, puree soup in batches until smooth. Return to saucepan, add milk and cream, and season with salt and pepper to taste. Reheat before serving.

3 CREAM OF ASPARAGUS SOUP

Prep: 10 minutes   Cook: 18 to 23 minutes   Serves: 4

Spring is the perfect time for buying and eating asparagus. Not only is it at its flavorful best in season, it is also least expensive. If the asparagus stalks are thin and tender, there is no need to peel their outer coating. However, if they are medium to large, sporting a thick fibrous peel, it is best to remove the skin with a swivel-bladed vegetable peeler before cooking. Cooking time will be shortened, and the asparagus will remain a beautiful bright green color.

3 tablespoons butter
2 pounds asparagus, trimmed and cut into 2-inch pieces; reserve 12 tips for garnish
1 medium leek (white part only), well rinsed and chopped, or 1 medium onion, chopped
1 medium red potato, peeled and diced
6 cups Chicken Stock (page 262) or reduced-sodium canned broth

1 bay leaf
1 sprig of fresh thyme or ½ teaspoon dried thyme leaves
1 cup light cream or half-and-half
1 teaspoon salt
¼ teaspoon pepper
¼ cup sour cream or nonfat plain yogurt
2 tablespoons minced fresh parsley

1. In a large saucepan, melt butter over medium-low heat. Add cut asparagus stalks, leek, and potato. Cook, stirring frequently, until crisp-tender, 5 minutes. Add chicken stock, bay leaf, and thyme. Bring to a boil, reduce heat to medium, and simmer, partially covered, stirring occasionally, until potato is soft, 10 to 15 minutes. Remove and discard bay leaf and thyme if using fresh sprig.

2. In a food processor, puree soup in batches until smooth; return to saucepan. Add reserved asparagus tips, cream, salt, and pepper. Bring soup to a boil. Reduce heat to medium-low and cook until tips are tender, about 3 minutes. Serve hot, garnished with a dollop of sour cream and a sprinkling of parsley.

4   BROCCOLI AND CHEDDAR CHEESE SOUP
Prep: 10 minutes   Cook: 32 to 38 minutes   Serves: 4

Broccoli is one of our favorite vegetables. Its versatility lends itself to countless combinations and pairings. Here we have combined it with the flavor of Cheddar cheese and crisp bacon. This is a very comforting soup for cold winter months.

3½ cups broccoli florets (about
       ¾ pound)
3 tablespoons vegetable oil
2 medium onions, minced
3 garlic cloves, minced
3 tablespoons flour
4½ cups Chicken Stock (page
       262) or reduced-sodium
       canned broth
1 sprig of fresh thyme or
       ½ teaspoon dried thyme
       leaves

1 bay leaf
1   cup milk
1 cup shredded sharp
       Cheddar cheese
   Salt and pepper
¼ cup crumbled crisply
       cooked bacon

1. In a large saucepan of boiling salted water, cook broccoli over medium-high heat 3 minutes. Drain and rinse under cold running water.

2. In another large saucepan, heat oil over medium heat. Add onions and garlic and cook, stirring frequently, until softened but not browned, 3 to 5 minutes. Add flour and cook, stirring constantly, 1 to 2 minutes without allowing to color. Whisk in chicken stock. Add thyme and bay leaf. Bring to a boil, reduce heat to low, and simmer 20 minutes. Remove and discard bay leaf and thyme if using fresh sprig.

3. In a food processor or blender, puree soup, in batches if necessary, until smooth. Return to saucepan and add broccoli. Bring to a boil, reduce heat to low, and simmer until broccoli is heated through, 3 to 5 minutes.

4. Remove pan from heat. Stir in milk. Gradually add cheese, ¼ cup at a time, stirring after each addition until melted. Return pan to stove and season with salt and pepper to taste. Cook over medium-low heat, stirring constantly, until heated through, 2 to 3 minutes. Garnish with bacon just before serving.

5 BUTTERNUT SQUASH SOUP WITH CHEESE TOASTS

Prep: 15 minutes   Cook: 43½ to 50½ minutes   Serves: 4

If you are looking for a hearty soup suitable as a main course this is a good choice. All it needs is some good bread and a tossed salad to make a meal.

1 (1½-pound) butternut squash
2 tablespoons butter
½ cup minced shallots
2 tablespoons flour
½ cup dry white wine
2 cups milk
2 cups Chicken Stock (page 262) or reduced-sodium canned broth

⅛ teaspoon grated nutmeg
   Salt and pepper
4 (½-inch-thick) slices of French or Italian bread, toasted
1 cup shredded Cheddar cheese (about 4 ounces)

1. Preheat oven to 350°F. Cut squash in half lengthwise, scoop out seeds and membranes, and place, cut sides down, on oiled baking sheet. Bake 30 to 35 minutes, or until tender. Let cool. Scoop squash from shell.

2. In a large nonreactive saucepan, melt butter over medium-low heat. Add shallots and cook, stirring frequently, until softened, about 2 minutes. Add flour and cook, stirring frequently, 1 to 2 minutes without allowing to color. Whisk in wine and boil 30 seconds. Stir in milk. Bring to a boil, reduce heat to low, and simmer 5 minutes.

3. In a food processor, combine reserved squash and hot milk mixture. Puree, in batches if necessary, until smooth. Return mixture to saucepan and stir in chicken stock and nutmeg. Season with salt and pepper to taste. Set over medium heat and cook, stirring often, until heated through, about 3 minutes.

4. Preheat broiler. Transfer soup to a large flameproof casserole or 4 flame-proof soup bowls. Float a slice of toast on top of each and cover each slice generously with about ¼ cup cheese. Place under broiler about 4 inches from heat until cheese is melted and golden, 2 to 3 minutes.

6   MISO SOUP WITH CABBAGE, TURNIP, AND CARROT

Prep: 10 minutes   Cook: 25 minutes   Serves: 6

This soup makes a nourishing lunch. You can vary the vegetables according to the season.

2 tablespoons vegetable oil
1 medium onion, minced
½ cup minced celery
2 garlic cloves, minced
1 tablespoon minced fresh ginger
2 medium carrots, peeled and sliced
3 small turnips (about ½ pound), peeled and diced

1 cup sliced napa or Savoy cabbage
6 cups Chicken Stock (page 262) or reduced-sodium canned broth
1 tablespoon dark miso (soybean paste)
Salt and pepper
¼ cup minced scallion green

1. In a large saucepan, heat oil over medium heat. Add onion, celery, garlic, and ginger and cook, stirring frequently, 5 minutes.

2. Add carrots, turnips, cabbage, chicken stock, and miso. Bring to a boil. Reduce heat to medium-low, cover, and simmer until vegetables are tender, about 20 minutes. Season with salt and pepper to taste. Serve garnished with scallion.

7   DILLED ARTICHOKE SOUP WITH LEMON

Prep: 10 minutes   Cook: 29 to 32 minutes   Serves: 6

Artichokes and fresh dill have an affinity for one another. When combined with freshly grated lemon zest (the colored part of the peel) and lemon juice, you have an unbeatable combination. For an added touch of flavor, the soup can be garnished with finely crumbled feta cheese.

3 tablespoons olive oil
2 cups chopped onions
1 large celery rib, chopped
3 garlic cloves, chopped
3 tablespoons flour
1 (14-ounce) can artichoke hearts, drained, rinsed, and coarsely chopped
6 cups Chicken Stock (page 262) or reduced-sodium canned broth

1 bay leaf
1 sprig of fresh thyme or ½ teaspoon dried thyme leaves
2 teaspoons grated lemon zest
½ teaspoon salt
¼ teaspoon black pepper
3 tablespoons minced fresh dill
2 teaspoons lemon juice

1. In a large nonreactive saucepan, heat oil over medium-low heat. Add onions, celery, and garlic, cover, and cook, stirring frequently, until softened, 5 to 7 minutes.

2. Add flour and cook, stirring constantly, 2 minutes without allowing to color. Add artichoke hearts, chicken stock, bay leaf, thyme, lemon zest, salt, and pepper. Bring to a boil. Reduce heat to medium and simmer, stirring frequently, 20 minutes. Remove and discard bay leaf and thyme if using fresh sprig.

3. In a food processor or blender, puree soup in batches until smooth; return to saucepan. Stir in dill and lemon juice. Cook over medium heat, stirring, until heated through, 2 to 3 minutes, and serve hot.

---

8   CABBAGE SOUP WITH CARAWAY SEED

Prep: 10 minutes   Cook: 46 to 48 minutes   Serves: 6 to 8

During the fall and winter months, cabbage is plentiful. While it was considered a mundane vegetable for years, its versatility now makes it all the rage—even with trendy chefs. It is particularly appealing during the winter doldrums. Here is a soup that is not only a flavorful repast, but a comforting staple to ward off the frigid winds of winter.

1 (14½-ounce) can Italian-style peeled tomatoes, juices reserved
2 tablespoons vegetable oil
1 medium onion, minced
3 garlic cloves, minced
5 cups shredded cabbage (about 1½ pounds)
1 medium carrot, peeled and sliced
6 cups Chicken Stock (page 262) or reduced-sodium canned broth

1 tablespoon caraway seed, lightly crushed
1 bay leaf
½ teaspoon salt
¼ teaspoon pepper
¼ cup sour cream or nonfat plain yogurt
2 tablespoons minced fresh dill

1. In a blender or food processor, puree tomatoes with their juices until smooth. Set aside.

2. In a large nonreactive saucepan, heat oil over medium heat. Add onion and garlic and cook, stirring frequently, until softened but not browned, 3 to 5 minutes.

3. Add cabbage and carrot and cook, stirring frequently, until crisp-tender, about 3 minutes. Add tomato puree, chicken stock, caraway seed, bay leaf, salt, and pepper. Bring to a boil. Reduce heat to low and simmer, stirring occasionally, 40 minutes.

4. Remove and discard bay leaf. Serve soup hot, garnished with sour cream and dill.

9   CREAMY CAULIFLOWER BISQUE
Prep: 10 minutes   Cook: 26 to 28 minutes   Serves: 6

The silky smooth texture of this soup makes it perfect as a first course for an elegant meal.

3 tablespoons butter
½ cup minced shallots
3 tablespoons flour
1 large head of cauliflower (2½ to 3 pounds), cut into florets
5 cups Chicken Stock (page 262) or reduced-sodium canned broth

1 bay leaf
1 cup milk or cream
⅛ teaspoon grated nutmeg
Salt and pepper

1. In a soup pot, melt butter over medium-low heat. Add shallots and cook, stirring frequently, until softened but not browned, 2 to 3 minutes. Add flour and cook, stirring constantly, 1 to 2 minutes without allowing to color. Add cauliflower, chicken stock, and bay leaf. Bring to a boil. Reduce heat to medium-low, partially cover, and cook until cauliflower is soft, about 20 minutes. Remove and discard bay leaf.

2. In a food processor or blender, puree soup in batches until smooth. Return to pan and stir in milk and nutmeg. Season with salt and pepper to taste. Bring to a boil, reduce heat to medium, and cook, stirring, until heated through, about 3 minutes, and serve.

10   CURRIED BUTTERNUT SQUASH SOUP
Prep: 10 minutes   Cook: 39 to 43 minutes   Serves: 6

Here curry powder adds a whole new dimension to an otherwise mild-tasting vegetable. In this light soup, it acts as a catalyst to bring out the subtle flavors of the squash.

2 tablespoons butter
1 medium onion, chopped
1 medium celery rib, chopped
3 garlic cloves, chopped
1 tablespoon minced fresh ginger
1 tablespoon Madras curry powder
1 (3-pound) butternut squash, peeled, seeded, and cubed

6 cups Chicken Stock (page 262) or reduced-sodium canned broth
1 bay leaf
1 tablespoon grated orange zest
Salt and pepper
¼ cup plain yogurt
2 tablespoons minced cilantro or fresh parsley

1. In a soup pot, melt butter over medium heat. Add onion, celery, garlic, and ginger. Cook, stirring occasionally, until vegetables are softened, 6 to 8 minutes.

2. Add curry powder and cook, stirring constantly, until fragrant and lightly toasted, 1 to 2 minutes. Add squash, chicken stock, bay leaf, and orange zest. Bring to a boil. Reduce heat to low, cover, and simmer 30 minutes. Remove and discard bay leaf.

3. In a food processor or blender, puree soup in batches until smooth. Return to pan. Cook over medium heat, stirring, until heated through, 2 to 3 minutes. Season with salt and pepper to taste. Garnish with yogurt and cilantro.

---

11   ORANGE-GINGER CARROT SOUP
Prep: 10 minutes   Cook: 38 to 41 minutes   Serves: 4

We both love glazed carrots with ginger and orange. It seemed only natural to combine these flavors in a soup. Buy fresh carrots whenever possible, and save their tops for flavoring stocks.

3 tablespoons vegetable oil
1 pound carrots, peeled and
   sliced
1 medium onion, finely
   chopped
6 garlic cloves, chopped
1 tablespoon minced fresh
   ginger
4½ cups Chicken Stock (page
   262) or reduced-sodium
   canned broth

2 teaspoons grated orange zest
1 bay leaf
½ cup fresh orange juice
   Salt and pepper
¼ cup sour cream or nonfat
   plain yogurt
2 tablespoons minced cilantro
   or fresh parsley

1. In a large saucepan, heat oil over medium heat. Add carrots, onion, garlic, and ginger and cook, stirring occasionally, until onion is golden, 6 to 8 minutes.

2. Add chicken stock, orange zest, and bay leaf. Bring to a boil. Reduce heat to medium-low, cover, and cook, stirring occasionally, until carrots are tender, about 30 minutes.

3. In a food processor or blender, puree soup in batches until smooth; return to saucepan. Stir in orange juice and season with salt and pepper to taste. Cook over medium heat, stirring occasionally, until heated through, 2 to 3 minutes. Garnish each soup bowl with a dollop of sour cream and a sprinkling of cilantro and serve.

12   CREAM OF CELERY SOUP
Prep: 10 minutes   Cook: 44 to 47 minutes   Serves: 6

Celery tops or leaves are wonderful additions to stocks and stews. Use them sparingly, though, since they are quite strong in flavor. The leaves also make a very pretty garnish.

3 **tablespoons butter**	3 **tablespoons flour**
1½ **pounds celery ribs, sliced (about 6 cups), 6 leaves reserved**	6 **cups Chicken Stock (page 262) or reduced-sodium canned broth**
2 **medium-large onions, chopped**	1 **bay leaf**
2 **large garlic cloves, minced**	1 **cup heavy cream or milk**
	Salt and white pepper

1. In a large saucepan, melt butter over medium-low heat. Add celery, onions, and garlic, cover, and cook, stirring frequently, until softened, about 10 minutes. Add flour and cook, stirring constantly, 1 to 2 minutes without allowing to color. Add chicken stock and bay leaf. Bring to a boil. Reduce heat to low, cover, and simmer 30 minutes. Remove and discard bay leaf.

2. In a food processor or blender, puree soup in batches until smooth. Add cream and salt and pepper to taste. Bring to a boil, reduce heat to low, and simmer until heated through, 3 to 5 minutes. Garnish with reserved celery leaves.

13   COUNTRY COLLARD GREEN SOUP WITH RED PEPPER AND POTATOES
Prep: 10 minutes   Cook: 1 hour 35 minutes   Serves: 6

The intense flavor of collard greens and the smokiness of the ham hock make the inclusion of stock unnecessary here. Only water is used as a base. The greens themselves produce a wonderfully robust and flavorful broth, which can be added to sauces and gravies accompanying roast pork, poultry, and game.

1 **ham hock (about ½ pound)**	¼ **teaspoon crushed hot red pepper**
2 **garlic cloves, thinly sliced**	4 **medium red potatoes, peeled and diced**
2 **tablespoons butter**	**Salt**
1 **medium onion, minced**	
1 **medium red bell pepper, diced**	
2 **pounds collard greens, trimmed, well rinsed, and coarsely chopped**	

1. In a soup pot, combine ham hock, garlic, and 8 cups cold water. Bring to a boil. Reduce heat to low, cover, and simmer 45 minutes. Remove ham hock and let cool. Remove meat from bone and dice.

2. In medium skillet, melt butter over medium heat. Add onion and bell pepper and cook, stirring frequently, until soft but not brown, about 5 minutes.

3. Add collards, onion and pepper mixture, and crushed hot pepper to ham broth in soup pot. Bring to a boil, reduce heat to low, and simmer 30 minutes. Add potatoes and reserved ham and simmer until potatoes are tender, about 15 minutes. Season with salt to taste before serving.

14 KALE AND MUSTARD GREEN SOUP WITH POTATOES AND WHITE BEANS
Prep: 10 minutes   Cook: 1 hour 35 minutes   Serves: 6

The pungency of mustard greens adds its distinctive flavor to this hearty soup. While it will look as if you have a mountain of greens, they will wilt dramatically when they cook.

2 tablespoons butter
2 medium onions, chopped
1 ham hock (about ½ pound)
3 garlic cloves, thinly sliced
1 bay leaf
1 pound kale, trimmed, well rinsed, and coarsely chopped
1 pound mustard greens, trimmed, well rinsed, and coarsely chopped

¼ to ½ teaspoon crushed hot red pepper
2 medium red potatoes, peeled and diced
1 (16-ounce) can cannellini beans, rinsed and drained
Salt

1. In a soup pot, melt butter over medium heat. Add onions and cook, stirring frequently, until tender, about 5 minutes. Remove onions from pot and set aside.

2. Place ham hock, garlic, bay leaf, and 8 cups cold water in pot. Bring to a boil. Reduce heat to low, cover, and simmer 45 minutes. Remove and discard bay leaf. Remove ham hock and let cool. Remove meat from bone and dice.

3. Add onions, kale, mustard greens, and hot pepper to liquid in pot. Bring to a boil, reduce heat to low, and simmer 30 minutes. Add potatoes, reserved meat, beans, and salt to taste. Simmer until potatoes are tender, about 15 minutes more, and serve.

15   KALE AND POTATO SOUP
Prep: 15 minutes   Cook: 30 minutes   Serves: 4 to 6

2 tablespoons olive oil
1 large onion, chopped
3 large garlic cloves, chopped
1 pound red potatoes, peeled
    and cut into 1-inch dice
6 cups Chicken Stock (page
    262) or reduced-sodium
    canned broth

¾ pound kale, trimmed, well
    rinsed, and sliced
½ teaspoon salt
¼ teaspoon pepper

1. In a large soup pot, heat olive oil over medium heat. Add onion and garlic and cook, stirring frequently, until soft but not brown, about 5 minutes. Add potatoes and chicken stock. Bring to a boil. Reduce heat to low, cover, and simmer until potatoes are just tender, about 10 minutes.

2. Add kale, salt, and pepper. Bring to a boil, reduce heat to low, and simmer, uncovered, until kale is just tender, about 15 minutes.

16   LEEK AND POTATO SOUP
Prep: 10 minutes   Cook: 30 minutes   Serves: 4

This classic soup is good hot or cold. If you do opt for chilling it, be sure to taste before serving, in case it needs more salt and pepper.

1½ pounds red potatoes, peeled
    and cut into 1-inch dice
1½ pounds leeks (white part
    only), well rinsed and
    chopped
1 large celery rib, sliced
7 cups Chicken Stock (page
    262) or reduced-sodium
    canned broth

1 cup sour cream, nonfat plain
    yogurt, or milk
½ teaspoon salt
¼ teaspoon pepper

1. In a large saucepan, combine potatoes, leeks, celery, and chicken stock. Bring to a boil. Reduce heat to medium-low, cover, and cook 30 minutes.

2. In a food processor or blender, puree soup in batches until smooth. Return to pan and stir in sour cream, salt, and pepper.

3. To serve hot, warm over medium-low heat, stirring, but do not let boil or sour cream may curdle. To serve cold, cover and refrigerate for at least 3 hours.

17 DILLED CUCUMBER AND LEEK SOUP
Prep: 10 minutes   Cook: 25 minutes   Serves: 6

3 tablespoons butter
3 cups chopped leeks (white
    and tender green, about
    4 medium leeks)
3 medium cucumbers,
    peeled, seeded, and diced
4½ cups Chicken Stock (page
    262) or reduced-sodium
    canned broth

1½ tablespoons cornstarch
½ cup heavy or light cream
2 teaspoons lemon juice
2 tablespoons minced fresh
    dill
½ teaspoon salt
¼ teaspoon pepper

1. In a large saucepan, melt butter over medium-low heat. Add leeks, cover, and cook, stirring frequently, 5 minutes. Add cucumbers and chicken stock. Bring to a boil, reduce heat to medium-low, and cook, partially covered, 15 minutes.

2. In a food processor or blender, puree soup in batches until smooth. Return to pan and bring to a boil.

3. In a small bowl, blend cornstarch with cream and stir into simmering soup. Simmer, stirring frequently, 5 minutes. Stir in lemon juice, dill, salt, and pepper.

18 FENNEL SOUP
Prep: 10 minutes   Cook: 22 minutes   Serves: 4 to 6

Fresh fennel, sometimes called "anise" in produce markets, has been a staple of Italian cooks for generations. An extremely versatile vegetable, it lends itself to being braised, stewed, and sautéed. It is also wonderful in salads and, of course, in soups.

2 tablespoons butter
½ pound fennel bulb,
    trimmed and minced,
    1 tablespoon chopped
    fronds reserved
1 medium onion, minced

2 tablespoons flour
5 cups Chicken Stock (page
    262) or reduced-sodium
    canned broth
2 teaspoons lemon juice
    Salt

1. In a large saucepan, melt butter over medium heat. Add minced fennel and onion and cook, stirring frequently, until soft but not brown, about 5 minutes. Reduce heat to low. Add flour and cook, stirring constantly, 2 minutes without allowing to color. Whisk in chicken stock. Bring to a boil, stirring occasionally. Reduce heat to medium-low, cover, and simmer 15 minutes.

2. Add lemon juice and season with salt to taste. Garnish with reserved fennel leaves.

19   ROASTED EGGPLANT SOUP
Prep: 1 hour   Cook: 1 hour 11 minutes   Serves: 4

When vegetables are roasted, their flavors intensify. This soup features the pure flavor of eggplant at its best.

1 medium-large eggplant (about 1½ pounds)	¼ teaspoon crushed hot red pepper
2 tablespoons olive oil	4 cups Chicken Stock (page 262) or reduced-sodium canned broth
1 large onion, chopped	
3 garlic cloves, crushed	
1 large red bell pepper, chopped	2 tablespoons minced cilantro
1 teaspoon salt	¼ cup nonfat plain yogurt or sour cream

1. Preheat oven to 375°F. Cut eggplant in half lengthwise. Brush cut sides with a little olive oil and arrange, cut sides down, on a greased baking sheet. Bake 30 minutes, or until tender. Let cool.

2. Meanwhile, in a large saucepan, heat remaining olive oil over medium heat. Add onion, garlic, bell pepper, salt, and hot pepper. Cook, stirring frequently, until softened, about 8 minutes. Add chicken stock. Bring to a boil. Reduce heat to low, cover, and simmer 30 minutes.

3. With a large spoon, scoop out eggplant and add to saucepan; discard skins. In a food processor or blender, puree soup in batches until smooth. Return to saucepan. Bring to a boil, reduce heat to low, and simmer 3 minutes. Add cilantro. Serve hot, with a dollop of yogurt on top.

20   CURRIED CAULIFLOWER SOUP
Prep: 10 minutes   Cook: 26 to 29 minutes   Serves: 6

Curry loves cauliflower, and the flavors blend beautifully for a soup. This one can be served either hot or cold.

3 tablespoons butter	1 medium head of cauliflower (2 to 2½ pounds), cut into florets, or 4 cups cauliflower florets
1 medium onion, chopped	
3 garlic cloves, chopped	
2 teaspoons minced fresh ginger	1 teaspoon grated lemon zest
1 tablespoon Madras curry powder, or more to taste	1 cup plain yogurt
	⅛ teaspoon cayenne
3 tablespoons flour	Salt
5 cups Chicken Stock (page 262) or reduced-sodium canned broth	2 tablespoons minced cilantro

1. In a large saucepan, melt butter over medium heat. Add onion, garlic, and ginger and cook, stirring frequently, until onion is golden, 5 to 7 minutes.

2. Add curry powder and flour and cook, stirring frequently, 1 to 2 minutes. Add chicken stock, cauliflower, and lemon zest. Bring to a boil. Reduce heat to medium-low, partially cover, and cook until cauliflower is soft, about 20 minutes.

3. In a food processor or blender, puree soup in batches until smooth. Return to pan and stir in yogurt and cayenne. Season with salt to taste. Heat just to a simmer. Garnish each soup bowl with cilantro and serve.

---

21 BACON, LETTUCE, AND TOMATO SOUP

Prep: 10 minutes   Cook: 27 to 30 minutes   Serves: 4

¼ **pound sliced bacon, chopped**
3 **tablespoons butter**
2 **cups chopped leeks (white and tender green, about 3 medium leeks)**
2 **garlic cloves, minced**
3 **tablespoons flour**
4 **cups Chicken Stock (page 262) or reduced-sodium canned broth**

2 **large heads of Boston lettuce, trimmed, rinsed, and shredded**
1 **bay leaf**
1 **cup light cream or milk**
   Salt and pepper
1 **medium tomato, diced**

1. In a large saucepan, cook bacon over medium heat until crisp, about 5 minutes. With a slotted spoon, transfer bacon to a plate lined with paper towels to drain. Pour off fat from pan.

2. In same saucepan, melt butter over medium heat. Add leeks and garlic and cook, stirring frequently, until softened but not browned, 3 to 5 minutes. Add flour and cook, stirring constantly, 1 to 2 minutes without allowing to color. Stir in chicken stock and lettuce. Add bay leaf. Bring to a boil. Reduce heat to medium-low, cover, and cook 15 minutes. Remove and discard bay leaf.

3. In a food processor or blender, puree soup in batches until smooth. Return to pan and stir in cream. Season with salt and pepper to taste. Cook over medium heat, stirring, until heated through, about 3 minutes. Stir in reserved bacon just before serving and garnish with diced tomato.

22   SUMMER MINESTRONE
Prep: 15 minutes   Cook: 43 to 48 minutes   Serves: 6

2   tablespoons olive oil
1   medium onion, chopped
2   garlic cloves, minced
4   cups Chicken Stock (page
        262) or reduced-sodium
        canned broth
4   large tomatoes, peeled,
        seeded, and chopped, or
        1 (28-ounce) can Italian-style
        peeled tomatoes, drained
        and chopped
1   sprig of fresh thyme or
        ½ teaspoon dried thyme
        leaves

1   bay leaf
½   cup small pasta shells
2   cups fresh corn kernels
        (from 3 or 4 ears)
1   medium zucchini, trimmed
        and diced
⅓   cup minced fresh basil
    Salt and pepper
    Grated Parmesan cheese

1. In a nonreactive soup pot, heat olive oil over medium heat. Add onion and garlic and cook, stirring frequently, until soft but not brown, 3 to 5 minutes. Add chicken stock, tomatoes, thyme, and bay leaf. Bring to a boil. Reduce heat to low, cover, and simmer, stirring frequently, 30 minutes.

2. Add pasta and corn. Simmer 5 minutes. Add zucchini and simmer until vegetables and pasta are just tender, 5 to 8 minutes longer. Add basil and season with salt and pepper to taste. Remove and discard bay leaf. Pass a bowl of Parmesan cheese on the side.

23   WINTER MINESTRONE
Prep: 10 minutes   Cook: 46 to 47 minutes   Serves: 6

2   tablespoons olive oil
2   medium onions, chopped
2   medium carrots, peeled and
        diced
2   medium celery ribs, diced
3   cups shredded cabbage
2   (14-ounce) cans Italian
        peeled tomatoes, juices
        reserved
8   cups Chicken Stock (page
        262) or reduced-sodium
        canned broth

½   teaspoon dried thyme leaves
½   teaspoon dried rosemary
1   bay leaf
¼   pound green beans, cut into
        1-inch pieces
1   cup elbow macaroni
1   cup kidney beans, rinsed
        and drained
2   garlic cloves, minced
3   tablespoons minced fresh
        parsley
⅔   cup grated Parmesan cheese

1. In a nonreactive soup pot, heat olive oil over medium heat. Add onions, carrots, and celery. Cook, stirring frequently, until softened, 5 minutes.

2. Add cabbage, tomatoes with their juices, chicken stock, thyme, rosemary, and bay leaf. Bring to a boil, reduce heat to low, cover, and simmer, stirring frequently, 30 minutes.

3. Add green beans and pasta to soup. Simmer 10 minutes, or until green beans and pasta are tender. Add kidney beans and garlic. Simmer, stirring frequently, until beans are heated through, 1 to 2 minutes. Remove and discard bay leaf. Stir in parsley and garnish each serving with Parmesan cheese.

24   SHIITAKE MUSHROOM AND BARLEY SOUP

Prep: 20 minutes   Stand: 10 minutes   Cook: 35 minutes   Serves: 8

Dried and fresh shiitake mushrooms give this soup a rich flavor. Buy dried shiitakes that look bright and whole, not pale and shriveled.

6 **dried shiitake mushrooms**
2 **tablespoons vegetable oil**
1 **large onion, chopped**
4 **garlic cloves, crushed through a press**
½ **cup pearl barley**
½ **teaspoon dried thyme leaves**
½ **teaspoon salt**
6 **cups Vegetable Stock (page 266) or canned broth**

1 **pound cultivated mushrooms, sliced**
½ **pound fresh shiitake mushrooms, stems discarded, caps sliced**
½ **teaspoon pepper**
2 **tablespoons chopped Italian (flat-leaf) parsley**

1. Place dried mushrooms in a medium heatproof bowl and cover with 1½ cups boiling water. Let stand 10 minutes. Remove mushrooms, discard stems, and finely chop mushroom caps. Reserve soaking liquid.

2. In a large soup pot, heat 1 tablespoon oil. Add onion and cook, stirring frequently, until golden, about 5 minutes. Stir in garlic, barley, thyme, salt, dried mushrooms, vegetable stock, and reserved mushroom soaking liquid and bring to a boil. Reduce heat to low, cover, and simmer until barley is tender, about 30 minutes.

3. Meanwhile, heat 1½ teaspoons oil in skillet over high heat. Add half of fresh mushrooms and cook, stirring frequently, until golden and tender, about 5 minutes. Transfer mushrooms to a bowl and repeat with remaining oil and mushrooms. When barley is cooked, stir cooked mushrooms, pepper, and parsley into soup and serve.

25 CREAMY CARROT SOUP WITH LEEKS AND THYME
Prep: 10 minutes   Cook: 28 to 30 minutes   Serves: 4

Here is a more traditional carrot soup flavored with fresh thyme. It makes a very elegant first course at a dinner party.

3 tablespoons butter
1 pound carrots, peeled and sliced
3 medium leeks (white part only), well rinsed and chopped
2 tablespoons flour
5½ cups Chicken Stock (page 262) or reduced-sodium canned broth

1 large sprig of fresh thyme or 1 teaspoon dried thyme leaves
1 bay leaf
½ cup heavy cream
Salt and pepper

1. In a large saucepan, melt butter over medium heat. Add carrots and leeks and cook, stirring frequently, until crisp-tender, about 5 minutes. Add flour and cook, stirring, 1 to 2 minutes without allowing to color. Add chicken stock, thyme, and bay leaf. Bring to a boil, reduce heat to medium-low, and cook, partially covered, until carrots are tender, about 20 minutes. Remove and discard fresh thyme and bay leaf.

2. In a food processor or blender, puree soup, in batches if necessary, until smooth. Return to saucepan and stir in cream. Season with salt and pepper to taste. Cook over medium heat, stirring, until heated through, 2 to 3 minutes. Serve, garnished with additional thyme leaves, if desired.

26 DRIED MUSHROOM SOUP
Prep: 10 minutes   Stand: 30 minutes   Cook: 32 minutes   Serves: 4

When fresh mushrooms are not at their best, try this dried mushroom version. It has a wonderfully earthy taste.

2 ounces dried mushrooms, such as porcini, cèpes, or Polish
3 tablespoons butter
½ cup minced shallots
2 garlic cloves, minced
3 tablespoons flour

4 cups Brown Beef Stock (page 264) or reduced-sodium canned broth
1 cup milk
Salt and pepper
2 tablespoons chopped fresh parsley

1. In a medium heatproof bowl, combine mushrooms and 2 cups hot water. Let stand 30 minutes. Drain mushrooms, reserving liquid, and chop. Strain mushroom liquid through a fine sieve or a coffee filter into a bowl.

2. In a large saucepan, melt butter over medium-low heat. Add shallots and garlic and cook, stirring, until soft and fragrant, about 2 minutes. Add chopped mushrooms and cook, stirring frequently, until tender, 5 minutes. Add flour and cook, stirring, 2 minutes, without allowing to color. Add reserved mushroom liquid and beef stock. Bring to a boil. Reduce heat to low, cover, and simmer 20 minutes.

3. In a food processor or blender, puree soup in batches until smooth. Return to pan and stir in milk. Season with salt and pepper to taste. Simmer 3 minutes. Garnish each serving with parsley.

27 ONION SOUP GRATINÉE

Prep: 15 minutes   Cook: 1 hour 14 minutes to 1 hour 22 minutes
Serves: 4

This soup makes a delicious meal. Serve it with a roasted vegetable salad and hearty bread.

3 tablespoons butter	½ teaspoon salt
1½ pounds Spanish onions, thinly sliced (about 6 cups)	¼ teaspoon pepper
	2 tablespoons cognac or brandy
¼ teaspoon sugar	8 (1-inch-thick) slices of French bread
3 tablespoons flour	
½ cup dry white wine	3½ tablespoons butter, melted
6 cups Brown Beef Stock (page 264) or reduced-sodium canned broth	1 garlic clove, halved
	1 cup shredded Gruyère or Swiss cheese (about 4 ounces)
½ teaspoon dried thyme leaves	
1 bay leaf	⅓ cup grated Parmesan cheese

1. In a large nonreactive saucepan, melt butter over medium-low heat. Stir in onions, cover, and cook, stirring occasionally, until softened, about 8 minutes. Add sugar and cook, uncovered, stirring frequently, until onions are golden, 3 to 5 minutes. Add flour and cook, stirring frequently, 2 minutes without allowing to color. Add wine, beef stock, thyme, bay leaf, salt, and pepper. Bring to a boil. Reduce heat to low, cover, and simmer, skimming surface and stirring occasionally, 30 minutes. Remove and discard bay leaf. Add cognac and season with additional salt and pepper to taste.

2. Preheat oven to 350°F. Brush both sides of bread lightly with some of the melted butter. Arrange on a baking sheet and bake, turning once, 15 minutes, or until bread is dry and lightly toasted. Rub bread with cut sides of garlic.

3. Transfer soup to a flameproof tureen or baking dish, cover with bread slices, and sprinkle Gruyère and Parmesan cheese on top. Drizzle remaining melted butter over cheeses. Bake 15 to 20 minutes, or until soup is simmering. Remove soup from oven and preheat broiler. Place dish 4 to 6 inches from heat source and broil until cheese is golden, 1 to 2 minutes.

28   CORN CHOWDER WITH PIMIENTO AND FRESH CHIVES

Prep: 10 minutes   Cook: 21 to 29 minutes   Serves: 4

2 tablespoons butter
1 cup minced scallions
1 medium celery rib, diced
3 cups fresh corn kernels
     (from 5 or 6 ears)
3 tablespoons flour
5½ cups Chicken Stock (page
     262) or reduced-sodium
     canned broth
1 fresh sprig of summer
     savory or ½ teaspoon
     dried

1 bay leaf
½ teaspoon salt
¼ teaspoon pepper
½ cup heavy or light cream
½ cup diced pimiento, drained
     and patted dry
2 tablespoons minced fresh
     chives

1. In a large saucepan, melt butter over medium heat. Add scallions and celery and cook, stirring frequently, until soft but not brown, 3 to 5 minutes. Add corn and cook, stirring frequently, 2 minutes. Add flour and cook, stirring constantly, 1 to 2 minutes without allowing to color. Add chicken stock, savory, bay leaf, salt, and pepper. Bring to a boil. Reduce heat to low, cover, and simmer until corn is very tender, about 15 to 20 minutes. Remove and discard savory if using fresh sprig and bay leaf.

2. In a food processor or blender, puree soup in batches until smooth. Return to saucepan and stir in cream and pimiento. Heat to simmering over medium heat. Garnish with minced chives.

29   MUSHROOM BISQUE

Prep: 10 minutes   Cook: 25 to 28 minutes   Serves: 4

3 tablespoons butter
1 pound mushrooms,
     chopped
½ teaspoon salt
⅛ teaspoon white pepper
3 tablespoons flour

4½ cups Chicken Stock (page
     262) or reduced-sodium
     canned broth
½ cup heavy cream
2 tablespoons minced fresh
     chives or scallion green

1. In a large saucepan, melt butter over medium heat. Add mushrooms, salt, and pepper and cook, stirring frequently, until softened, 6 to 8 minutes. Reduce heat to low, add flour, and cook, stirring constantly, 2 minutes without allowing to color. Stir in chicken stock. Bring to a boil. Reduce heat to low, cover, and simmer 15 minutes.

2. In a food processor or blender, puree soup in batches until smooth. Return to pan and stir in cream. Bring to a boil, reduce heat to low, and simmer, stirring frequently, until heated through, 2 to 3 minutes. Garnish each serving with chives.

30   FRESH PEA SOUP WITH MINT

Prep: 15 minutes   Cook: 20 to 22 minutes   Serves: 4

Tender fresh peas should be used to prepare this soup. If they are out of season, frozen peas can be substituted.

2 tablespoons butter
½ cup minced shallots
2 tablespoons flour
3½ cups Chicken Stock (page 262) or reduced-sodium canned broth
4 cups shelled peas (about 4 pounds)

3 tablespoons chopped fresh mint, plus whole leaves for garnish
½ teaspoon sugar
½ cup light cream or milk
Salt and pepper
¼ cup sour cream

1. In a large saucepan, melt butter over medium heat. Add shallots and cook, stirring frequently, until softened, about 2 minutes. Add flour and cook, stirring constantly, 1 to 2 minutes without allowing to color. Stir in chicken stock, peas, 2 tablespoons chopped mint, and sugar. Bring to a boil, reduce heat to medium-low, and cook, partially covered, stirring frequently, until peas are tender, about 15 minutes.

2. In a food processor or blender, puree soup in batches until smooth. Return to pan and stir in cream and remaining 1 tablespoon chopped mint. Season with salt and pepper to taste. Simmer, stirring frequently, until heated through, 2 to 3 minutes. Top each serving with a dollop of sour cream and garnish with mint leaves.

31   CREAM OF ONION SOUP

Prep: 10 minutes   Cook: 55 to 57 minutes   Serves: 6

Here's an old-fashioned soup that's often overlooked, which is a shame because it goes well before practically any meat, poultry, or fish entree. Serve with herbed biscuits or toasted croutons.

3 tablespoons butter
2 pounds Spanish onions, sliced (about 8 cups)
½ cup dry white wine
6 cups Chicken Stock (page 262) or reduced-sodium canned broth

¼ cup long-grain white rice
1 cup heavy cream or milk
Salt and white pepper
3 tablespoons minced fresh chives or scallion green

1. In a nonreactive soup pot, melt butter over medium-low heat. Add onions, cover, and cook, stirring frequently, until golden, 6 to 8 minutes. Add wine and boil 1 minute. Add chicken stock and rice. Bring to a boil. Reduce heat to low, cover, and simmer, stirring occasionally, 45 minutes.

2. In a food processor or blender, puree soup in batches until smooth. Return to pan and stir in cream. Season with salt and pepper to taste. Simmer, stirring frequently, to heat through, 3 minutes. Garnish with chives.

32   GINGERED PARSNIP AND ORANGE SOUP
Prep: 10 minutes   Cook: 35 to 38 minutes   Serves: 6

Parsnips, a member of the root vegetable family, are often overlooked and underrated. Slightly sweet, they are delicious braised, stewed, and sautéed, and they make wonderful additions to stews and soups. Here they are flavored with orange and ginger for an unbeatable combination.

3 tablespoons butter
1 medium onion, chopped
1 tablespoon minced fresh ginger
2½ pounds parsnips, peeled and diced
1 medium red potato, peeled and diced
7 cups Chicken Stock (page 262) or reduced-sodium canned broth

1 tablespoon grated orange zest
¼ teaspoon cinnamon
1 bay leaf
2 cups light cream or milk
2 teaspoons lemon juice
Salt and pepper

1. In a soup pot, melt butter over medium heat. Add onion and ginger and cook, stirring frequently, until onion is soft but not brown, 3 to 5 minutes. Add parsnips, potato, chicken stock, orange zest, cinnamon, and bay leaf. Bring to a boil. Reduce heat to low, cover, and simmer, stirring occasionally, 30 minutes. Remove and discard bay leaf.

2. In a food processor or blender, puree soup in batches until smooth. Return to pan and stir in cream and lemon juice. Season with salt and pepper to taste. Simmer, stirring occasionally, until heated through, 2 to 3 minutes, and serve.

33   SWEET POTATO CHOWDER WITH BACON AND TOMATOES
Prep: 15 minutes   Cook: 24 to 31 minutes   Serves: 6

Serve this homey soup with warm corn bread and a crisp spinach salad.

4 slices of bacon, coarsely chopped
1 small red onion, chopped
1 small red bell pepper, chopped
1 large sweet potato (about ¾ pound), peeled and cut into ½-inch dice
½ teaspoon dried thyme leaves

1 (14½-ounce) can diced peeled tomatoes in puree
3 cups Chicken Stock (page 262) or reduced-sodium canned broth
¼ cup heavy cream
½ teaspoon black pepper
Salt

1. In a large nonreactive saucepan, cook bacon over medium heat, stirring occasionally, until crisp, about 4 minutes. With a slotted spoon, transfer bacon to paper towels to drain.

2. Add onion and bell pepper to saucepan and cook, stirring occasionally, until vegetables are softened, 3 to 5 minutes. Stir in sweet potato, thyme, tomatoes, and chicken stock. Bring to a boil, reduce heat to medium, and cook, partially covered, until sweet potato is soft, 15 to 20 minutes.

3. With a slotted spoon, transfer about 2 cups of solids from soup to a blender or food processor. Puree until smooth; return puree to soup. Stir in bacon, cream, and pepper and simmer 2 minutes longer. Season with salt to taste.

---

34 RIBOLLITA

Prep: 30 minutes   Cook: 3 hours 38 minutes   Serves: 12

This traditional Italian soup is found throughout Tuscany.

½ cup extra-virgin olive oil
1 large onion, chopped
2 medium celery ribs, thinly sliced
3 carrots, peeled and chopped
4 garlic cloves, minced
¼ teaspoon crushed hot red pepper
3 sprigs of fresh thyme or ½ teaspoon dried thyme leaves
4 fresh sage leaves, chopped, or ¼ teaspoon dried
1½ teaspoons salt
¾ teaspoon pepper
1 (14½-ounce) can diced peeled tomatoes, juices reserved

½ head of Savoy cabbage, shredded
1 bunch of spinach (about ¾ pound), well rinsed, tough stems removed, and leaves shredded
2 (15-ounce) cans cannellini or Great Northern beans, undrained
1 pound small red potatoes, cut into ½-inch dice
4 slices of country or Italian bread, cut into 1-inch chunks

1. In a large nonreactive soup pot, heat olive oil over medium-high heat. Add onion, celery, carrots, garlic, hot pepper, thyme, sage, salt, and pepper. Cook, stirring frequently, until vegetables are softened, about 8 minutes.

2. Stir in tomatoes with their juices, cabbage, spinach, beans and liquid, potatoes, and enough water to cover. Bring to a boil, reduce heat to low, and simmer, partially covered, 3 hours.

3. Stir in bread, bring to a boil, and simmer until bread dissolves into soup, about 30 minutes longer. Stir before serving.

35   SWISS CHARD SOUP
Prep: 10 minutes   Cook: 1 hour 18 minutes   Serves: 4

This is a refreshing pale green soup—perfect as a first course or luncheon dish.

2 pounds Swiss chard, trimmed and well rinsed	6 cups Chicken Stock (page 262) or reduced-sodium canned broth
3 tablespoons butter	½ teaspoon dried thyme leaves
2 medium onions, chopped	1 bay leaf
2 medium celery ribs, sliced	2 teaspoons lemon juice
2 garlic cloves, minced	Salt and pepper
3 tablespoons flour	

1. Cut leaves from chard and chop. Cut stalks into 1-inch pieces. In a large saucepan, melt butter over medium heat. Add onions, celery, and garlic. Cook, stirring frequently, until softened, about 5 minutes. Add chard, cover, and cook over medium-low heat 5 minutes. Add flour and cook, stirring constantly, 3 minutes without allowing to color. Add chicken stock, thyme, and bay leaf. Bring to a boil, reduce heat to low, and simmer 1 hour. Remove and discard bay leaf.

2. In a food processor or blender, puree soup in batches until smooth. Return to pan and stir in lemon juice. Simmer 5 minutes. Season with salt and pepper to taste.

36   CREAM OF TOMATO SOUP
Prep: 10 minutes   Cook: 22 to 27 minutes   Serves: 4 to 6

2 tablespoons butter	2 cups Brown Beef Stock (page 264) or reduced-sodium canned broth
1 medium onion, chopped	1 tablespoon tomato paste
1 small carrot, peeled and finely diced	½ teaspoon dried basil
2 tablespoons flour	½ teaspoon dried thyme leaves
2 pounds fresh tomatoes, peeled, seeded, and chopped, or 1 (28-ounce) can crushed tomatoes, juices reserved	1 bay leaf
	1 cup light cream or milk
	Salt and pepper

1. In a large nonreactive saucepan, melt butter over medium heat. Add onion and carrot and cook, stirring frequently, until softened, 3 to 5 minutes. Add flour and cook, stirring constantly, 1 to 2 minutes without allowing to color. Add tomatoes with their juices, beef stock, tomato paste, basil, thyme, and bay leaf. Bring to a boil. Reduce heat to low, cover, and simmer, stirring frequently, 15 minutes. Remove and discard bay leaf.

2. In a food processor or blender, puree soup in batches until smooth. Return to pan and stir in cream. Season with salt and pepper to taste. Simmer until heated through, 3 to 5 minutes, and serve.

37 FRESH TOMATO SOUP WITH PISTOU
Prep: 5 minutes   Cook: 30 minutes   Serves: 6

This soup is at its best when prepared with fresh summer tomatoes and basil. However, canned Italian-style plum tomatoes can be substituted during those months when fresh tomatoes are unavailable.

2 tablespoons olive oil
2 medium onions, chopped
1 medium celery rib, chopped
3 garlic cloves, chopped
3 pounds tomatoes, peeled,
    seeded, and chopped
5 cups Chicken Stock (page
    262) or reduced-sodium
    canned broth

2 teaspoons tomato paste
1 sprig of fresh thyme or
    ½ teaspoon dried thyme
    leaves
1 bay leaf
    Salt and pepper
    Pistou (recipe follows)

1. In a large nonreactive soup pot, heat oil over medium heat. Add onions, celery, and garlic. Cook, stirring frequently, until tender, about 8 minutes. Add tomatoes, chicken stock, tomato paste, thyme, and bay leaf. Bring to a boil, reduce heat to low, and simmer 20 minutes. Remove and discard bay leaf.

2. In a food processor or blender, puree soup in batches until smooth. Return to saucepan and season with salt and pepper to taste. Simmer until heated through, about 2 minutes. Serve topped with Pistou.

38 PISTOU
Prep: 15 minutes   Cook: none   Makes: about 1 cup

Pistou is the French version of the classic recipe for pesto.

3 garlic cloves, crushed
    through a press
1½ cups packed basil leaves
⅔ cup grated Parmesan cheese

Freshly ground black
    pepper
⅔ cup extra-virgin olive oil
    Salt

In a food processor or blender, preferably a small model, combine garlic, basil, Parmesan cheese, and pepper. With machine on, add oil in a stream and puree until well blended. Season with salt to taste.

39   SWEET POTATO SOUP
Prep: 10 minutes   Cook: 38 minutes   Serves: 4

This is a wonderful soup to begin Thanksgiving dinner. Garnish each serving with a dollop of sour cream or nonfat yogurt and pass a basket of Cheddar cheese corn sticks on the side.

2   tablespoons butter
1   medium onion, chopped
1   tablespoon minced fresh
      ginger
1½ pounds sweet potatoes,
      peeled and chopped
6   cups Chicken Stock (page
      262) or reduced-sodium
      canned broth

1   teaspoon grated orange zest
½   teaspoon cinnamon
¼   teaspoon ground allspice
1   cup light cream or
      half-and-half
Salt and pepper

1. In a large saucepan, melt butter over medium heat. Add onion and ginger and cook, stirring frequently, until softened but not browned, about 3 minutes. Add sweet potatoes, chicken stock, orange zest, cinnamon, and allspice. Bring to a boil. Reduce heat to medium-low, cover, and cook 30 minutes.

2. In a food processor or blender, puree soup in batches until smooth. Return to pan and stir in cream. Season with salt and pepper to taste. Simmer until heated through, about 5 minutes, and serve.

40   OLD-FASHIONED CHUNKY VEGETABLE SOUP
Prep: 10 minutes   Cook: 36 to 38 minutes   Serves: 4

3   tablespoons butter
1   large onion, chopped
1   medium celery rib, sliced
2   medium carrots, peeled and
      sliced
5   cups Chicken Stock (page
      262) or reduced-sodium
      canned broth

1   bay leaf
1   cup broccoli florets
1   yellow summer squash,
      sliced ¼ inch thick
Salt and pepper
3   tablespoons minced fresh
      parsley

1. In a large saucepan, melt butter over medium heat. Add onion, celery, and carrots. Reduce heat to low, cover, and cook, stirring frequently, 10 minutes.

2. Add chicken stock and bay leaf. Bring to a boil, reduce heat to medium-low, and cook 20 minutes. Add broccoli and squash. Simmer until vegetables are tender, 6 to 8 minutes. Season with salt and pepper to taste. Stir in parsley just before serving.

41   CREAM OF VEGETABLE SOUP
Prep: 10 minutes   Cook: 40 minutes   Serves: 4

3 tablespoons butter
2 medium onions, chopped
2 medium carrots, peeled and
   sliced
2 medium celery ribs, sliced
4½ cups Chicken Stock (page
   262) or reduced-sodium
   canned broth

1 large red potato, peeled and
   diced
3 garlic cloves, minced
1 bay leaf
½ teaspoon dried thyme leaves
½ cup heavy cream
   Salt and pepper

1. In a large saucepan, melt butter over medium heat. Add onions, carrots, and celery. Cook, stirring occasionally, until vegetables are softened, about 5 minutes. Add chicken stock, potato, garlic, bay leaf, and thyme. Bring to a boil. Cover, reduce heat to low, and simmer 30 minutes. Remove and discard bay leaf.

2. In a food processor or blender, puree soup in batches until smooth. Return to pan and stir in cream. Season with salt and pepper to taste. Simmer until heated through, about 5 minutes, and serve.

42   ITALIAN TOMATO AND BREAD SOUP
Prep: 15 minutes   Stand: 5 minutes   Cook: 25 minutes   Serves: 4

Make this thick soup in the middle of winter to remind yourself of the summer sun.

½ cup extra-virgin olive oil
3 garlic cloves, minced
5 slices of day-old country or
   Italian bread, cut into
   1-inch pieces
¼ teaspoon crushed hot red
   pepper
1 (28-ounce) can crushed
   tomatoes in thick puree

½ teaspoon salt
4 cups Vegetable Stock (page
   266), Chicken Stock (page
   262), or canned vegetable
   broth
16 basil leaves, shredded

1. In a large nonreactive soup pot, heat olive oil over medium-high heat. Add garlic and bread and cook, stirring constantly, until bread is lightly toasted, about 5 minutes.

2. Stir in red pepper, tomatoes, salt, and vegetable stock. Bring to a boil, reduce heat to low, and simmer until thickened, about 20 minutes. Stir in basil and let stand 5 minutes. Serve warm (not hot).

43 ROASTED VEGETABLE SOUP

Prep: 10 minutes   Cook: 1 hour 18 minutes   Serves: 6

Roasted or slightly charred vegetables intensify the flavor of soups and stews and add a pleasing smoky note. The vegetables themselves are easy to prepare and basically cook unattended. The result is well worth the additional cooking time.

1 medium eggplant (about 1 pound), halved lengthwise
2 large onions, quartered
3 tablespoons olive oil
1 large red bell pepper, quartered, cored, and seeded
6 plum tomatoes, halved and seeded

4 garlic cloves
1 teaspoon dried thyme leaves
½ teaspoon dried rosemary
6 cups Chicken Stock (page 262) or reduced-sodium canned broth
Salt and pepper
3 tablespoons minced fresh parsley

1. Preheat oven to 425°F. In a shallow nonreactive baking pan, place eggplant and onions, cut sides down, and brush with half of oil. Bake 30 minutes. Add bell pepper, tomatoes, and garlic. Brush with remaining olive oil and sprinkle with thyme and rosemary. Bake 30 minutes longer, or until vegetables are tender. Chop vegetables and transfer to a large soup pot.

2. Add chicken stock to soup pot and bring to a boil. Reduce heat to medium-low, cover, and cook, stirring frequently, 15 minutes.

3. In a food processor or blender, puree soup in batches until smooth. Return to soup pot and season with salt and pepper to taste. Simmer until heated through, about 3 minutes. Stir in parsley just before serving.

Chapter 2

Chicken and Meat Soups

Lighter than stews but more substantial than vegetable or first-course soups, these wonderful chicken- and meat-based soups make perfect light meals.

One of my fondest childhood memories is of midwinter school lunches featuring my favorite soup—piping hot. I can still smell the comforting aroma of chicken noodle soup as I poured it from my lunch box thermos. I also remember the envy in the eyes of all around me. I would sit in class most of the morning waiting for the lunch bell to ring—with great expectation. There is nothing more inviting than a steaming bowl of soup on a cold winter's day.

Equally good as adult fare, serve these soups accompanied by a salad and good wholesome bread—warmed or toasted. What would make a finer lunch than Portuguese Chicken Soup with Lemon and Mint or Italian Meatball Soup followed by a grilled vegetable salad—perhaps with a sprinkling of some feta cheese—and some crusty bread? These soups are ideal for light suppers as well.

44 CHICKEN NOODLE SOUP WITH CARROTS AND PARSNIPS
Prep: 25 minutes   Cook: 12 to 14 minutes   Serves: 6

Try this updated version of an old favorite.

2 tablespoons olive oil
2 shallots, minced
2 medium carrots, peeled and chopped
2 medium parsnips, peeled and chopped
1 (1-inch) piece of fresh ginger, peeled and grated
1 teaspoon ground cumin

Pinch of cayenne
6 cups Chicken Stock (page 262) or reduced-sodium canned broth
1 cup fine egg noodles
1½ cups diced cooked chicken
2 teaspoons grated lemon zest
1 tablespoon lemon juice

1. In a soup pot, heat oil over medium-high heat. Add shallots, carrots, and parsnips and cook, stirring occasionally, 5 minutes. Stir in ginger, cumin, cayenne, and chicken stock and bring to a boil.

2. Stir in noodles and cook until tender but still firm, 5 to 7 minutes. Stir in chicken, lemon zest, and lemon juice. Simmer 2 minutes to heat through and serve.

45 CURRIED CHICKEN SOUP WITH RICE NOODLES

Prep: 20 minutes   Cook: 33 to 37 minutes   Serves: 4

This soup was inspired by a great Vietnamese soup restaurant in New York's Chinatown.

1 tablespoon vegetable oil
1 pound chicken thighs, skinned
½ teaspoon ground cumin
½ teaspoon ground coriander
¼ teaspoon ground turmeric
⅛ teaspoon crushed hot red pepper
1 (1-inch) piece of fresh ginger, peeled and grated

3 garlic cloves, chopped
3 shallots, thinly sliced
6 cups Chicken Stock (page 262) or reduced-sodium canned broth
½ pound red potatoes, peeled and cut into 1-inch dice
¼ pound rice noodles (dried rice sticks)
½ teaspoon salt

1. In a large saucepan, heat oil over medium-high heat. Add chicken and cook, turning occasionally, until browned on both sides, 6 to 8 minutes. With a slotted spoon, transfer chicken to a plate.

2. In a small bowl, combine cumin, coriander, turmeric, hot pepper, ginger, garlic, and shallots. Add to saucepan and cook over medium-high heat, stirring constantly, 1 minute. Add chicken stock and bring to a boil.

3. Cut chicken into 1-inch cubes. Add chicken and potatoes to soup. Reduce heat to medium-low, partially cover, and cook until potatoes are tender, about 20 minutes. Add noodles and salt, simmer until noodles are tender but still firm, 6 to 8 minutes, and serve.

46 CHICKEN ALPHABET SOUP

Prep: 40 minutes   Cook: 1 hour 3 minutes   Serves: 8

Kids will love this simple chicken soup.

1 whole chicken (about 3 pounds), quartered
3 large carrots, peeled
6 garlic cloves, peeled
1 bay leaf
1 cup alphabet pasta
¾ teaspoon salt

½ teaspoon pepper
1 cup frozen peas, thawed
4 plum tomatoes, seeded and chopped
3 tablespoons chopped fresh mint

1. In a large soup pot, combine chicken, 10 cups water, carrots, garlic, and bay leaf. Bring to a boil, skimming occasionally. Reduce heat to medium-low and cook 45 minutes. With a slotted spoon, remove carrots from stock and cut into ½-inch-thick slices. Remove chicken from stock and set aside to cool. Meanwhile, remove and discard garlic and bay leaf from stock and simmer 10 minutes longer to reduce slightly.

2. Remove skin and bones from chicken. Tear chicken into bite-size pieces.

3. Bring chicken soup to a boil. Stir in pasta, salt, and pepper and boil until pasta is tender but still firm, about 5 minutes. Stir in peas, tomatoes, carrots, chicken, and mint, reduce heat, and simmer 3 minutes. Serve hot.

---

47   CHICKEN TORTILLA SOUP
Prep: 10 minutes   Cook: 33 to 34 minutes   Serves: 4

1 (14½-ounce) can Italian peeled tomatoes, juices reserved
3 tablespoons vegetable oil, plus additional for frying
1 whole skinless, boneless chicken breast, halved
1 medium onion, chopped
3 garlic cloves, minced
2 teaspoons chili powder
2 teaspoons ground cumin
6 cups Chicken Stock (page 262) or reduced-sodium canned broth

1 tablespoon tomato paste
1 (4-ounce) can chopped mild green chiles, drained
1 tablespoon minced seeded jalapeño peppers (about 2), or to taste
4 corn tortillas, cut into ½-inch-wide strips
2 tablespoons chopped cilantro
Salt and pepper
2 tablespoons grated Parmesan cheese

1. In a food processor or blender, puree tomatoes with their juices until smooth.

2. In a large nonreactive saucepan, heat 2 tablespoons oil over medium heat. Add chicken and cook 3 minutes on each side, or until golden brown on both sides. Transfer chicken to a plate. Heat remaining 1 tablespoon oil in saucepan. Add onion and cook, stirring frequently, until golden, about 5 minutes. Add garlic, chili powder, and cumin and cook, stirring frequently, 1 minute. Add chicken stock, pureed tomatoes, tomato paste, chiles, and jalapeño peppers.

3. Return chicken to saucepan and bring to a boil. Reduce heat to low, cover, and simmer 20 minutes. Transfer chicken to a cutting board, cut into strips, and return to saucepan.

4. In a large skillet, heat ½ inch of vegetable oil over medium-high heat. Add tortilla strips in batches and cook, stirring frequently, until crisp, 1 to 2 minutes. Transfer tortilla strips to a plate lined with paper towels.

5. Skim surface of soup and stir in cilantro. Season with salt and pepper to taste. Divide tortillas among 4 soup bowls and ladle soup over tortillas. Serve sprinkled with cheese.

48   CHICKEN SOUP PRIMAVERA

Prep: 20 minutes   Cook: 21 to 23 minutes   Serves: 6

Vary the vegetables according to the season, substituting fresh asparagus, fresh peas, or fresh mushrooms for the squash.

2 tablespoons olive oil	6 ounces egg noodles
1 medium onion, chopped	1 pound skinless, boneless
1 large red bell pepper, chopped	chicken thighs, cut into ½-inch dice
1 large carrot, peeled and chopped	1 zucchini, trimmed, cut in half lengthwise, and sliced
2 garlic cloves, minced	sliced
5 cups Chicken Stock (page 262) or reduced-sodium canned broth	1 yellow squash, trimmed, cut in half lengthwise, and sliced
1 (8-ounce) can tomato sauce	2 tablespoons chopped fresh basil or parsley
½ teaspoon dried thyme leaves	basil or parsley
½ teaspoon dried rosemary	Salt and black pepper

1. In a soup pot, heat olive oil over medium heat. Add onion, bell pepper, carrot, and garlic. Cook, stirring occasionally, until softened, about 5 minutes. Add chicken stock, tomato sauce, thyme, and rosemary. Bring to a boil, reduce heat to low, and simmer, stirring occasionally, 5 minutes. Add noodles and simmer 5 minutes longer.

2. Add chicken, zucchini, and yellow squash to soup pot and return to a boil. Reduce heat to medium-low and simmer, stirring occasionally, until chicken is no longer pink in center, 6 to 8 minutes. Stir in basil and season with salt and pepper to taste.

49   CHICKEN SOUP WITH MATZO BALLS

Prep: 15 minutes   Cook: 35 to 40 minutes   Chill: 2 hours   Serves: 6

The addition of seltzer to the matzo ball mix here results in a lighter dumpling.

3 eggs, separated	1 cup matzo meal
3 tablespoons minced fresh parsley	1 large carrot, peeled and sliced
⅓ cup seltzer	1 medium celery rib, sliced
¼ cup vegetable oil	8 cups Chicken Stock (page
½ teaspoon salt	262) or reduced-sodium
¼ teaspoon pepper	canned broth

1. In a medium bowl, whisk together egg yolks, parsley, seltzer, 3 tablespoons oil, ¼ teaspoon salt, and ⅛ teaspoon pepper until well blended. In another small bowl, beat egg whites until stiff peaks form. Stir matzo meal into egg yolk mixture and fold in whites. Cover and refrigerate until well chilled, at least 2 hours.

2. With dampened hands, shape matzo mixture into 12 balls. Cover and refrigerate until ready to cook.

3. In a large saucepan, heat remaining 1 tablespoon oil over medium heat. Add carrot and celery and cook, stirring occasionally, until softened, about 5 minutes. Add chicken stock and remaining ¼ teaspoon salt and ⅛ teaspoon pepper. Bring to a boil and reduce heat to low. Add matzo balls, cover, and simmer until matzo balls puff up, rise to surface of soup, and are cooked through, 30 to 35 minutes. Serve hot.

50 MOROCCAN SPICED LENTIL SOUP WITH CHICKEN AND LAMB

Prep: 25 minutes   Cook: 1 hour 11 minutes to 1 hour 25 minutes
Serves: 6

This is a version of the famous Moroccan soup Harira, eaten at sunset every day during Ramadan. It is substantial enough to eat as a main course.

<table>
<tr><td>

2 tablespoons butter
2 large onions, chopped
2 celery ribs with leaves, chopped
½ cup chopped parsley
½ teaspoon ground turmeric
½ teaspoon cinnamon
¼ teaspoon saffron threads, crushed
1 pound chicken thighs, skinned

</td><td>

½ pound lamb shoulder, cut into ½-inch chunks
1 cup lentils, rinsed and picked over
1 cup tomato puree
1 teaspoon salt
¼ cup chopped cilantro
1 cup fine egg noodles
½ teaspoon pepper
6 lemon slices

</td></tr>
</table>

1. In a large soup pot, melt butter over medium heat. Add onions, celery, and ¼ cup parsley and cook, stirring occasionally, until vegetables are softened but not browned, 3 to 5 minutes. Stir in turmeric, cinnamon, saffron, chicken, and lamb. Cook, stirring occasionally, until meat is no longer pink, 8 to 10 minutes.

2. Stir in lentils, tomato puree, salt, 2 tablespoons cilantro, and 6 cups water. Simmer, partially covered, until both lamb and lentils are tender, 50 to 60 minutes.

3. Add noodles, pepper, and remaining ¼ cup parsley and 2 tablespoons cilantro. Simmer 10 minutes longer.

4. To serve, ladle soup into bowls and top each serving with a lemon slice.

51 SENEGALESE CREAMY CURRIED CHICKEN SOUP

Prep: 10 minutes   Cook: 3 to 4 minutes   Chill: 2 hours   Serves: 4

Senegalese is the traditional name for this classic, chilled chicken soup flavored with curry.

2 tablespoons butter
3 shallots, minced
1 tablespoon flour
1 tablespoon curry powder
¼ teaspoon ground cumin
   Pinch of cayenne
3 cups Chicken Stock (page 262) or reduced-sodium canned broth

2 egg yolks
½ cup heavy cream
1 skinless, boneless chicken breast, cooked and cut into bite-size pieces
½ cup sprigs of fresh watercress

1. In a medium saucepan, melt butter over medium heat. Add shallots and cook, stirring, until softened, about 2 minutes. Stir in flour, curry powder, cumin, and cayenne. Cook, stirring constantly, 1 to 2 minutes without allowing to color. Gradually whisk in chicken stock and bring to a boil.

2. In a small bowl, whisk together egg yolks and cream. Remove saucepan from heat and slowly pour egg mixture into saucepan, whisking constantly. Return saucepan to heat and bring just to a simmer.

3. Remove soup from heat and let cool slightly. Stir in chicken, cover, and refrigerate until well chilled, at least 2 hours. To serve, ladle soup into bowls and garnish each serving with watercress.

52 PORTUGUESE CHICKEN SOUP WITH LEMON AND MINT

Prep: 15 minutes   Cook: 32 to 38 minutes   Serves: 6

6 cups Chicken Stock (page 262) or reduced-sodium canned broth
1 pound chicken thighs
1 large onion, chopped
2 garlic cloves
3 sprigs of fresh parsley
½ teaspoon salt

3 (2 x 1-inch) strips of lemon zest
1½ cups cooked long-grain white rice
2 teaspoons lemon juice
½ cup chopped fresh mint or cilantro
½ teaspoon pepper

1. In a large saucepan, combine chicken stock, chicken, onion, garlic, parsley, and salt. Bring to a boil, reduce heat to medium-low, and cook until chicken is no longer pink in center, 30 to 35 minutes. Strain soup through a fine sieve and discard all solids except chicken. Remove skin and bones from chicken; cut meat into bite-size pieces.

2. Return soup to saucepan and bring to a boil. Return chicken to saucepan. Reduce heat to low. Add rice, lemon juice, mint, and pepper. Simmer until heated through, 2 to 3 minutes longer, and serve.

---

53 CHINESE SMOKED CHICKEN AND NOODLE SOUP

Prep: 20 minutes   Stand: 15 minutes   Cook: 10 minutes   Serves: 4

Smoked chicken gives this soup a delicate, smoky flavor. Or if you prefer, use 1 cup chopped ham instead.

6 dried shiitake mushrooms
2 teaspoons vegetable oil
4 cups Chicken Stock (page 262) or reduced-sodium canned broth
½ pound fresh Chinese noodles or capellini or thin spaghetti
½ smoked chicken breast, boned, skinned, and torn into bite-size pieces (about 1½ cups)

1 cup trimmed fresh snow peas (about 2 ounces)
2 cups shredded bok choy
2 tablespoons reduced-sodium soy sauce
1 tablespoon dry sherry
2 scallions, thinly sliced

1. In a medium heatproof bowl, cover mushrooms with 1 cup boiling water and let stand 15 minutes. Drain mushrooms; discard liquid. Cut off and discard mushroom stems and slice caps.

2. In a large saucepan, heat oil over medium-high heat. Add mushrooms and cook, stirring, until tender, 2 minutes. Add chicken stock and bring to a boil. Add noodles, reduce heat to low, and simmer 3 minutes.

3. Stir in chicken, snow peas, bok choy, soy sauce, sherry, and scallions, cook until heated through, about 5 minutes longer, and serve.

54 SPICY CHICKEN NOODLE SOUP WITH CORN AND CUMIN

Prep: 20 minutes   Cook: 10 minutes   Serves: 4

The robust flavors of the Southwest are featured in this chunky soup. For a change of pace, make it with turkey instead of chicken.

1 cup corn kernels (1 or 2 ears)
1 tablespoon vegetable oil
1 medium onion, chopped
4 garlic cloves, minced
½ teaspoon ground cumin
½ teaspoon dried marjoram
½ teaspoon minced canned chipotle chile or ¼ to ½ teaspoon cayenne, to taste

½ teaspoon sugar
6 cups Chicken Stock (page 262) or reduced-sodium canned broth
1 cup broken capellini or thin spaghetti
1½ cups diced cooked chicken
1 medium zucchini, cut in half lengthwise and thinly sliced

1. Cut kernels off corn cobs. Reserve kernels and discard cobs. In a large saucepan, heat oil over medium-high heat. Add onion and cook, stirring occasionally, 5 minutes. Stir in garlic, cumin, marjoram, chile, sugar, and chicken stock and bring to a boil.

2. Add capellini, corn, chicken, and zucchini. Reduce heat to low and simmer 5 minutes.

55 TURKEY CHOWDER

Prep: 10 minutes   Cook: 36 to 39 minutes   Serves: 4 to 6

¼ pound lean bacon, cut into 1-inch pieces
3 tablespoons butter
1 medium onion, chopped
2 medium celery ribs, chopped
1½ cups fresh or thawed frozen corn kernels
3 tablespoons flour
4 cups Chicken Stock (page 262) or reduced-sodium canned broth

½ teaspoon dried thyme leaves
1 bay leaf
2 cups chopped cooked turkey
1 cup light cream or milk
½ teaspoon salt
½ teaspoon pepper
2 tablespoons chopped parsley

1. In a large soup pot, cook bacon over medium heat, stirring occasionally, until crisp, 4 to 5 minutes. With a slotted spoon, transfer bacon to paper towels to drain. Pour off fat from pot.

2. Add butter to same pot and melt over medium heat. Add onion and celery and cook, stirring frequently, until softened but not browned, 3 to 5 minutes. Stir in corn and cook 2 minutes longer.

3. Add flour and cook, stirring constantly, about 2 minutes without allowing to brown. Add chicken stock, thyme, and bay leaf. Bring to a boil, reduce heat to medium, and cook, stirring occasionally, 20 minutes.

4. Add turkey, bacon, cream, salt, and pepper to soup. Simmer 5 minutes. Remove and discard bay leaf. Sprinkle soup bowls with parsley and serve.

56 TURKEY AND WILD RICE SOUP
Prep: 10 minutes   Cook: 36 to 37 minutes   Serves 4 to 6

This is a wonderful way to use up leftover Thanksgiving turkey.

3 tablespoons butter
1 medium onion, chopped
1 medium celery rib, chopped
1 medium carrot, peeled and
   chopped
2 garlic cloves, minced
2 tablespoons flour
5 cups Chicken Stock (page
   262) or reduced-sodium
   canned broth

1 cup milk
1 bay leaf
1½ teaspoons minced fresh sage
   or ½ teaspoon dried
2 cups chopped cooked
   turkey
1 cup cooked wild rice
   Salt and pepper

1. In a large saucepan, melt butter over medium heat. Add onion, celery, carrot, and garlic. Cook, stirring frequently, until onion is softened, about 5 minutes.

2. Add flour and cook, stirring constantly, 1 to 2 minutes without allowing to brown. Add chicken stock, milk, bay leaf, and sage. Bring to a boil, stirring often, until slightly thickened. Reduce heat to medium-low, cover, and cook 20 minutes.

3. Add turkey and wild rice. Season with salt and pepper to taste and simmer, stirring occasionally, until heated through, about 10 minutes. Remove and discard bay leaf before serving.

57 OLD-FASHIONED BEEF AND VEGETABLE SOUP

Prep: 10 minutes   Cook: 1 hour 3 minutes to 1 hour 10 minutes
Serves: 4

2 tablespoons vegetable oil
1 pound boneless beef chuck,
   cut into 1-inch pieces
1 teaspoon salt
½ teaspoon pepper
2 medium onions, sliced
3 celery ribs, sliced
3 garlic cloves, minced
1 (14½-ounce) can Italian
   peeled tomatoes,
   chopped, juices reserved
4 cups Chicken Stock (page
   262) or reduced-sodium
   canned broth

1 teaspoon dried thyme leaves
½ teaspoon dried rosemary
1 bay leaf
3 medium potatoes, peeled
   and cut into ½-inch dice
1 large carrot, peeled and
   sliced
1½ cups shredded cabbage
3 tablespoons chopped
   parsley

1. In a large flameproof casserole, heat oil over medium heat. Add meat and season with ½ teaspoon salt and ¼ teaspoon pepper. Cook, stirring occasionally, until browned all over, about 5 minutes. With slotted spoon, transfer meat to a plate.

2. Add onions and celery to casserole and cook, stirring occasionally, until softened, 3 to 5 minutes. Add garlic, tomatoes with their juices, chicken stock, thyme, rosemary, bay leaf, and remaining ½ teaspoon salt and ¼ teaspoon pepper. Return meat to casserole. Bring to a boil, reduce to low, and simmer 30 minutes.

3. Add potatoes, carrot, and cabbage to soup. Bring to a boil, reduce heat to low, cover, and simmer until vegetables and meat are tender, 25 to 30 minutes. Remove and discard bay leaf. Stir in parsley and season with additional salt and pepper to taste.

58   BEEFY BORSCHT

Prep: 10 minutes   Cook: 2 hours 53 minutes to 2 hours 55 minutes
Serves: 6 to 8

This is one of our favorite soups—a meaty version of the classic beet soup. With a simple salad and some warm crusty rolls, it makes a perfect Sunday night supper, particularly during the cold weather months.

2 pounds beef short ribs
5 medium onions—3 whole stuck with 2 whole cloves each, 2 thinly sliced
2 carrots, peeled and quartered
1 large celery rib, thickly sliced
1 bay leaf
2 sprigs of fresh thyme or 1 teaspoon dried thyme leaves
3 tablespoons butter

2 garlic cloves, minced
2 pounds beets, peeled and shredded
1 medium potato, peeled and shredded
3 tablespoons red wine vinegar
2 teaspoons salt
½ teaspoon pepper
¼ cup minced fresh dill
Sour cream and sprigs of fresh dill

1. In a large soup pot, combine short ribs, whole onions stuck with cloves, carrots, celery, bay leaf, thyme, and 3 quarts water. Bring to a boil, reduce heat to low, and simmer, skimming occasionally, 2 hours.

2. Remove ribs and stock from soup pot. Rinse out pot. Cut meat into small slivers and discard bones and fat. Strain stock through a fine sieve back into pot. Boil over medium-high heat until stock is reduced to 8 cups, 5 to 7 minutes.

3. In a large saucepan, melt butter over medium heat. Add sliced onions and garlic and cook, stirring frequently, until onions are golden, about 8 minutes. Add beets, potato, reserved stock, vinegar, salt, and pepper. Bring to a boil, reduce heat to medium-low, and cook 20 minutes.

4. Add reserved meat and simmer 20 minutes longer. Stir in minced dill and season with additional salt and pepper to taste. Garnish each serving with a dollop of sour cream and dill sprigs.

59 POTATO, CABBAGE, AND SMOKED SAUSAGE SOUP

Prep: 15 minutes   Cook: 30 minutes   Serves: 4

2 tablespoons vegetable oil
2 medium onions, sliced
½ pound knockwurst or smoked kielbasa, sliced ¼-inch thick
1 pound red potatoes, peeled and cut into 1-inch dice
4 cups Simple Beef Stock (page 264) or reduced-sodium canned broth

1 teaspoon caraway seed
¼ teaspoon salt
¼ teaspoon pepper
2 cups shredded cabbage
¼ cup sour cream
¼ teaspoon minced fresh dill

1. In a large flameproof casserole, heat oil over medium heat. Add onions and cook, stirring occasionally, until golden, 5 minutes. Add sausage and cook, turning occasionally, until lightly browned all over, about 5 minutes. Add potatoes, beef stock, caraway seed, salt, and pepper. Bring to a boil. Reduce heat to low, cover, and simmer 10 minutes.

2. Add cabbage and simmer until vegetables are tender, about 10 minutes. Garnish each serving with a dollop of sour cream and a sprinkling of dill.

60 VIETNAMESE ONE-POT BEEF SOUP WITH LEMONGRASS AND RICE NOODLES

Prep: 15 minutes   Cook: 10 minutes   Freeze: 15 minutes   Serves: 4

This hearty one-pot soup is a staple of Vietnamese cuisine.

2 tablespoons coarsely chopped peanuts
¼ pound round steak
6 cups Simple Beef Stock (page 264) or reduced-sodium canned broth
2 stalks of lemongrass
1 star anise pod
1 (2-inch) piece of cinnamon stick

4 thin slices of peeled fresh ginger
¼ pound rice noodles (dried rice sticks)
2 tablespoons Thai fish sauce *(nam pla)* or soy sauce
¼ cup cilantro leaves
½ cup fresh basil
½ cup fresh mint

1. In a small skillet, toast peanuts over medium heat, stirring constantly, until lightly browned, about 5 minutes. Set aside.

2. Meanwhile, freeze the beef for 15 minutes. Slice as thinly as possible and set aside.

3. Trim off tops of lemongrass stalks. Remove and discard outer leaves. Cut lemongrass into 1-inch pieces. Crush lightly with flat side of a large knife.

4. In a large saucepan, combine beef stock, anise pod, cinnamon stick, ginger, and lemongrass and bring to a boil. Stir in rice noodles and fish sauce. Reduce heat to low and simmer until noodles are tender, about 5 minutes.

5. Place meat slices in soup bowls. Pour soup and noodles over meat (this cooks the meat). Sprinkle with cilantro, basil, mint, and peanuts.

---

61   CHINESE HOT AND SOUR SOUP

Prep: 25 minutes   Stand: 15 minutes   Cook: 23½ to 26 minutes
Serves: 4

The Chinese ingredients used in this wonderfully warming soup can be found at Asian markets, specialty food shops, and in many large supermarkets.

6 dried black Chinese
   mushrooms
⅓ cup tree ear mushrooms
3 tablespoons cider vinegar or
   red wine vinegar
2 teaspoons sugar
3 tablespoons soy sauce
2 tablespoons cornstarch
½ teaspoon freshly ground
   pepper
1 tablespoon vegetable oil

¼ pound shredded pork
5 cups Chicken Stock (page
   262) or reduced-sodium
   canned broth
4 scallions, sliced
⅓ cup bamboo shoots
1 egg, lightly beaten
1 (3-inch) square of firm bean
   curd, diced
1 tablespoon Asian sesame oil

1. In a medium heatproof bowl, cover dried mushrooms and tree ears with boiling water and let stand 15 minutes; drain and discard liquid. Cut off and discard stems from mushrooms; slice caps.

2. In a small bowl, combine vinegar, sugar, soy sauce, cornstarch, 3 tablespoons water, and pepper. Stir to dissolve sugar and blend well.

3. In a large saucepan, heat vegetable oil over medium-high heat. Add pork and stir-fry until no longer pink, 2 to 3 minutes. Add chicken stock, sliced mushrooms, tree ears, scallions, and bamboo shoots. Bring to a boil, reduce heat to medium-low, and cook 20 minutes.

4. Stir reserved cornstarch mixture and add to hot soup. Bring to a boil, stirring, until thickened, 1 to 2 minutes. Stir in beaten egg in a thin stream. Cook, stirring constantly, just until egg sets, 30 to 60 seconds. Stir in bean curd and sesame oil. Serve at once.

62   OXTAIL SOUP

Prep: 10 minutes   Cook: 3 hours 15 minutes to 3 hours 20 minutes
Serves: 4

Oxtails are extremely flavorful and produce a wonderfully robust broth. Although the cooking time is long, it is virtually unattended.

2 **pounds lean oxtail, cut into 2½-inch lengths**
4 **cups Simple Beef Stock (page 264) or reduced-sodium canned broth**
1 **large onion, stuck with 4 whole cloves**
2 **medium celery ribs, sliced**
1 **large carrot, peeled and sliced**

¼ **pound mushrooms, sliced**
1 **teaspoon dried thyme leaves**
1 **large bay leaf**
6 **black peppercorns**
1 **teaspoon salt**
¼ **cup pastina or other tiny pasta**

1. Place oxtails in a soup pot. Add enough cold water to cover. Bring to a boil. Reduce heat to medium and cook 5 minutes. Drain oxtails and discard liquid. Rinse oxtails and return to soup pot. Add beef stock, 4 cups water, onion stuck with cloves, celery, carrot, mushrooms, thyme, bay leaf, peppercorns, and salt. Bring to a boil. Reduce heat to medium-low, cover, and cook until meat is tender, about 3 hours.

2. With a slotted spoon, transfer oxtails to a cutting board. As soon as it is cool enough to handle, remove meat from bones and cut into 1-inch pieces. Discard bones. Skim fat and peppercorns from cooking liquid. Remove and discard bay leaf.

3. In a food processor, puree liquid with vegetables in batches until smooth. Strain through a medium sieve, pressing hard on solids to extract as much liquid as possible. Discard liquid. Return puree to soup pot and add meat. Bring to a boil. Add pastina and cook over medium heat, stirring frequently, until pasta is tender but still firm, 5 to 7 minutes.

63   ITALIAN MEATBALL SOUP
Prep: 20 minutes   Cook: 50 to 52 minutes   Serves: 6

2 tablespoons olive oil
2 medium onions, chopped
2 medium celery ribs, chopped
1 small carrot, peeled and chopped
5 garlic cloves, minced
1 (28-ounce) can crushed tomatoes, juices reserved
8 cups Chicken Stock (page 262) or reduced-sodium canned broth
1 teaspoon dried basil
1 bay leaf

1½ teaspoons salt
½ teaspoon pepper
2 slices of white bread, crusts removed
½ cup milk
2 tablespoons butter
½ pound ground veal
1 egg, lightly beaten
3 tablespoons minced fresh parsley
⅓ cup flour
4 ounces spaghettini, broken into 2-inch lengths

1. In a nonreactive soup pot, heat oil over medium-low heat. Add ¾ cup onion, celery, carrot, and 1 tablespoon garlic. Cover and cook, stirring occasionally, until vegetables are crisp-tender, 10 minutes. Add tomatoes with their juices, chicken stock, basil, bay leaf, ½ teaspoon salt, and ¼ teaspoon pepper. Bring to a boil, reduce heat to medium-low, and cook, partially covered, stirring occasionally, 20 minutes. Remove and discard bay leaf.

2. Meanwhile, in a small bowl, soak bread in milk until soft. Gently squeeze bread dry, discarding liquid.

3. In a small skillet, melt butter over medium heat. Add remaining onion and garlic and cook, stirring occasionally, until onion is golden, about 5 minutes. Transfer onion and garlic to a medium bowl. Add softened bread, veal, egg, 1 tablespoon parsley, remaining 1 teaspoon salt, and ¼ teaspoon pepper to bowl. Mix with hands until well blended and form into meatballs about 1 inch in diameter. Dredge to coat lightly with flour; shake off excess flour.

4. Carefully drop meatballs into simmering broth and cook 10 minutes. Add spaghettini and cook until tender but still firm, 5 to 7 minutes. Stir in remaining 2 tablespoons parsley just before serving.

64 SCOTCH BROTH

Prep: 30 minutes   Cook: 2 to 2½ hours   Serves: 6

This soup is particularly good on a cold winter's day when served with toasted whole grain bread.

2 **pounds lean lamb neck, cut into 2-inch pieces**
2 **medium onions, minced**
2 **medium carrots, peeled and chopped**
1 **small turnip, chopped**
1 **medium leek (white and tender green), well rinsed and sliced**

½ **cup medium pearl barley**
8 **cups Lamb Stock (page 265), Simple Beef Stock (page 264), or reduced-sodium canned beef broth**
2 **teaspoons salt**
½ **teaspoon pepper**
3 **tablespoons minced fresh parsley**

1. In a soup pot, combine lamb, onions, carrots, turnip, leek, barley, lamb stock, salt, and pepper. Bring to a boil. Reduce heat to low, cover, and simmer, skimming surface and stirring occasionally, until meat and vegetables are tender, 2 to 2½ hours.

2. Remove meat from bones. Discard bones and return to meat pan. Simmer to heat through, 2 to 3 minutes. Sprinkle each serving with parsley.

65 PORTUGUESE GREEN SOUP

Prep: 10 minutes   Cook: 42 to 47 minutes   Serves: 4

Bright green in color and very satisfying, this showstopping *caldo gallego* becomes a meal when served with a crusty bread.

¼ **cup olive oil**
2 **medium onions, finely chopped**
3 **garlic cloves, minced**
4 **medium red potatoes, peeled and cut into 1-inch dice**
6 **cups Chicken Stock (page 262) or reduced-sodium canned broth**

½ **pound chorizo or kielbasa, thinly sliced**
½ **teaspoon salt**
¼ **teaspoon pepper**
1 **pound greens, such as kale, collards, or turnip greens, well rinsed, trimmed, and thinly shredded**

1. In a large saucepan, heat 3 tablespoons oil over medium-high heat. Add onions and cook, stirring constantly, until golden, about 5 minutes. Add garlic and cook, stirring constantly, until fragrant, about 1 minute. Add potatoes and cook, stirring frequently, 5 minutes longer. Stir in chicken stock and 2 cups water and bring to a boil. Reduce heat to medium-low, cover, and simmer until potatoes are softened, about 15 minutes.

2. In a large nonstick skillet, heat remaining 1 tablespoon oil over medium heat. Add sausage and cook, turning occasionally, until golden, 6 to 8 minutes. Remove sausage to paper towels to drain.

3. With a potato masher, mash potatoes directly in saucepan. Add sausage, salt, and pepper. Bring to a boil, reduce heat to low, and simmer 5 minutes. Add greens and simmer until tender, about 5 to 8 minutes longer.

66 BEEF CONSOMMÉ

Prep: 10 minutes   Cook: 20 minutes   Makes: 6 cups

A consommé is a stock or broth that has been cooked down, resulting in a more concentrated flavor. A genuine consommé includes crushed eggshells, egg whites, and raw meat, all of which help to clarify the finished recipe. Be sure to remove the fat from the basic beef stock before preparing this consommé for a lower-fat version.

8 cups defatted Brown Beef
   Stock (page 264)
   Crushed shells from 4 large
   eggs
4 large egg whites, lightly
   beaten
2 whole leeks (white and
   green parts), well rinsed
   and sliced

2 tomatoes, chopped
1 large carrot, peeled and
   diced
1 celery rib, sliced
½ pound ground beef
¼ teaspoon salt

1. In a nonreactive soup pot, combine beef stock, eggshells, egg whites, leeks, tomatoes, carrot, celery, ground beef, and salt. Bring to a boil, stirring frequently. Reduce heat to low and simmer, undisturbed, 20 minutes.

2. Ladle stock through a fine sieve lined with a double thickness of rinsed and squeezed cheesecloth. Serve hot.

Variation

CHICKEN CONSOMMÉ

Prepare recipe as directed, but substitute Chicken Stock (page 262) for beef stock and ground chicken for ground beef.

Chapter 3

Short-Cut Soups

For many people, finding the time to make soup seems about as likely as squeezing the soup from a stone—in their minds, next to impossible. Plus, homemade soup has a reputation for being long-cooking and time consuming. At the end of a long day, most people head for the can opener and make do with less-than-satisfying canned soups. In this chapter, we offer some delicious soup solutions to the ever-present no-time-to-cook problem.

If you're throwing a simple dinner party and want a first course that won't keep you in the kitchen for hours, try the Cauliflower and Cheddar Soup or the Cream of Watercress Soup. Both simple and quite elegant, either can be quickly thrown together. Get home late and need to get a fast dinner on the table? Try the Sausage, Potato, and Cabbage Soup. Add some store-bought focaccia or corn bread and a green salad and dinner is served.

For a great summery soup, try the Quick Three-Bean Soup with Fresh Tomato Salsa. Or for wintry dinners, try the Parsnip Chowder with warm rolls and a steamed vegetable. This chapter offers living proof: combine a small amount of chopping, some canned broth and select ingredients, and a great homemade soup can be served up in no time at all.

67 ITALIAN EGG DROP SOUP
Prep: 3 minutes   Cook: 2 minutes   Serves: 4

Serve this soup with Parmesan Toasts (page 236).

5 cups Chicken Stock (page 262) or reduced-sodium canned broth
2 eggs
¼ cup grated Parmesan cheese
¼ cup minced Italian (flat-leaf) parsley
Salt and pepper

1. In a large saucepan, bring stock to a boil.

2. In a medium bowl, beat eggs with a fork until foamy. Mix in Parmesan cheese and parsley.

3. Reduce heat to low. Drizzle eggs into stock while stirring gently to make ribbons. Cook just until eggs are set, about 2 minutes. Season with salt and pepper to taste. Serve at once.

68   CHINESE EGG DROP SOUP
Prep: 5 minutes   Cook: 17 to 18 minutes   Serves: 4

Pure and simple—an all-time favorite with us.

6 cups Chicken Stock (page
      262) or reduced-sodium
      canned broth
1 (1-inch) piece of fresh
      ginger, peeled and thinly
      sliced

3 large garlic cloves, minced
2 tablespoons soy sauce
4 teaspoons cornstarch
2 eggs, lightly beaten
      Minced scallions

1. In a large saucepan, combine chicken stock, ginger, and garlic. Bring to a boil, reduce heat to low, and simmer 15 minutes. Strain broth through a fine sieve and return stock to pan.

2. Bring stock to a boil again, reduce heat to low, and add soy sauce. In a small bowl, blend cornstarch with 2 tablespoons water. Stir into broth and return to a boil, stirring constantly until thickened, 1 to 2 minutes. Reduce heat to low.

3. Drizzle eggs into soup, stirring gently. Simmer until drops are set, about 1 minute. Garnish each serving with scallions and serve at once.

69   GREEK EGG AND LEMON SOUP
Prep: 5 minutes   Cook: 3 minutes   Serves: 4

Avgolemono is the traditional name for this soup. To prepare a more robust soup version, use lamb stock and stir in 1½ cups cooked orzo, tiny rice-shaped pasta, at the end of the cooking time.

5 cups Chicken Stock (page
      262) or reduced-sodium
      canned broth
3 eggs, lightly beaten

¼ cup lemon juice
1 tablespoon minced fresh
      dill
      Salt and pepper

1. In a nonreactive saucepan, bring chicken stock to a boil. Reduce heat to medium-low.

2. In a small bowl, whisk together eggs and lemon juice until foamy. Gradually whisk in 1 cup hot stock in a stream. Whisk stock and egg mixture back into pan.

3. Cook soup over medium-low heat, stirring constantly, until slightly thickened, about 3 minutes. Stir in dill and season with salt and pepper to taste. Serve at once.

70   QUICK THREE-BEAN SOUP WITH FRESH TOMATO SALSA

Prep: 5 minutes   Cook: 12 minutes   Serves: 4

Make this fresh-tasting soup when tomatoes are at their peak of flavor.

1 (10-ounce) can garbanzo beans, undrained
1 (10-ounce) package frozen cut green beans, thawed
3 cups Vegetable Stock (page 266) or canned broth

1 (10-ounce) package frozen baby peas
Fresh Tomato Salsa (recipe follows)

1. In a large soup pot, combine garbanzo beans, green beans, and vegetable stock and bring to a boil. Reduce heat to medium-low and cook 7 minutes.

2. Stir in frozen peas and cook 5 minutes longer. Ladle soup into bowls and top each serving with Fresh Tomato Salsa.

71   FRESH TOMATO SALSA

Prep: 25 minutes   Cook: none   Serves: 4 to 6

6 plum tomatoes, halved and seeded
½ medium red onion, cut into chunks
4 garlic cloves, smashed
½ cup fresh basil

¼ cup parsley sprigs
3 tablespoons extra-virgin olive oil
¼ teaspoon salt
¼ teaspoon pepper

Place tomatoes, red onion, garlic, basil, parsley, olive oil, salt, and pepper in a food processor. Pulse, turning machine quickly on and off, until chopped; do not puree. Use at once or set aside at room temperature for up to 2 hours.

72   LIMA BEAN AND ALMOND SOUP
Prep: 7 minutes   Cook: 18 to 21 minutes   Serves: 4

The combination of almonds and limas makes a rich puree. By sautéing the almonds, they become lightly toasted, enhancing their flavor.

2 **tablespoons olive oil**	½ **teaspoon salt**
1 **medium onion, chopped**	½ **teaspoon pepper**
⅓ **cup whole almonds**	2 **(10-ounce) packages baby**
4 **garlic cloves, minced**	**lima beans, thawed**
½ **teaspoon dried thyme leaves**	4 **cups Vegetable Stock (page**
¼ **teaspoon dried sage**	**266) or canned broth**

1. In a large saucepan, heat oil over medium-high heat. Add onion and cook, stirring occasionally, until softened, 3 to 5 minutes. Add almonds and cook, stirring constantly, until lightly browned, about 3 minutes. Stir in garlic, seasonings, lima beans, and vegetable stock and bring to a boil. Reduce heat to low and simmer 10 minutes.

2. Add soup in batches to food processor or blender and puree until smooth. Return to saucepan and cook over medium heat until heated through, 2 to 3 minutes. Serve hot.

73   ORIENTAL NAPA CABBAGE SOUP
Prep: 10 minutes   Cook: 7 minutes   Serves: 6

The simplicity and purity of Asian soups is very appealing. They are light, refreshing, and low in calories. It is not surprising their popularity has grown. Extend this basic soup with the addition of cellophane noodles, shrimp, and snow peas, and you have a complete meal.

7 **cups Quick Brown Chicken**	½ **cup sliced scallions**
Stock (page 262) or	2 **tablespoons rice wine or dry**
reduced-sodium canned	**sherry**
broth	2 **tablespoons minced cilantro**
½ **pound napa cabbage, thinly**	**Salt**
sliced	
½ **pound firm bean curd, cut**	
into 1-inch cubes	

1. In a large nonreactive saucepan, bring stock to a boil. Add cabbage. Reduce heat to medium and cook, stirring frequently, 3 minutes.

2. Add tofu and scallions. Reduce heat to medium-low and cook until cabbage is crisp-tender, about 4 minutes. Before serving, stir in rice wine and cilantro and season with salt to taste.

74   CORN AND HAM CHOWDER
Prep: 12 minutes   Cook: 12 to 15 minutes   Serves: 6

1 tablespoon vegetable oil
1 medium onion, chopped
1 poblano pepper, seeded and
  chopped
1 cup chopped ham
1 tablespoon flour
½ teaspoon dried thyme leaves

½ teaspoon dried oregano
½ teaspoon black pepper
2 medium red potatoes, cut
  into ½-inch dice
1 (10-ounce) package frozen
  corn kernels
3 cups milk

1. In a large soup pot, heat oil over medium-high heat. Add onion, poblano pepper, and ham and cook, stirring occasionally, until softened, 3 to 4 minutes.

2. Stir in flour and cook, stirring constantly, 1 minute without allowing to brown. Stir in thyme, oregano, pepper, potatoes, corn, and milk and bring to a boil. Reduce heat to medium and cook until potatoes are tender, 8 to 10 minutes.

75   QUICK MANHATTAN CLAM CHOWDER
Prep: 10 minutes   Cook: 14 to 16 minutes   Serves: 6

Since we always think of Manhattan clam chowder as having Italian roots, this version contains fresh fennel, a popular Italian ingredient.

3 tablespoons extra-virgin
  olive oil
1 large sweet onion, chopped
1 large fennel bulb or celery
  rib, chopped,
  2 tablespoons chopped
  fronds reserved
½ medium red bell pepper,
  chopped
2 medium red potatoes,
  peeled and cut into
  ½-inch dice

1 teaspoon fennel seed,
  lightly crushed
¼ teaspoon crushed hot red
  pepper
2 (14½-ounce) cans diced
  peeled tomatoes, juices
  reserved
2 (8-ounce) bottles clam juice
2 (6½-ounce) cans chopped
  clams, juices reserved
2 tablespoons chopped
  parsley

1. In a large nonreactive saucepan, heat oil over medum-high heat. Add onion, chopped fennel, and bell pepper. Cook, stirring occasionally, until vegetables are softened, about 5 minutes.

2. Stir in potatoes, fennel seed, crushed red pepper, tomatoes with their juices, and clam juice. Bring to a boil, reduce heat to medium, and cook until potatoes are tender, 8 to 10 minutes.

3. Stir in clams with their liquid, parsley, and reserved chopped fennel fronds and simmer 1 minute longer, just to heat through. Serve at once.

76   JAPANESE CLEAR SOUP WITH MUSHROOMS AND BEAN CURD

Prep: 5 minutes   Stand: 10 minutes   Cook: 10 minutes   Serves: 4

Kombu (dried kelp) can be purchased at oriental markets or specialty food shops.

1   (5-inch) square of kombu (dried kelp)
6   mushrooms, trimmed and thinly sliced
1   (3-inch) square of firm bean curd, cut into 1-inch cubes

¼   cup dark miso (soybean paste)
1½   tablespoons soy sauce
1   tablespoon dry sherry
    Salt
3   tablespoons thinly sliced scallions

1. Place kombu in a large saucepan. Cover with 5 cups cold water. Bring just to a boil over medium heat. Remove from heat and let stand 10 minutes. Discard kombu.

2. Add mushrooms and bean curd to broth. Bring to a boil. Reduce heat to medium-low and cook 5 minutes.

3. Stir in miso, soy sauce, and sherry. Season with salt to taste and simmer 3 minutes. Garnish soup bowls with scallions and serve.

77   PARSNIP CHOWDER

Prep: 15 minutes   Cook: 14 to 15 minutes   Serves: 4

If you like the flavor of sweet parsnips, you'll love this simple chowder.

4   slices of bacon, coarsely chopped
2   shallots, minced
½   large yellow or red bell pepper, chopped
1   tablespoon flour

1   pound parsnips, peeled and cut into ¼-inch dice
3   cups milk
½   teaspoon freshly ground black pepper
1   cup frozen peas

1. In a large saucepan, cook bacon over medium heat, stirring occasionally, until crisp, about 4 minutes. With a slotted spoon, transfer bacon to paper towels to drain.

2. Add shallots and bell pepper to soup pot and cook, stirring occasionally, until shallots are softened, about 2 minutes. Stir in flour and cook, stirring constantly, 1 minute without allowing to color. Stir in parsnips and milk. Bring to a boil, reduce heat to medium, and cook until parsnips are softened, 5 to 6 minutes.

3. Stir in black pepper and peas and simmer 2 minutes longer. Add bacon just before serving.

78 CAULIFLOWER AND CHEDDAR SOUP

Prep: 7 minutes   Cook: 18 to 21 minutes   Serves: 6

To save time here, purchase the cauliflower already cut into florets in the produce department of your supermarket.

2 tablespoons butter
1 large onion, chopped
2 garlic cloves, minced
1 tablespoon flour
4 cups cauliflower florets (about 1 pound)
4 cups Chicken Stock (page 262) or reduced-sodium canned broth

2 imported bay leaves
½ teaspoon salt
Pinch of cayenne
1 cup shredded sharp Cheddar cheese (about 4 ounces)

1. In a large soup pot, melt butter over medium-high heat. Add onion and garlic and cook, stirring occasionally, until onion is softened but not brown, about 3 minutes. Stir in flour and cook, stirring constantly, 1 minute without allowing to brown.

2. Add cauliflower, chicken stock, bay leaves, salt, and cayenne to soup pot and bring to a boil. Reduce heat to medium, cover, and cook until cauliflower is very soft, 12 to 15 minutes.

3. Remove and discard bay leaves. Remove 2 cups of the solids from the soup, place in a food processor or blender, and puree until smooth.

4. Return puree to soup pot. Add cheese and cook, stirring constantly, until melted, about 2 minutes.

79 EASY PUMPKIN BISQUE

Prep: 5 minutes   Cook: 21 to 22 minutes   Serves: 4 to 6

This is a very easy to prepare soup that uses frozen or canned pumpkin puree. Be sure not to confuse pumpkin puree with pumpkin pie filling, which has added spices and flavorings.

1½ cups pumpkin puree
2 (14½-ounce) cans reduced-sodium chicken broth
2 tablespoons flour
½ teaspoon ground ginger

⅛ teaspoon grated nutmeg
1 cup heavy cream
Salt and pepper
1 cup shredded Gruyère or Swiss cheese

1. In a large saucepan, whisk together pumpkin puree, chicken broth, flour, ginger, and nutmeg. Bring to a boil, reduce heat to medium-low, and cook, stirring occasionally, 20 minutes.

2. Stir cream into soup and season with salt and pepper to taste. Simmer, stirring constantly, or until heated through, 1 to 2 minutes. Remove from heat, stir in cheese, and serve.

80   SPANISH GARLIC SOUP
Prep: 7 minutes   Cook: 20 to 21 minutes   Serves: 4

¼ cup olive oil
4 large garlic cloves, thinly
    sliced
4 (1-inch-thick) slices of
    Italian or French bread
5 cups Brown Beef Stock
    (page 264), Chicken Stock
    (page 262), or reduced-
    sodium canned beef
    broth

1 tablespoon sweet paprika
½ teaspoon ground cumin
3 tablespoons minced cilantro
Salt
4 eggs

1. Preheat oven to 425°F. In a large saucepan, heat oil over medium heat. Add garlic and cook, stirring frequently, until golden, about 2 minutes. Remove and reserve garlic.

2. Add bread slices to saucepan. Cook, turning over once, until golden on both sides, 3 to 4 minutes. Transfer to a plate.

3. Carefully add reserved garlic, beef stock, paprika, and cumin to sauce-pan, mashing garlic with back of a spoon. Bring to a boil over medium heat. Reduce heat to low and simmer 10 minutes. Stir in cilantro. Season with salt to taste.

4. Place toasts in 4 heatproof soup bowls and top each toast with an egg. Carefully ladle soup into bowls and bake 5 minutes, or until eggs are set.

81   PEAR AND CELERY ROOT SOUP
Prep: 10 minutes   Cook: 14 to 20 minutes   Serves: 6

Pears and celery root seem to have a special affinity for each other. Make this wonderful soup in the late fall when pears are at their finest.

2 tablespoons butter
2 shallots, minced
1 small celery root, peeled and
    chopped
2 ripe pears, peeled, cored,
    and chopped
1 sprig of fresh thyme or
    ½ teaspoon dried thyme
    leaves

½ teaspoon salt
½ teaspoon pepper
4 cups Vegetable Stock (page
    266) or canned broth
2 tablespoons chopped fresh
    chervil

1. In a large soup pot, melt butter over medium heat. Add shallots and cook, stirring frequently, until softened, 1 to 2 minutes. Add celery root, pears, thyme, salt, pepper, and vegetable stock. Bring to a boil, reduce heat to medium, and cook, partially covered, until celery root is tender, 10 to 15 minutes.

2. With a slotted spoon, remove solids from soup. Add in batches to food processor and puree until smooth. Return to soup pot and whisk together. Cook, stirring occasionally, until heated through, about 3 minutes. Serve sprinkled with chervil.

82   SAUSAGE, POTATO, AND CABBAGE SOUP

Prep: 10 minutes   Cook: 23 to 28 minutes   Serves: 4

Many supermarkets now offer packaged shredded cabbage. It's a real time-saver. For a very quick winter meal, serve this filling soup with toasted bread, flavorful cheese, and fresh fruit.

1 tablespoon vegetable oil	1 cup milk
½ pound veal or pork sausage	2 cups Chicken Stock (page
1 large onion, chopped	262) or reduced-sodium
3 garlic cloves, minced	canned broth
4 cups shredded cabbage	½ teaspoon salt
(about ½ pound)	Pinch of cayenne
1 tablespoon flour	2 tablespoons chopped
2 medium red potatoes,	parsley
peeled and cut into	2 tablespoons chopped fresh
½-inch dice	dill or 2 teaspoons dried

1. In a large saucepan, heat oil over medium-high heat. Add sausage and cook, stirring occasionally, until evenly browned, 6 to 8 minutes. Remove sausage to a plate and cut into ½-inch-thick slices.

2. Add onion to oil remaining in saucepan and cook, stirring occasionally, until softened, 3 minutes. Add garlic and cabbage and cook, stirring frequently, until cabbage is wilted, about 5 minutes. Stir in flour and cook, stirring constantly, 1 to 2 minutes without allowing to brown.

3. Stir in potatoes, milk, chicken stock, salt, and cayenne and bring to a boil. Reduce heat to medium and cook until potatoes are tender, 8 to 10 minutes. Stir in parsley and dill just before serving.

83   CREAM OF SORREL SOUP
Prep: 10 minutes   Cook: 18 minutes   Serves: 4

Sorrel has a very intense lemony flavor. We have added potato to temper the tartness and also to act as a thickener. This soup can be served either hot or cold.

3 tablespoons butter
1 medium onion, chopped
¾ pound sorrel leaves, well rinsed and chopped (about 2 cups)
1 medium baking potato, peeled and cut into ½-inch dice

4 cups Chicken Stock (page 262) or reduced-sodium canned broth
1 cup heavy or light cream
Salt and pepper
⅓ cup sour cream
2 tablespoons minced fresh chives

1. In a large nonreactive saucepan, melt butter over medium heat. Add onion and cook, stirring frequently, until softened, about 4 minutes. Add sorrel and cook, stirring constantly, until wilted, about 2 minutes. Add potato and stock. Bring to a boil, reduce heat to medium, and cook, partially covered, until potato is soft, about 10 minutes.

2. In a food processor or blender, puree soup in batches until smooth. Return to saucepan and stir in heavy cream. Season with salt and pepper to taste. Simmer, stirring frequently, until heated through, about 2 minutes. Top each serving with a dollop of sour cream and a generous sprinkling of chives.

84   ROASTED RED PEPPER SOUP WITH CHIVE CREAM
Prep: 5 minutes   Cook: 18 to 21 minutes   Serves: 6

3 tablespoons butter
2 medium onions, chopped
3 garlic cloves, minced
6 cups Chicken Stock (page 262) or reduced-sodium canned broth
3 (7-ounce) jars roasted red peppers, drained

2 teaspoons lemon juice
½ teaspoon salt
⅛ teaspoon cayenne
1 cup sour cream
¼ cup minced fresh chives

1. In a large saucepan, melt butter over medium-low heat. Add onions and garlic, cover, and cook, stirring occasionally, until softened, 6 to 8 minutes. Add chicken stock and roasted peppers. Bring to a boil. Reduce heat to medium-low, cover, and cook 10 minutes.

2. In a food processor or blender, puree soup in batches until smooth. Return to saucepan and cook until heated through, 2 to 3 minutes. Stir in lemon juice, salt, and cayenne.

3. In a small bowl, stir together sour cream and chives. Season with additional salt to taste. Serve soup hot, with a dollop of chive cream on top of each bowl.

---

85   CREAM OF SPINACH SOUP
Prep: 5 minutes   Cook: 13 to 19 minutes   Serves: 6

Ready-to-use fresh spinach, packaged in 10- or 12-ounce bags, is easy to find in many supermarkets these days. It's a real time-saver.

1 **pound rinsed, trimmed fresh spinach**
2 **tablespoons butter**
½ **cup minced shallots**
1 **medium red potato, peeled and diced**
5 **cups Chicken Stock (page 262) or reduced-sodium canned broth**

1 **cup heavy or light cream**
⅛ **teaspoon grated nutmeg**
½ **teaspoon salt**
¼ **teaspoon pepper**

1. In a large saucepan of boiling water, place spinach and boil 1 minute. Drain, rinse under cold water, and squeeze dry.

2. In a large saucepan, melt butter over medium heat. Add shallots and cook, stirring frequently, until softened, 2 to 3 minutes. Add spinach, potato, and stock. Bring to a boil, reduce heat to medium-low, and cook, partially covered, until potatoes are tender, 10 to 15 minutes.

3. In a food processor or blender, puree soup in batches until smooth. Return to pan and stir in cream, nutmeg, salt, and pepper. Heat through before serving.

86 TEX-MEX VEGETABLE SOUP
Prep: 15 minutes   Cook: 16 to 18 minutes   Serves: 6

Serve this Southwestern soup with broiled quesadillas made with Monterey Jack cheese and scallions sprinkled on flour tortillas.

2 tablespoons vegetable oil
1 large onion, chopped
1 large sweet potato (about
    ¾ pound), peeled,
    quartered lengthwise,
    and thinly sliced
1 teaspoon ground cumin
½ teaspoon salt
1 (4-ounce) can chopped
    peeled mild chiles, juices
    reserved
1 cup frozen lima beans

1 (14½-ounce) can chopped
    peeled tomatoes with
    Mexican seasonings,
    juices reserved
3 cups Chicken Stock (page
    262) or reduced-sodium
    canned broth
1 cup frozen corn kernels
½ teaspoon pepper
2 scallions, finely chopped
2 tablespoons chopped
    cilantro

1. In a soup pot, heat oil over medium-high heat. Add onion and cook, stirring occasionally, until softened, about 3 minutes. Stir in sweet potato, cumin, salt, chiles with their juices, lima beans, tomatoes with their juices, and chicken stock. Bring to a boil, reduce heat to medium, and cook, partially covered, until potato is softened, 8 to 10 minutes.

2. Stir in corn and pepper and simmer 5 minutes longer. Stir in scallions and cilantro just before serving.

87 QUICK VEGETABLE BEEF SOUP
Prep: 5 minutes   Cook: 26 to 27 minutes   Serves: 6

1 tablespoon olive oil
1 pound sirloin tip or round
    steak, cut into ½-inch dice
½ teaspoon salt
½ teaspoon pepper
1 large onion, chopped
3 garlic cloves, minced
2 tablespoons flour
4 cups Simple Beef Stock
    (page 264) or
    2 (14½-ounce) cans
    reduced-sodium broth

1 (14½-ounce) can diced
    peeled tomatoes, juices
    reserved
½ teaspoon dried thyme leaves
1 (16-ounce) package frozen
    mixed vegetables
    (preferably broccoli, corn,
    red pepper mix)
3 tablespoons chopped fresh
    basil

1. In a soup pot, heat olive oil over medium-high heat. Season beef with salt and pepper. Add to soup pot in 2 batches and cook, stirring occasionally, until browned on all sides, about 5 minutes per batch. With a slotted spoon, transfer beef to a bowl.

2. Add onion and garlic to soup pot and cook, stirring occasionally, until onion is golden, about 5 minutes. Add flour and cook, stirring constantly, 1 minute without allowing to brown. Stir in beef stock, tomatoes with their juices, and thyme. Bring to a boil, reduce heat to medium, and cook 5 minutes.

3. Stir in vegetables and basil and cook 3 minutes. Return beef to soup pot and cook until vegetables are tender, 2 to 3 minutes longer.

---

88 CREAM OF WATERCRESS SOUP
Prep: 7 minutes   Cook: 24 minutes   Serves: 6

Watercress has a mildly bitter taste. The leaves are blanched to remove some of the bitterness, which produces a soup that is subtle in flavor.

1 **pound watercress, large stems removed**	1 **cup heavy or light cream**
3 **tablespoons butter**	⅛ **teaspoon grated nutmeg**
⅓ **cup minced shallots**	½ **teaspoon salt**
1 **medium red potato, peeled and diced**	¼ **teaspoon pepper**
5 **cups Chicken Stock (page 262) or reduced-sodium canned broth**	

1. Reserve 6 sprigs of watercress for garnish. In a large saucepan of boiling water, cook remaining watercress 1 minute. Drain, rinse under cold running water until cool, and squeeze dry.

2. In a large saucepan, melt butter over medium heat. Add shallots, cooked watercress, and potato and cook, stirring frequently, 10 minutes. Add chicken stock. Bring to a boil, reduce heat to low, and simmer until potato is tender, about 10 minutes longer.

3. In a food processor or blender, puree soup in batches until smooth. Return to saucepan and stir in cream and nutmeg. Season with salt and pepper and cook over medium-low heat, stirring frequently, until heated through, about 3 minutes.

Chapter 4

Cold Vegetable and Fruit Soups

On a hot, humid summer night, nothing is more cooling than an icy, chilled soup. This chapter offers plenty of delicious relief, whether you desire it in the form of a first course, main course, or even as a dessert.

As an elegant appetizer, a classic vichyssoise with a twist is offered. This American soup (with a very French pedigree) is a chilled potato-leek soup, served here with a parsleyed puree swirled into the top. It's super easy to make and very impressive to serve.

As a main course, serve either the Cold Zucchini Soup with Cilantro Pesto or the Chilled Caribbean Yam Soup. Both are quick to make, the most work being done by your refrigerator as they sit and chill.

For dessert, try one of the many fruit soups offered. These are unusual and, on a hot, sultry day, surprisingly delightful. Just be sure to serve them ice cold. Choose a soup according to the season. In the early spring, try the Rhubarb-Strawberry Soup, a classic combination; in late summer, a berry or stone fruit soup, like the Blackberry Buttermilk or Gingered Plum Soup. Keep your options open as you shop and look for the ripest and most flavorful fruit you can find. You'll be amply rewarded with the rich results.

89 COLD BEET SOUP WITH DILL AND CHIVES
Prep: 10 minutes   Cook: 28 to 40 minutes   Chill: 2 hours   Serves: 4

Here is a quick and simple beet soup, which can be served either cold or hot.

2 tablespoons butter
1 medium onion, minced
2 garlic cloves, minced
2 tablespoons flour
3 cups minced peeled beets
   (about 4 medium beets)
5 cups Simple Beef Stock
   (page 264) or reduced-
   sodium canned broth

1 bay leaf
1 teaspoon salt
½ teaspoon pepper
1 cup plain yogurt
1½ tablespoons minced fresh
   dill
1½ tablespoons minced fresh
   chives or scallion green

1. In a large saucepan, melt butter over medium-low heat. Add onion and garlic and cook, stirring occasionally, until onion is soft but not brown, about 5 minutes. Add flour and cook, stirring constantly, 1 to 2 minutes without allowing to brown. Add beets, beef stock, bay leaf, salt, and pepper. Bring to a boil, reduce heat to medium, and cook, partially covered, stirring frequently, until beets are soft, 20 to 30 minutes. Remove and discard bay leaf.

2. In a food processor or blender, puree soup in batches until smooth. Return soup to saucepan and stir in yogurt. Cook over medium heat, stirring frequently, until heated through, 2 to 3 minutes. Let cool, then cover and refrigerate until chilled, at least 2 hours. Sprinkle with dill and chives just before serving.

90 CHILLED AVOCADO SOUP WITH CUCUMBER AND TOMATO
Prep: 20 minutes   Cook: none   Serves: 4 to 6

2 medium avocados, peeled,
   pitted, and quartered
1⅔ cups cold Chicken Stock
   (page 262) or reduced-
   sodium canned broth
1 cup milk
⅔ cup sour cream
¼ cup minced shallot
⅓ cup crushed ice
2 teaspoons lemon juice

½ teaspoon salt
⅛ teaspoon freshly ground
   pepper
1 tablespoon minced fresh
   dill
1 medium tomato, peeled,
   seeded, and diced
⅔ cup diced, seeded, peeled
   cucumber

1. In a food processor or blender, combine avocados, chicken stock, milk, sour cream, shallot, and crushed ice. Puree soup until smooth.

2. Pour soup into serving bowl. Add lemon juice, salt, and pepper. Stir in dill, tomato, and cucumber just before serving.

91 ICED AVOCADO SOUP WITH LIME
Prep: 20 minutes   Cook: none   Serves: 4 to 6

This is a wonderfully refreshing soup for warm-weather months. For a Southwestern accent, substitute cilantro for the chives and add ground toasted cumin seed for flavor.

2 medium avocados, peeled, pitted, and quartered
1½ cups Chicken Stock (page 262) or reduced-sodium canned broth
1 cup milk
½ cup sour cream
⅓ cup chopped scallion (white part only)

⅓ cup crushed ice
2 to 3 teaspoons lime juice
½ teaspoon salt
⅛ teaspoon white pepper
  Mixed fresh chives and lime slices

1. In a food processor or blender, combine avocados, chicken stock, milk, sour cream, scallion, and crushed ice. Puree soup until smooth.

2. Pour soup into a serving bowl; stir in lime juice, salt, and pepper. If not serving immediately, cover and chill. Before serving, garnish with chives and lime slices.

92 CHILLED ROAST CARROT AND CHILE SOUP
Prep: 20 minutes   Cook: 45 minutes   Chill: 3 hours   Serves: 6

2 tablespoons vegetable oil
1½ pounds carrots, peeled and cut into 1-inch chunks
1 large Spanish onion, cut into 1-inch wedges
1 large poblano pepper, seeded and cut into 1-inch dice
4 garlic cloves

1½ teaspoons sugar
½ teaspoon salt
  Pinch of cayenne
5 cups Chicken Stock (page 262) or reduced-sodium canned broth
⅓ cup sour cream
¼ cup chopped cilantro

1. Preheat oven to 450°F. In a large bowl, combine oil, carrots, onion, poblano pepper, and garlic. Stir in sugar, salt, and cayenne. Spread onto a large cookie sheet and roast 30 minutes. Remove garlic and continue roasting until vegetables are browned and soft, about 15 minutes longer.

2. Transfer garlic and vegetables to a food processor or blender and process until smooth. With machine on, pour in chicken stock. Refrigerate at least 3 hours.

3. To serve, ladle soup into bowls and top with a dollop of sour cream and a sprinkling of chopped cilantro.

93   PARSLEYED VICHYSSOISE
Prep: 15 minutes   Cook: 25 minutes   Chill: 3 hours
Serves: 6

Here's a variation on vichyssoise—a truly classic chilled soup.

2   tablespoons butter
3   medium leeks (white and tender green parts only), well rinsed and thinly sliced
2   large shallots, thinly sliced
2   garlic cloves, finely chopped
2   medium red potatoes, peeled and chopped

4   cups Chicken Stock (page 262) or reduced-sodium canned broth
¾   teaspoon salt
¼   teaspoon freshly ground black pepper
¾   cup light or heavy cream
½   cup chopped Italian (flat-leaf) parsley

1. In a soup pot, melt butter over medium heat. Add leeks and shallots and cook, stirring occasionally, until very soft but not browned, about 4 minutes. Add garlic and cook, stirring constantly, 1 minute. Stir in potatoes, chicken stock, salt, and pepper and simmer until potatoes are very soft, about 20 minutes.

2. Place mixture in a food processor or blender and process until very smooth. With machine on, pour in cream and process until well blended. Transfer soup to a bowl. Remove 1 cup soup and place in food processor or blender with parsley. Puree until smooth. Refrigerate both portions of soup at least 3 hours.

3. To serve, ladle uncolored soup into serving bowls and swirl parsleyed soup on top.

94   CHILLED CORN CHOWDER
Prep: 10 minutes   Cook: 35 minutes   Chill: 3 hours   Serves: 4

2   teaspoons ground cumin seed
3   tablespoons vegetable oil
1   medium onion, minced
1   small red bell pepper, finely chopped
1   medium celery rib, finely diced
3   cups fresh corn kernels (5 to 6 ears)
3   garlic cloves, minced

3   tablespoons flour
5   cups Chicken Stock (page 262) or reduced-sodium canned broth
1   bay leaf
1   sprig of fresh thyme or ½ teaspoon dried thyme leaves
1   cup plain yogurt or sour cream
    Salt and black pepper

1. In a small skillet, cook cumin seed over medium heat, stirring frequently, until lightly toasted and fragrant, 3 to 5 minutes.

2. In a large saucepan, heat oil over medium heat. Add onion, bell pepper, and celery. Cook, stirring frequently, until vegetables are soft but not brown, about 5 minutes. Add corn and garlic and cook, stirring constantly, 3 minutes. Add flour and cumin seed. Cook, stirring constantly, 1 to 2 minutes without allowing to brown. Add chicken stock, bay leaf, and thyme. Bring to a boil. Reduce heat to low, cover, and simmer, stirring occasionally, 20 minutes. Remove and discard bay leaf and fresh thyme sprig.

3. Let soup cool, then cover and refrigerate until cold, at least 3 hours or overnight.

4. Skim off any fat from top of soup. Stir in yogurt and season with salt and black pepper to taste. Serve chilled.

95 ROASTED YELLOW PEPPER SOUP WITH SCALLION CREAM

Prep: 40 minutes   Cook: 46 to 53 minutes   Chill: 1 hour   Serves: 8

6 medium yellow bell
  peppers
2 tablespoons extra-virgin
  olive oil
1 medium onion, chopped
1 medium carrot, peeled and
  chopped
1 celery rib, chopped
2 garlic cloves, minced
1 medium red potato, peeled
  and cut into ½-inch dice

1½ teaspoons salt
¾ teaspoon black pepper
  Pinch of powdered saffron
2 teaspoons sugar
1 cup sour cream
¼ cup thinly sliced scallion
  greens
⅛ teaspoon cayenne

1. Place bell peppers directly over gas burners set on high and roast, turning occasionally, until blackened on all sides, about 10 minutes. Place peppers in a paper bag and set aside to cool. (Alternately, if you have an electric stove, preheat broiler. Place bell peppers on cookie sheet and broil 2 to 3 inches from heat source, turning occasionally, until blackened all over, about 15 minutes. Place peppers in paper bag to cool.)

2. When peppers are cool, scrape off blackened skin with back of paring knife or with fingers. Seed and chop peppers.

3. In a large soup pot, heat olive oil over medium-high heat. Add onion, carrot, and celery and cook, stirring frequently, until softened, 6 to 8 minutes. Stir in garlic, potato, roasted peppers, salt, black pepper, saffron, sugar, and 5 cups water. Bring to a boil, reduce heat to low, and simmer 30 minutes. Transfer soup to a food processor or blender and puree until smooth. Pour soup into a large bowl, cover, and refrigerate until well chilled, at least 1 hour.

4. In a small bowl, combine sour cream, scallion greens, and cayenne. Season lightly with salt. To serve, ladle soup into bowls and swirl in scallion cream.

96   GAZPACHO
Prep: 20 minutes   Cook: none: Chill: 1 hour   Serves: 4

This warm-weather favorite can be garnished with diced avocado, minced scallion, and croutons.

1½ cups tomato juice
 3 tablespoons extra-virgin
     olive oil
 2 tablespoons sherry wine
     vinegar or red wine
     vinegar
 1 medium-large Spanish
     onion, quartered
 2 garlic cloves, minced
 5 large ripe tomatoes (about
     2½ pounds), peeled,
     seeded, and chopped

 1 large cucumber, peeled,
     seeded, and chopped
 1 small red bell pepper,
     chopped
 1 small green bell pepper,
     chopped
 2 tablespoons minced cilantro
     Salt and freshly ground
     pepper

1. In a food processor or blender, combine tomato juice, olive oil, vinegar, onion, and garlic. Puree until smooth.

2. Transfer puree to a large bowl. Stir in tomatoes, cucumber, bell peppers, and cilantro. Season with salt and black pepper to taste. Cover and refrigerate until well chilled, at least 1 hour, before serving.

97   WHITE GAZPACHO
Prep: 10 minutes   Cook: 15 minutes   Chill: 1 hour   Serves: 4

Although most people are familiar with the red gazpacho made from tomatoes, there is a traditional white version that stems from Málaga, Spain, based on almonds, bread, and grapes. It is wonderfully refreshing.

 1 cup blanched almonds
 2 garlic cloves, chopped
 3 slices of day-old white
     bread, crusts removed
 4 cups cold Chicken Stock
     (page 262) or reduced-
     sodium canned broth

 ¼ cup extra-virgin olive oil
 3 tablespoons white wine
     vinegar
 ½ teaspoon salt
 1 cup halved seedless grapes
 ½ cup croutons

1. Preheat oven to 350°F. Place almonds in a shallow baking pan and bake, stirring occasionally, 15 minutes, or until lightly toasted. Cool slightly.

2. In a food processor or blender, process almonds and garlic until finely ground.

3. In a small bowl, soak bread in about ¼ cup cold water and squeeze dry. Add bread to processor and process until well blended. Add chicken stock, olive oil, vinegar, and salt and puree until smooth.

4. Pass soup through medium blade of a food mill or strain through a medium sieve, pressing on solids to extract as much as liquid as possible. Discard solids. Cover and refrigerate until well chilled, at least 1 hour. Stir in grapes just before serving and garnish with croutons.

98   ICED DOUBLE TOMATO SOUP
Prep: 10 minutes   Stand: 20 minutes   Cook: 32 to 33 minutes
Chill: 3 hours   Serves: 6

12 sun-dried tomato halves (not packed in oil)
 3 tablespoons extra-virgin olive oil
 4 large shallots, thinly sliced
 2 garlic cloves, minced
 1 (28-ounce) can Italian-style plum tomatoes, seeded and chopped, juices reserved
 2 teaspoons sugar
 3 (2 x 1-inch) strips of orange zest
 2 bay leaves
 ½ teaspoon salt
 ½ teaspoon pepper
 1 cup Vegetable Stock (page 266), Chicken Stock (page 262), or canned vegetable broth
 ⅓ cup plain yogurt
 ¼ cup minced fresh chives

1. Place sun-dried tomatoes in a heatproof bowl and cover with 1 cup boiling water. Let stand 20 minutes. Drain, reserving liquid. Coarsely chop tomatoes.

2. In a soup pot, heat oil over medium-high heat. Add shallots and garlic and cook, stirring constantly, 2 to 3 minutes. Stir in plum tomatoes with their juices, dried tomatoes and soaking liquid, sugar, orange zest, bay leaves, salt, pepper, and vegetable stock. Bring to a boil, reduce heat to low, and simmer 30 minutes. Remove and discard bay leaves and orange strips. Transfer soup to a food processor or blender and process until smooth. Refrigerate at least 3 hours.

3. To serve, ladle soup into bowls and top with a dollop of yogurt and a sprinkling of chives.

99 COLD ZUCCHINI SOUP WITH CILANTRO PESTO

Prep: 10 minutes   Cook: 15 minutes   Chill: 3 hours   Serves: 4

This soup is equally good chilled or warm.

2　tablespoons olive oil
1　small onion, chopped
1　pound small zucchini
　　(about 3 medium), cut
　　into ½-inch pieces
¼　teaspoon salt
¼　teaspoon pepper

1½　cups Vegetable Stock (page
　　266), Chicken Stock (page
　　262), or canned broth
Cilantro Pesto (recipe
　　follows)

1. In a large saucepan, heat olive oil over medium-high heat. Add onion and cook until softened but not browned, 5 minutes. Add zucchini, salt, pepper, and vegetable stock and simmer 10 minutes.

2. Transfer soup to a food processor or blender and puree until smooth. Pour soup into a medium bowl, cover, and refrigerate until well chilled, at least 3 hours.

3. To serve, ladle soup into bowls and top with Cilantro Pesto.

100 CILANTRO PESTO

Prep: 10 minutes   Cook: none   Serves: 4

1　cup cilantro leaves
4　scallions, cut into 1-inch
　　lengths
1　large garlic clove, coarsely
　　chopped

2　teaspoons lime juice
2　tablespoons butter, softened
2　tablespoons olive oil

In a blender or food processor, combine cilantro, scallions, garlic, and lime juice. Process until finely chopped. With machine on, drop in butter and olive oil and puree until smooth. Serve at once.

101 CHILLED CARIBBEAN YAM SOUP

Prep: 15 minutes   Cook: 20 minutes   Chill: 3 hours   Serves: 8

This soup tastes equally good hot or cold, and made with either yams or sweet potatoes.

3 tablespoons butter
1 large Spanish onion, chopped
½ teaspoon ground allspice
½ teaspoon dried thyme leaves
3 medium yams or sweet potatoes, peeled and cut into ½-inch dice

4 cups Chicken Stock (page 262) or reduced-sodium canned broth
½ teaspoon salt
 Pinch of cayenne
½ cup plain yogurt
2 scallions, thinly sliced

1. In a soup pot, melt butter over medium heat. Add onion and cook, stirring occasionally, until golden, 3 to 4 minutes. Stir in allspice, thyme, yams, chicken stock, and salt and bring to a boil. Reduce heat to low and simmer until potatoes are very soft, about 15 minutes.

2. Transfer soup to a food processor or blender. Add cayenne and process until smooth. Refrigerate at least 3 hours.

3. To serve, ladle soup into bowls and top with a dollop of yogurt and a sprinkling of scallions.

102 CHILLED CUCUMBER SOUP WITH SHRIMP AND SCALLIONS

Prep: 15 minutes   Cook: none   Chill: 1 hour   Serves: 6

Here's a quick and easy low-fat summer soup.

3 medium cucumbers, trimmed, peeled, and sliced
1 garlic clove, minced
1 teaspoon salt
½ teaspoon pepper
¼ pound small shrimp, shelled, cooked, and coarsely chopped

2 plum tomatoes, seeded and chopped
3 scallions, finely chopped
1 small jalapeño pepper, seeded and minced
2 tablespoons finely chopped cilantro
1 tablespoon olive oil
2 tablespoons lime juice

1. In a food processor or blender, combine cucumbers, garlic, salt, and pepper and process until smooth. Refrigerate at least 1 hour.

2. In a medium bowl, combine shrimp, tomatoes, scallions, jalapeño pepper, cilantro, olive oil, and lime juice. Refrigerate until ready to serve.

3. To serve, ladle soup into serving bowls and top with shrimp mixture.

103   APPLE-CARDAMOM SOUP
Prep: 10 minutes   Cook: 15 minutes   Chill: 2 hours   Serves: 4

Simply omit the water to transform this full-flavored soup into a tasty applesauce side dish.

4 large Granny Smith or other large tart apples, peeled, cored, and thinly sliced	¼ teaspoon ground cardamom
	¼ teaspoon white pepper
	2 cups apple juice
¾ cup packed brown sugar	1 teaspoon lemon juice

1. In a large saucepan, combine apples, brown sugar, cardamom, pepper, apple juice, and 2 cups water. Bring to a boil, reduce heat to low, and simmer, stirring frequently, until apples are softened, about 15 minutes.

2. Transfer soup to a food processor or blender and puree until smooth. Stir in lemon juice, cover, and refrigerate until chilled, at least 2 hours.

104   BANANA COCONUT MILK SOUP
Prep: 10 minutes   Cook: none   Serves: 4

3 chilled, very ripe bananas	1 teaspoon vanilla extract
1 cup chilled coconut milk	Pinch of salt
3 tablespoons brown sugar	

Place bananas in blender or food processor and puree until smooth. With machine on, pour in coconut milk, brown sugar, vanilla, and salt. Process until well blended and serve.

105   BLACKBERRY BUTTERMILK SOUP
Prep: 10 minutes   Cook: 5 minutes   Chill: 2 hours   Serves: 4

4 pints blackberries, rinsed	1 cup buttermilk
½ cup dry red wine	2 tablespoons chopped fresh mint
¼ teaspoon ground allspice	
½ cup sugar	

1. In a large nonreactive saucepan, combine blackberries, wine, allspice, and sugar. Bring to a boil, reduce heat to low, and simmer 5 minutes.

2. Transfer soup to food processor or blender and puree until smooth. Pass soup through medium blade of a food mill or strain through a medium sieve, pressing on solids to extract as much liquid as possible. Place in a medium bowl, cover, and refrigerate until well chilled, at least 2 hours.

3. When ready to serve, stir in buttermilk. Ladle soup into bowls and sprinkle with mint.

106 NORTHWEST BERRY SOUP

Prep: 10 minutes   Cook: 12 to 13 minutes   Chill: 1 hour   Serves: 4

Experiment with any combination of berries when making this wonderfully refreshing dessert soup.

4 cups mixed berries (blueberries, raspberries, strawberries, and/or blackberries) ½ cup sugar	1 tablespoon cornstarch 2 tablespoons framboise or raspberry-flavored liqueur 1 pint vanilla frozen yogurt

1. In a large saucepan, combine berries, sugar, and 1 cup water. Bring to a boil, reduce heat to low, and simmer, stirring frequently, until berries are softened, about 10 minutes.

2. In a small bowl, blend cornstarch with 2 tablespoons cold water. Add to saucepan and simmer until soup is thickened, 2 to 3 minutes. Pass soup through medium blade of a food mill or strain through a medium sieve, pressing on solids to extract as much liquid as possible. Discard solids. Transfer soup to a medium bowl and stir in framboise. Cover and refrigerate soup until well chilled, at least 1 hour.

3. When ready to serve, divide frozen yogurt into serving bowls and ladle soup around yogurt.

107 CURRIED MANGO SOUP

Prep: 15 minutes   Cook: 3 minutes   Chill: 1 hour   Serves: 6

Serve this first-course soup at your next party. Your guests will find its unique blend of flavors refreshing.

1 tablespoon butter
1 medium shallot, minced
1 teaspoon curry powder
¼ teaspoon ground cumin
⅛ teaspoon black pepper
    Pinch of cayenne
    Pinch of salt
1 cup Chicken Stock (page 262), reduced-sodium canned broth, or water
	2 ripe mangoes, peeled and cut into ½-inch chunks
	½ teaspoon lemon juice
	⅓ cup plain yogurt
	2 tablespoons chopped fresh chives

1. In a soup pot, heat butter over medium-high heat. Add shallot and cook, stirring frequently, until golden, about 2 minutes. Add curry powder, cumin, black pepper, cayenne, and salt and cook, stirring constantly, 1 minute. Stir in chicken stock and bring to a boil

2. Transfer soup to a food processor or blender. Add mangoes and lemon juice and puree until smooth. Cover and refrigerate until well chilled, at least 1 hour. Garnish each serving with yogurt and chives.

108 CHERRY-LIME SOUP

Prep: 10 minutes   Cook: none   Chill: 1 hour   Serves: 4

Just a touch of sweetness makes this in-a-minute soup a perfect ending to a great meal.

- 2 (17-ounce) cans pitted dark sweet cherries in syrup
- 1 tablespoon sugar
- 2 tablespoons lime juice
- ¼ cup vanilla yogurt

1. Drain cherries, reserving ½ cup liquid. In a food processor or blender, combine cherries, sugar, and lime juice and puree until smooth. Transfer soup to a medium bowl and stir in reserved cherry liquid. Cover and refrigerate until well chilled, at least 1 hour.

2. To serve, ladle soup into bowls and serve topped with dollops of yogurt.

109 GINGERED PLUM SOUP

Prep: 10 minutes   Cook: 45 minutes   Chill: 1 hour   Serves: 4

For best flavor, prepare this refreshing soup in August, when your plum trees are bursting with ripe fruit.

- 2 pounds purple plums, pitted and sliced
- ⅔ cup sugar
- 2 teaspoons minced fresh ginger
- ¼ cup dry red wine
- Pinch of salt
- ⅓ cup heavy cream

1. In a large soup pot, combine plums, sugar, ginger, wine, salt, and 2 cups water. Bring to a boil, reduce heat to low, and simmer 10 minutes. Uncover and simmer until plums are very soft, about 35 minutes longer.

2. Transfer plum mixture to food processor or blender and puree until smooth. Pour into medium bowl, cover, and refrigerate until well chilled, at least 1 hour.

3. When ready to serve, transfer 1 cup plum mixture to small bowl; stir in cream. Ladle remaining soup into serving bowls and drizzle in cream mixture.

110   TWO-MELON SOUP

Prep: 20 minutes   Cook: none   Chill: 1 hour   Serves: 4

½ large honeydew melon, cut
   into 1-inch chunks
3 tablespoons lime juice
½ teaspoon pepper
1 small cantaloupe, cut into
   1-inch chunks

1 tablespoon sugar
1 tablespoon orange juice
2 tablespoons chopped fresh
   mint

1. In a food processor or blender, combine honeydew, lime juice, and pepper and puree until smooth. Transfer mixture to a medium bowl, cover, and refrigerate until well chilled, at least 1 hour.

2. Meanwhile, wash out processor bowl. Add cantaloupe, sugar, and orange juice and puree until smooth. Transfer mixture to another medium bowl, cover, and refrigerate until well chilled, at least 1 hour.

3. When ready to serve, ladle about ½ cup of each soup into soup bowls, pouring both mixtures into bowl at same time. Gently swirl soup with knife to create marbleized design. Garnish with mint.

111   RHUBARB-STRAWBERRY SOUP

Prep: 10 minutes   Cook: 5 minutes   Chill: 1 hour   Serves: 4

A pretty and refreshing dessert soup, perfect for late spring.

2 cups thinly sliced rhubarb
¼ cup port
¼ cup sugar
   Pinch of salt
1 cup sliced strawberries, plus
   4 whole strawberries for
   garnish

¼ cup heavy cream, lightly
   whipped

1. In a large nonreactive saucepan, combine rhubarb, port, 2 tablespoons water, sugar, and salt. Bring to a boil, cover, and cook until rhubarb is softened, about 5 minutes.

2. Transfer soup to blender or food processor. Add sliced strawberries and puree until smooth. Cover and refrigerate until well chilled, at least 1 hour.

3. To serve, ladle soup into bowls. Top with whipped cream and reserved whole strawberries.

112 BLUEBERRY SOUP WITH CINNAMON AND VANILLA

Prep: 5 minutes   Cook: 5 to 6 minutes   Chill: 1 hour   Serves: 4

This thick and creamy soup also doubles as a sauce for ice cream.

1 pint blueberries
¼ cup maple syrup
⅛ teaspoon cinnamon
1 tablespoon cornstarch

2 tablespoons heavy cream, half-and-half, or milk
1 teaspoon vanilla extract

1. In a nonreactive saucepan, combine blueberries, maple syrup, cinnamon, and ½ cup water. Bring to a boil, reduce heat to low, and simmer, stirring occasionally, 3 minutes. In a small bowl, blend cornstarch with 1 tablespoon cold water and add to saucepan. Return mixture to a boil and simmer until thickened, 2 to 3 minutes.

2. Transfer soup to food processor or blender and puree until smooth. Transfer to a medium bowl and stir in cream and vanilla. Cover and refrigerate until well chilled, at least 1 hour.

113 FIVE-SPICE PEACH SOUP

Prep: 20 minutes   Cook: 15 minutes   Chill: 1 hour   Serves: 4

For a slightly sweeter, more intense flavor, substitute nectarines for the peaches.

2 pounds ripe peaches, pitted and sliced
½ teaspoon Chinese five-spice powder

½ cup packed brown sugar
¼ cup dry white wine

1. In a Dutch oven or large nonreactive saucepan, combine peaches, five-spice powder, brown sugar, wine, and 1½ cups water. Bring to a boil, reduce heat to low, and simmer, stirring frequently, until fruit is softened, about 15 minutes.

2. Transfer soup to a food processor or blender and puree until smooth. Pour soup into a medium bowl, cover, and refrigerate until well chilled, at least 1 hour.

Chapter 5

Pasta Soups

Every culture has its own treasure chest of universally loved pasta dishes. And everywhere pasta is found, you'll be sure to find pasta in soups. What better way to use noodles than to fill a satisfying broth with chopped vegetables, lovely bits of meat or fish, and pleasing—and filling—pasta shapes?

These days, when we mention the word *pasta*, it's usually Italian pasta that comes to mind. And Italians do use lots of pasta in soups, whether it be a traditional Pasta e Fagiole, Tortellini Soup with Spinach and Parmesan Cheese, or a simple Escarole and Pasta Soup with Tomatoes and Romano Cheese. But don't overlook the other cultures that favor noodles. In this chapter, we have quite a variety—from the French-inspired Garlic Soup with Orzo and Green Beans (a simple soup that's great for a cold) as well as Moroccan Zucchini and Couscous Soup with Lemon and Cilantro (couscous is made from semolina, the same hard wheat used to make good-quality Italian pasta). The Middle East is represented with a Turkish Capellini and Lemon Soup as well as the Orient with Sesame-Scented Broth with Watercress and Tofu.

One of pasta's most endearing qualities is its ability to cook very quickly. Usually, pasta is thrown in at the end of a soup's cooking time to prevent overcooking. Since the pasta simply absorbs the soup broth to cook (instead of water), a pasta soup can become quite thick during the cooking (also due to starch released from the pasta). You can always adjust the soup with more stock if it becomes too thick for your liking.

One point to remember: though these soups reheat beautifully for several days afterward, freezing is not quite as successful. Pasta tends to disintegrate after freezing. To make these soups to freeze ahead, just omit the pasta until reheating. Then add the pasta as if you were cooking the soup for the first time.

114   BUCATINI, FENNEL, AND TOMATO SOUP
Prep: 20 minutes   Cook: 21 to 22 minutes   Serves: 6

2 tablespoons extra-virgin
  olive oil
1 medium onion, chopped
1 medium celery rib, chopped
1 large fennel bulb, chopped,
  tough stalks removed,
  fronds reserved
¼ cup chopped parsley
2 garlic cloves, minced
1 teaspoon crushed fennel
  seed

1 (14½-ounce) can Italian
  peeled tomatoes, drained
  and chopped
¾ teaspoon salt
½ teaspoon pepper
1½ cups broken bucatini or
  spaghetti
½ cup grated Parmesan cheese
2 tablespoons chopped fresh
  basil

1. In a large soup pot, heat oil over medium heat. Add onion, celery, fennel, and parsley and cook, stirring occasionally, until vegetables are softened, about 8 minutes. Add garlic, fennel seed, tomatoes, salt, and pepper and simmer 4 minutes. Add 6 cups water and bring to a boil.

2. Add bucatini and cook until tender but still firm, 9 to 10 minutes. Chop 2 tablespoons of reserved fennel fronds, stir in along with Parmesan cheese and basil, and serve.

115   TURKISH CAPELLINI AND LEMON SOUP
Prep: 10 minutes   Cook: 14 to 15 minutes   Serves: 4

Turkish soups are commonly enriched with egg yolks. Make sure to whisk the yolks well when mixing with the broth.

2 tablespoons butter
1 small onion, minced
4 plum tomatoes, peeled,
  seeded, and chopped
4 cups Chicken Stock (page
  262) or reduced-sodium
  canned broth

½ teaspoon salt
1 cup broken dried capellini
  or spaghettini
½ cup chopped parsley
½ teaspoon pepper
2 egg yolks
2 tablespoons lemon juice

1. In a large saucepan, melt butter over medium heat. Add onion and cook, stirring occasionally, 2 minutes. Add tomatoes and cook, stirring occasionally, 5 minutes longer. Stir in chicken stock and salt and bring to a boil. Reduce heat to medium.

2. Stir in capellini and cook, stirring occasionally, 5 minutes. Stir in parsley and pepper.

3. In a small bowl, beat egg yolks with lemon juice. Remove ½ cup hot broth from saucepan and whisk into egg yolk mixture. Add to saucepan, whisking constantly. Serve hot.

116 CAPELLINI AND SAUSAGE SOUP WITH RED WINE

Prep: 15 minutes   Cook: 19½ minutes   Serves: 4

1 pound mild Italian sausage, cut into ½-inch dice
2 tablespoons extra-virgin olive oil
1 medium onion, minced
1 garlic clove, minced
½ teaspoon dried thyme leaves
½ teaspoon dried oregano
½ cup dry red wine

4 cups Chicken Stock (page 262) or reduced-sodium canned broth
¼ pound fresh capellini
1 medium zucchini, shredded
2 tablespoons chopped parsley
½ cup grated Parmesan cheese

1. In a large saucepan, cook sausage over medium heat, turning occasionally, until browned on all sides, about 10 minutes. With a slotted spoon, transfer sausage to a plate. Drain and discard fat from saucepan.

2. Heat olive oil in same saucepan. Add onion and cook, stirring frequently, until softened, about 4 minutes. Add garlic, thyme, and oregano and cook, stirring constantly, 30 seconds. Stir in wine and simmer 3 minutes longer.

3. Add chicken stock and bring to a boil. Reduce heat to medium. Stir in capellini and zucchini and cook until capellini is tender but still firm, about 2 minutes. Stir in parsley and Parmesan cheese just before serving.

117 CAVATELLI AND SWISS CHARD SOUP

Prep: 15 minutes   Cook: 15½ minutes   Serves: 4

Cavatelli is a shell pasta that is a natural for homemade soups. The "bowl" shape does a great job catching all the flavors.

4 garlic cloves, crushed through a press
½ teaspoon salt
1 tablespoon extra-virgin olive oil
4 cups Vegetable Stock (page 266) or canned broth
1 cup dried cavatelli

2 cups chopped fresh Swiss chard
2 tablespoons chopped parsley
½ teaspoon grated nutmeg
½ teaspoon pepper
⅓ cup grated Asiago or Parmesan cheese

1. In a small bowl, combine garlic and salt; mix well to form a paste.

2. In a large soup pot, heat olive oil over medium-high heat. Add garlic paste and cook, stirring constantly, 30 seconds. Stir in vegetable stock and bring to a boil. Stir in cavatelli, reduce heat to low, and simmer until cavatelli is tender but still firm, about 10 minutes. Stir in Swiss chard and simmer until wilted, 5 minutes. Stir in parsley, nutmeg, and pepper. To serve, ladle soup into bowls and sprinkle with cheese.

118   FETTUCCINE, POTATO, AND PEA SOUP
Prep: 20 minutes   Cook: 18 to 19 minutes   Serves: 6

1 tablespoon butter
2 tablespoons extra-virgin
   olive oil
1 small onion, chopped
1 pound red potatoes, peeled
   and cut into ½-inch dice
1 garlic clove, minced
6 cups Vegetable Stock (page
   266) or canned broth

½ teaspoon dried thyme leaves
½ teaspoon salt
½ teaspoon pepper
1 cup (2-inch) fettuccine
   pieces
1 cup frozen tiny peas

1. In a large soup pot, melt butter in oil over medium-high heat. Add onion and cook, stirring occasionally, until softened, 3 to 4 minutes. Add potatoes and garlic and cook, stirring occasionally, 5 minutes longer.

2. Stir in vegetable stock, thyme, salt, and pepper and bring to a boil. Reduce heat to low and simmer until potatoes are softened, about 6 minutes. Stir in fettuccine and peas, cook until fettuccine is tender but still firm, about 4 minutes, and serve.

119   ASPARAGUS SOUP WITH DITALINI AND FRESH BASIL
Prep: 20 minutes   Cook: 18 minutes   Serves: 4

Ditalini is a small tubelike pasta. If you wish, you can substitute any small pasta.

½ teaspoon salt
1 pound asparagus, trimmed
   and cut into 1-inch
   lengths
2 tablespoons butter
1 tablespoon extra-virgin
   olive oil
1 small onion, finely chopped
1 large garlic clove, minced

2 tablespoons chopped
   parsley
4 plum tomatoes, peeled,
   seeded, and chopped
1 cup ditalini
2 tablespoons chopped fresh
   basil
½ teaspoon pepper
⅓ cup grated Parmesan cheese

1. In a large nonreactive saucepan, bring 6 cups water and salt to a boil. Add asparagus and cook until crisp but tender, about 6 minutes. Pour through a strainer set in a large bowl, reserving both asparagus and liquid.

2. In same saucepan, melt butter in oil over medium-high heat. Add onion, garlic, and parsley and cook, stirring occasionally, until onion is softened, about 5 minutes. Stir in tomatoes and reserved cooking liquid from asparagus and bring to a boil. Reduce heat to medium.

3. Add ditalini and cook until tender but still firm, about 5 minutes. Stir in asparagus, basil, and pepper and cook 2 minutes longer. Ladle soup into bowls and serve sprinkled with Parmesan cheese.

120 ESCAROLE AND PASTA SOUP WITH TOMATOES AND ROMANO CHEESE

Prep: 20 minutes   Cook: 12 minutes   Serves: 5

2 tablespoons extra-virgin olive oil
1 small onion, minced
4 thin slices of pancetta or bacon, chopped
2 garlic cloves, minced
¼ cup chopped parsley
4 plum tomatoes, peeled, seeded, and chopped

6 cups Chicken Stock (page 262) or reduced-sodium canned broth
6 cups chopped escarole
1 cup (½-inch lengths) fresh fettuccine pieces
½ cup grated Romano cheese
½ teaspoon pepper

1. In a large nonreactive soup pot, heat oil over medium-high heat. Add onion, pancetta, garlic, and parsley and cook, stirring occasionally, 5 minutes. Stir in tomatoes and chicken stock and bring to a boil.

2. Add escarole, reduce heat to medium, and cook 5 minutes. Stir in fettuccine and cook until fettuccine is tender but still firm, about 2 minutes longer. Stir in Romano cheese and pepper just before serving.

121 MOROCCAN ZUCCHINI AND COUSCOUS SOUP WITH LEMON AND CILANTRO

Prep: 15 minutes   Cook: 16½ to 20½ minutes   Serves: 4

2 tablespoons unsalted butter
1 medium onion, minced
½ teaspoon ground cumin
¼ teaspoon ground ginger
¼ teaspoon ground turmeric
⅛ teaspoon cayenne
½ cup quick-cooking couscous

5 cups Chicken Stock (page 262) or reduced-sodium canned broth
3 small zucchini, chopped
1 tablespoon lemon juice
2 tablespoons chopped cilantro

1. In a large soup pot, melt 1 tablespoon butter over medium-high heat. Add onion and cook, stirring occasionally, until softened, 2 to 3 minutes. Add spices and cayenne and cook, stirring constantly, 30 seconds. Add couscous and 1 cup chicken stock and bring to a boil. Remove from heat and set aside.

2. In a large skillet, melt remaining 1 tablespoon butter over medium-high heat. Add zucchini and cook, stirring occasionally, until lightly browned, about 3 minutes. Add 1 cup chicken stock and simmer until zucchini is tender, 3 to 4 minutes.

3. Add contents of skillet to saucepan along with remaining 3 cups chicken stock. Bring to a boil, reduce heat to low, and simmer until heated through, 8 to 10 minutes. Stir in lemon juice and cilantro just before serving.

122 FUSILLI, ARTICHOKE, AND POTATO SOUP
Prep: 30 minutes   Cook: 30 minutes   Serves: 4

Trimming artichokes can take a few minutes, but it's worth the work for this special soup.

2 tablespoons butter	5 cups Vegetable Stock (page 266) or canned broth
2 tablespoons extra-virgin olive oil	½ teaspoon salt
1 medium onion, finely chopped	1 cup fusilli
3 garlic cloves, minced	2 tablespoons chopped parsley
1 pound red potatoes, peeled and cut into ½-inch dice	1 tablespoon chopped fresh mint
2 large artichokes, top 1 inch cut off, outer leaves discarded, choke removed, and thinly sliced	½ teaspoon pepper
	⅓ cup grated Parmesan cheese

1. In a large saucepan, melt butter in oil over medium-high heat. Add onion and cook, stirring occasionally, until softened, about 5 minutes. Add garlic, potatoes, artichokes, vegetable stock, and salt and bring to a boil. Reduce heat to low and simmer 20 minutes.

2. Stir in fusilli and cook 10 minutes longer. Stir in parsley, mint, pepper, and Parmesan cheese just before serving.

123 SPINACH FUSILLI SOUP WITH CHICKEN, ARUGULA, AND HERBS
Prep: 20 minutes   Cook: 57 to 58 minutes   Serves: 4

Arugula is a type of salad green with a peppery, mustard flavor. When cooked, it loses its peppery quality and becomes nutty and mellow.

1 pound chicken thighs, skinned	1 cup spinach fusilli
5 cups Chicken Stock (page 262) or reduced-sodium canned broth	¼ teaspoon salt
	2 cups chopped arugula
2 garlic cloves, lightly crushed	¼ cup chopped mixed fresh herbs (chives, thyme, savory, parsley, or tarragon)
1 small onion, chopped	
1 bay leaf	

1. In a large soup pot, combine chicken, chicken stock, garlic, onion, and bay leaf and bring to a boil, skimming any foam from surface. Reduce heat to low and simmer until chicken is no longer pink in center, about 45 minutes. Remove and discard bay leaf. Remove chicken from stock and place on cutting board. When cool enough to handle, remove skin and bones from chicken and discard. Tear chicken into bite-size pieces and set aside.

2. Return stock to a boil and add fusilli and salt. Cook, stirring occasionally, until fusilli is tender but still firm, about 8 minutes. Return chicken to soup pot along with arugula and herbs. Simmer until heated through, 4 to 5 minutes.

124 PASTA E FAGIOLE

Prep: 20 minutes   Stand: 12 hours   Cook: 1 hour 5 minutes
Serves: 4

One of Italy's best-known dishes, the name simply means pasta and beans. Remember to put the dried beans up to soak the night before.

1 cup dried cranberry beans or cannellini beans, rinsed and picked over
3 tablespoons extra-virgin olive oil
1 small onion, finely chopped
1 medium celery rib, finely chopped
1 medium carrot, peeled and finely chopped
3 garlic cloves, minced
2 sprigs of fresh thyme or 1 teaspoon dried thyme leaves

1 small ham bone
6 cups Chicken Stock (page 262), Simple Beef Stock (page 264), or reduced-sodium canned chicken broth
½ teaspoon salt
½ teaspoon pepper
1 (14½-ounce) can tomatoes, chopped, juices reserved
1 cup elbow macaroni
⅓ cup grated Parmesan cheese

1. Place cranberry beans in a large bowl and add enough water to cover by at least 2 inches. Let stand at least 12 hours or overnight. Drain and rinse beans before using.

2. In a large saucepan, heat oil over medium-high heat. Add onion, celery, carrot, garlic, thyme, and ham bone. Cook, stirring occasionally, about 5 minutes. Add beans and chicken stock and bring to a boil. Reduce heat to medium-low and cook 30 minutes.

3. Stir in salt, pepper, and tomatoes with their juices and cook 20 to 30 minutes longer, or until beans are soft. Stir in macaroni and cook until macaroni is tender, about 10 minutes longer. Ladle soup into bowls, sprinkle with cheese, and serve.

125   GARLIC SOUP WITH ORZO AND GREEN BEANS

Prep: 20 minutes   Cook: 28 to 30 minutes   Serves: 4

2 large heads of garlic, cloves
   lightly crushed
2 bay leaves
2 tablespoons extra-virgin
   olive oil
½ teaspoon salt
6 cups Vegetable Stock (page
   266), Chicken Stock (page
   262), or canned vegetable
   broth

1 cup orzo
½ pound fresh green beans,
   trimmed and cut into
   1-inch lengths
1 tablespoon chopped fresh
   tarragon or ½ teaspoon
   dried
½ teaspoon pepper

1. In a large saucepan, combine garlic, bay leaves, olive oil, salt, and vegetable stock. Bring to a boil, reduce heat to medium-low, and simmer 20 minutes.

2. Strain the soup. Remove bay leaves and discard. Push the solids through a sieve. Return the solids to stock and bring back to a boil. Stir in orzo and beans. Reduce heat to medium and cook until tender, 8 to 10 minutes. Stir in tarragon and pepper just before serving.

126   ROASTED ONION SOUP WITH WHOLE WHEAT ROTELLE

Prep: 15 minutes   Cook: 1 hour 38 minutes   Serves: 4

Slow roasting brings out the natural sweetness in these onions.

2 tablespoons butter
2 large onions, thinly sliced
1 cup dry white wine
6 cups Vegetable Stock (page
   266) or canned vegetable
   broth

½ teaspoon salt
½ teaspoon pepper
½ teaspoon sugar
2 cups whole wheat rotelle or
   elbow macaroni
¼ cup grated Romano cheese

1. Preheat oven to 350°F. In a shallow baking dish, place butter, onions, wine, 1 cup vegetable stock, ¼ teaspoon salt, and ¼ teaspoon pepper. Bake 1½ hours, or until onions are very soft and liquid is mostly absorbed.

2. In a large saucepan, bring remaining 5 cups vegetable stock, salt, pepper, and sugar to a boil over high heat. Add pasta and cook until tender but still firm, about 8 minutes. Stir in onions. Ladle soup into bowls and serve sprinkled with Romano cheese.

127   ORZO, SPINACH, AND CAULIFLOWER SOUP

Prep: 20 minutes   Cook: 23 to 26 minutes   Serves: 4

2 tablespoons butter
2 tablespoons olive oil
1 medium onion, finely chopped
2 garlic cloves, minced
   Pinch of ground saffron
   Pinch of crushed hot red pepper
2 cups chopped cauliflower florets

6 cups Vegetable Stock (page 266) or canned broth
1 cup canned peeled tomatoes, chopped
½ cup orzo
⅛ teaspoon salt
2 cups chopped fresh spinach

1. In a large saucepan, melt butter in olive oil over medium-high heat. Add onion and cook, stirring occasionally, until onion is softened, 2 to 3 minutes. Add garlic, saffron, and hot red pepper and cook, stirring constantly, 1 minute. Stir in cauliflower and 2 cups vegetable stock and simmer until cauliflower is crisp-tender, 10 minutes.

2. Stir in tomatoes and remaining 4 cups vegetable stock and bring to a boil. Reduce heat to low, add orzo and salt, and simmer until orzo is tender, 8 to 10 minutes. Stir in spinach, simmer 2 minutes longer, and serve.

128   FENNEL-SAFFRON SOUP WITH TINY PASTA

Prep: 20 minutes   Cook: 1 hour 17 minutes   Serves: 4

2 fennel bulbs, outer stalks removed, trimmed, cut lengthwise in half, and thinly sliced
1 medium onion, thinly sliced
3 garlic cloves, thinly sliced
2 tablespoons butter
1 cup dry white wine
2 tablespoons licorice-flavored liqueur

6 cups Vegetable Stock (page 266), Chicken Stock (page 262), or canned vegetable broth
½ teaspoon salt
⅛ teaspoon ground saffron
1 cup orzo semi de melone
2 tablespoons chopped parsley

1. Preheat oven to 400°F. In a shallow baking pan, place fennel, onion, garlic, butter, wine, liqueur, and 1 cup vegetable stock. Bake 1 hour, or until vegetables are softened and liquid is absorbed.

2. In a large saucepan, bring remaining 5 cups vegetable stock, salt, and saffron to a boil. Reduce heat to medium. Add orzo and cook until orzo is tender but still firm, about 7 minutes. Stir in fennel mixture and parsley, simmer 10 minutes longer, and serve.

129 HEARTY LENTIL AND PASTA SOUP WITH HAM AND POTATOES

Prep: 30 minutes   Cook: 25 minutes   Serves: 6

Try this satisfying soup—you won't be disappointed.

2 tablespoons extra-virgin olive oil
3 shallots, minced
1 medium carrot, peeled and finely chopped
1 medium celery rib, finely chopped
½ cup lentils, rinsed and picked over
6 cups Chicken Stock (page 262) or reduced-sodium canned broth

½ pound red potatoes, cut into ½-inch dice
1½ cups cubed ham or smoked duck
3 lasagne noodles, broken into 1-inch lengths
Parsley Puree (recipe follows)

1. In a soup pot, heat olive oil over medium-high heat. Add shallots, carrot, and celery and cook, stirring occasionally, until vegetables are softened, about 5 minutes. Stir in lentils and chicken stock and bring to a boil. Reduce heat to low, cover, and simmer 10 minutes.

2. Stir in potatoes, ham, and lasagne noodles, cover, and simmer until potatoes are softened, 10 minutes longer. To serve, ladle soup into bowls and swirl in Parsley Puree.

PARSLEY PUREE
Makes: about ⅓ cup

3 garlic cloves
¼ teaspoon salt

½ teaspoon pepper
⅓ cup minced fresh parsley

Combine garlic, salt, pepper, and parsley in a blender or food processor (preferably small model) and process until pureed.

130 CHICKPEA AND PASTA SHELL SOUP WITH ESCAROLE AND TOMATOES

Prep: 15 minutes   Cook: 10 minutes   Serves: 4

5 cups Vegetable Stock (page 266), Chicken Stock (page 262), or canned vegetable broth
1 (10½-ounce) can chickpeas, liquid reserved
½ teaspoon salt
1 cup small shell macaroni
4 cups chopped escarole (light inner leaves only)

2 medium tomatoes, peeled, seeded, and chopped
1 teaspoon grated lemon zest
1 tablespoon lemon juice
¼ cup chopped parsley
1 tablespoon chopped fresh thyme or ¾ teaspoon dried thyme leaves

1. In a large nonreactive saucepan, bring vegetable stock, beans with their liquid, and salt to a boil. Add macaroni, reduce heat to medium-low, and cook until macaroni is almost tender, about 7 minutes.

2. Stir in escarole, tomatoes, lemon zest and juice, parsley, and thyme, simmer until heated through, about 3 minutes longer, and serve.

131 FUSILLI AND BROCCOLI SOUP

Prep: 10 minutes   Cook: 13½ minutes   Serves: 6

1 small onion, peeled and cut into quarters
1 medium head of broccoli, washed, stems sliced, and florets cut into bite-size pieces
3 tablespoons extra-virgin olive oil
4 anchovy fillets, minced
⅛ teaspoon crushed hot red pepper

3 garlic cloves, chopped
½ teaspoon salt
5 cups Vegetable Stock (page 266) or canned broth
1 cup fusilli
2 tablespoons chopped fresh basil
1 teaspoon grated lemon zest
½ cup grated Romano cheese

1. In a food processor fitted with steel blade, process onion and broccoli stems together until finely chopped.

2. In a large skillet, heat oil over medium-high heat. Add anchovies, hot red pepper, and garlic and cook, stirring constantly, 30 seconds. Stir in broccoli mixture and salt. Reduce heat to medium, cover, and cook, stirring occasionally, 5 minutes.

3. Meanwhile, in a soup pot, bring vegetable stock to a boil. Reduce heat to low, add fusilli, and simmer 4 minutes. Stir in broccoli florets and chopped broccoli mixture and simmer until fusilli is tender but still firm, about 4 minutes longer. Stir in basil, lemon zest, and Romano cheese just before serving.

132   SEASAME-SCENTED BROTH WITH WATERCRESS AND TOFU

Prep: 10 minutes   Cook: 9 to 10 minutes   Serves: 2

Japanese soba noodles are made with buckwheat flour. If you can't find them, substitute udon or spaghetti. Mirin is sold in Japanese markets and in the Asian foods section of many supermarkets

1 tablespoon sesame seeds
3 cups dashi or 2 cups
    Chicken Stock (page 262)
    diluted with 1 cup water
¼ pound dried soba noodles
½ pound tofu (bean curd), cut
    into ½-inch cubes

1 bunch of watercress, tough
    stems removed
1 tablespoon grated fresh
    ginger
1 tablespoon mirin
1 tablespoon soy sauce
1 teaspoon Asian sesame oil

1. Place sesame seeds in a small skillet and cook over medium heat, stirring frequently, until lightly toasted, 3 to 4 minutes. Remove from skillet and set aside.

2. In a large saucepan, bring dashi to a boil. Add noodles, reduce heat to low, and cook until noodles are tender but still firm, about 5 minutes. Stir in tofu, watercress, ginger, mirin, soy sauce, and sesame oil and simmer 1 minute. Serve sprinkled with sesame seeds.

133   CHEESE RAVIOLI IN BROTH WITH MIXED MUSHROOMS

Prep: 20 minutes   Stand: 10 minutes   Cook: 12 to 15 minutes Serves: 4

½ ounce dried porcini, morel,
    or chanterelle
    mushrooms
2 tablespoons butter
1 tablespoon olive oil
1 medium onion, minced
¼ cup chopped parsley
2 garlic cloves, chopped
½ pound mixed fresh wild
    (cremini, chanterelle,
    oyster, or morel) and
    cultivated mushrooms,
    sliced

4 cups Chicken Stock (page
    262), Simple Beef Stock
    (page 264), or reduced-
    sodium canned broth
½ pound fresh cheese ravioli
¼ cup grated Parmesan cheese

1. In a medium heatproof bowl, cover dried mushrooms with 1 cup boiling water. Let stand 10 minutes, or until softened. Remove mushrooms, coarsely chop, and set aside. Strain soaking liquid through a paper towel-lined sieve or coffee filter. Discard strained solids and set liquid aside.

2. In a large saucepan, melt butter in oil over medium-high heat. Add onion, 2 tablespoons parsley, and garlic and cook, stirring constantly, 2 minutes. Add dried and fresh mushrooms and cook, stirring frequently, until mushrooms are tender, 5 to 8 minutes. Stir in chicken stock and bring to a boil. Reduce heat to low and keep warm.

3. In a large skillet, bring 4 cups water to a boil. Add ravioli, reduce heat to medium, and cook until ravioli is tender but still firm, about 5 minutes. With a slotted spoon, transfer ravioli to bowls. Ladle mushroom soup over ravioli and sprinkle with remaining 2 tablespoons parsley and Parmesan cheese.

134 MUSHROOM MARSALA SOUP WITH WHOLE WHEAT SPAGHETTI

Prep: 20 minutes   Stand: 10 minutes   Cook: 29 to 31 minutes
Serves: 4

¼ ounce dried porcini mushrooms
2 tablespoons unsalted butter
4 shallots, minced
2 garlic cloves, minced
1 tablespoon olive oil
1 pound fresh cremini or white button mushrooms, sliced

⅓ cup tomato puree
5 cups Vegetable Stock (page 266) or canned broth
1½ cups broken whole wheat spaghetti
2 tablespoons marsala

1. In a medium heatproof bowl, cover dried mushrooms with 1 cup boiling water. Let stand until softened, about 10 minutes. Remove mushrooms from liquid and chop mushrooms. Strain mushroom liquid through a paper towel-lined sieve or a coffee filter. Set mushrooms and soaking liquid aside.

2. In a large nonreactive saucepan, melt 1 tablespoon butter over medium heat. Add shallots and garlic and cook, stirring occasionally, until softened, 2 to 3 minutes. Transfer shallot mixture to a bowl.

3. Melt remaining 1 tablespoon butter in olive oil in same saucepan. Add fresh mushrooms in batches, if necessary, and cook, stirring frequently, until browned, about 5 minutes. Add shallot mixture and dried mushrooms to saucepan along with tomato puree, vegetable stock, and mushroom soaking liquid and cook 10 minutes.

4. Meanwhile, bring a large pot of salted water to a boil. Add spaghetti and stir well. Reduce heat to medium-low and cook until spaghetti is tender but still firm, about 10 minutes. Drain spaghetti well and stir into saucepan along with marsala. Simmer until heated through, 2 to 3 minutes, and serve.

135 TORTELLINI SOUP WITH SPINACH AND PARMESAN CHEESE

Prep: 25 minutes   Cook: 14 minutes   Serves: 4

If you can't find pancetta, use a couple of slices of ham or bacon.

2 tablespoons extra-virgin olive oil	5 cups Simple Beef Stock (page 264), Chicken Stock (page 262), or reduced-sodium canned broth
4 thin slices of pancetta or ham or bacon	
1 medium onion, chopped	2 cups fresh meat- or cheese-filled tortellini
1 small carrot, peeled and chopped	2 cups chopped fresh spinach
1 medium celery rib, chopped	½ teaspoon salt
2 plum tomatoes, peeled, seeded, and chopped	½ teaspoon pepper
2 garlic cloves, minced	¼ cup grated Parmesan cheese
1 sprig of fresh rosemary or ¼ teaspoon dried	

1. In a large nonreactive saucepan, heat oil over medium-high heat. Add pancetta, onion, carrot, and celery and cook, stirring frequently, until vegetables are softened, about 5 minutes. Add tomatoes, garlic, and rosemary and cook, stirring frequently, 2 minutes longer.

2. Add beef stock and bring to a boil. Stir in tortellini and cook 5 minutes, or until tender but still firm. Stir in spinach, salt, and pepper and cook 2 minutes longer. To serve, ladle soup into bowls and sprinkle with cheese.

136 HEARTY PASTA AND BEAN SOUP WITH PARSLEY-WALNUT PESTO

Prep: 20 minutes   Cook: 19 to 20 minutes   Serves: 4

For optimum flavor, add the pesto to the soup just before serving.

2 tablespoons olive oil	2 garlic cloves, minced
4 thin slices pancetta or bacon, chopped	5 cups Vegetable Stock (page 266) or canned broth
1 medium onion, chopped	1 cup dried tubetti or other small pasta
1 (10-ounce) can cannellini beans, liquid reserved	½ teaspoon salt
1 (14½-ounce) can diced tomatoes, juices reserved	¼ cup Parsley-Walnut Pesto (recipe follows)

1. In a large nonreactive saucepan, heat olive oil over medium-high heat. Add pancetta and onion and cook, stirring occasionally, 4 minutes. Add cannellini with their liquid, tomatoes with their juices, garlic, and vegetable stock and bring to a boil. Reduce heat to low and simmer 10 minutes.

2. Stir in tubetti and salt and cook until pasta is tender but still firm, 5 to 6 minutes. To serve, ladle soup into bowls, top with Parsley-Walnut Pesto, and swirl gently with a spoon.

137 PARSLEY-WALNUT PESTO
Prep: 10 minutes   Cook: 10 to 12 minutes   Serves: 4

1 tablespoon chopped walnuts	⅛ teaspoon salt
1½ cups packed Italian (flat-leaf) parsley leaves	⅛ teaspoon pepper
1 large garlic clove	3 tablespoons grated Parmesan cheese
	¼ cup olive oil

1. Preheat oven to 350°F. Place walnuts in a shallow baking pan. Bake, stirring occasionally, until lightly toasted, 10 to 12 minutes. Cool slightly.

2. In a food processor or blender, place walnuts, parsley, garlic, salt, pepper, and cheese and process until well blended. With machine on, drizzle in oil and puree until smooth.

138 MEXICAN VERMICELLI IN ROASTED TOMATO BROTH
Prep: 15 minutes   Cook: 51 to 55 minutes   Serves: 4

This hearty soup, full of roasted tomato flavor, is a dinner soup commonly served in Mexico.

8 plum tomatoes	5½ cups Chicken Stock (page 262), Vegetable Stock (page 266), or reduced-sodium canned broth
1 small onion, coarsely chopped	
2 garlic cloves	
3 tablespoons vegetable oil	½ teaspoon salt
¼ pound very fine vermicelli, broken into 4-inch lengths	½ teaspoon black pepper
	½ teaspoon cayenne

1. Preheat oven to 400°F. Place tomatoes in a shallow pan and roast until blackened, about 35 minutes. Transfer tomatoes with their juices to a food processor. With motor running, add onion and garlic and puree until smooth.

2. In a large nonreactive saucepan, heat oil over medium-high heat. Add vermicelli and cook, stirring constantly, until golden brown, about 2 minutes.

3. Add tomato mixture and cook, stirring constantly, until mixture is very dry, 6 to 8 minutes. Stir in chicken stock, salt, black pepper, and cayenne and bring to a boil. Reduce heat to medium and simmer until vermicelli is tender but still firm, 8 to 10 minutes.

Chapter 6

Bean, Rice, and Grain Soups

Since the new USDA Food Pyramid recommends basing our diets on grains, carbohydrates, and rice (6 to 11 servings a day) and adding more legumes and eating less meat for protein, this chapter can come in quite handy when planning meals. Since most of these recipes use only small amounts of meat, fish, or poultry, they fit right into these current nutritional guidelines.

Supermarket shelves are now packed with a wide variety of grains, such as the quinoa used in the Quinoa Soup with Beets and Beet Greens. Quinoa (pronounced KEEN-WAH) is an ancient South American grain that has a subtle nutty taste and is high in protein. If quinoa seems a bit too exotic for your taste, stay on more familiar ground with the Barley, Carrot, and Broccoli Soup, or for a truly economical soup, try the Mexican Oatmeal Soup with Roasted Tomatoes.

This chapter also uses a variety of rices, most of which you'll be able to purchase in any well-stocked supermarket. From the Celery, Rice, and Prosciutto Soup (which uses Italian Arborio rice, a short-grain white rice), to Indian-Spiced Tomato Soup with Basmati Rice (a long-grain aromatic rice), you'll be amazed at the tastes and aromas of different rice varieties. For a special occasion, try the Wild Rice and Mushroom Soup, which uses wild rice (technically a seed from a native American grass, not a rice at all). Wild rice expands at a greater volume than true rices—four times its volume instead of three times—and is cooked through when the brown grains burst open and the fluffy white insides are exposed.

As for cooking with beans, this chapter takes advantage of dried beans that require soaking overnight as well as lentils, green and yellow split peas, and canned beans. All are wonderful, low-fat proteins that are very versatile. Try Lentil, Turkey, and Wild Rice Soup for a great way to use left-over turkey or Jamaican Yellow Split Pea Soup for a new way to eat yellow split peas. Red lentils (widely available in health food stores) have a wonderful hue and break down into a lovely puree when cooked in the Turkish Red Lentil Soup with Mint. Even the Lima Bean and Corn Soup with Chipotle Chiles is relatively quick once the limas are presoaked.

Tip: While the dried bean recipes in this chapter call for soaking the beans overnight, you can use a quick method if you forget. Place the beans in a large pot with enough cold water to cover by at least 2 inches. Bring to a boil, remove from the heat, cover, and let stand 1 to 2 hours, until softened. Drain and rinse the beans before using.

139   BARLEY, CARROT, AND BROCCOLI SOUP

Prep: 20 minutes   Cook: 1 hour 23 minutes to 1 hour 25 minutes
Serves: 6

Whole barley, commonly found at health food stores, has much more flavor than the more common pearl barley.

1   cup whole kernel barley
2   tablespoons olive oil
1   large onion, finely chopped
1   medium bunch of broccoli, stems chopped, florets reserved
3   medium carrots, peeled and diced
2   garlic cloves, minced
2   sprigs of fresh thyme or ½ teaspoon dried thyme leaves

1   bay leaf
6   cups Vegetable Stock (page 266) or canned broth
½   teaspoon salt
½   teaspoon pepper
2   tablespoons chopped parsley

1. Place barley in a large heavy soup pot over medium heat. Stir and shake pan 12 minutes, or until barley is lightly browned. Remove to a small bowl to cool.

2. In same pot, heat oil over medium-high heat. Add onion, broccoli stems, and carrots and cook, stirring occasionally, until softened, 6 to 8 minutes. Stir in garlic, thyme, bay leaf, vegetable stock, barley, salt, and pepper and bring to a boil. Reduce heat to medium-low, cover, and simmer 1 hour, or until barley is tender.

3. Chop reserved broccoli florets into ½-inch pieces. Stir into soup along with parsley, simmer 5 minutes longer, and serve.

140   BLACK BEAN AND ROASTED GARLIC SOUP

Prep: 15 minutes   Cook: 1 hour 5 minutes   Serves: 4

2   heads of garlic, loose skins removed
1   tablespoon olive oil
1   large onion, chopped
1   medium carrot, peeled and chopped
1   medium parsnip, peeled and chopped
¼   teaspoon ground coriander

⅛   teaspoon ground cloves
½   teaspoon salt
½   teaspoon pepper
    Pinch of cayenne
5   cups Vegetable Stock (page 266) or canned broth
2   (15-ounce) cans black beans, drained and rinsed

1. Preheat oven to 400°F. Wrap garlic in foil and bake 40 minutes, or until very soft.

2. Meanwhile, in a large saucepan, heat oil over medium-high heat. Add onion, carrot, and parsnip and cook, stirring occasionally, about 5 minutes. Stir in coriander, cloves, salt, pepper, cayenne, vegetable stock, and beans and bring to a boil. Reduce heat to medium-low and simmer until vegetables are softened, 20 minutes.

3. When garlic is done, cut 1 inch off tops and squeeze puree into a small bowl. Stir into soup and serve.

141 LIMA BEAN AND CORN SOUP WITH CHIPOTLE CHILES
Prep: 15 minutes   Stand: 12 hours   Cook: 50 to 51 minutes
Serves: 8

Cooking the soup with the corn cobs bolsters the flavor of this soup. Try to get the freshest corn you can find and shuck it just before using. Remember to put the lima beans up to soak the night before.

1 cup large dried lima beans, rinsed and picked over
2 tablespoons vegetable oil
1 large onion, chopped
2 carrots, peeled and diced
6 garlic cloves, chopped
½ teaspoon dried oregano
½ teaspoon dried thyme leaves
½ teaspoon ground cumin

2 ears of corn, kernels cut from the cob, cobs reserved
½ teaspoon minced canned chipotle chile in adobo sauce
1½ teaspoons sugar
½ teaspoon salt

1. Place lima beans in a large bowl and add enough water to cover by at least 2 inches. Let stand at least 12 hours or overnight. Drain and rinse beans before using.

2. In a soup pot, heat oil over medium-high heat. Add onion and carrots and cook, stirring occasionally, until onion is softened, 4 to 5 minutes. Add garlic and cook, stirring constantly, until fragrant, 1 minute. Stir in oregano, thyme, and cumin. Add beans, corn cobs, and 5 cups water. Bring to a boil. Reduce heat to medium-low and simmer 30 minutes. Remove and discard cobs.

3. Stir in chipotle chile, corn kernels, sugar, and salt, simmer until corn is tender, 15 minutes longer, and serve.

142   WALLA WALLA ONION SOUP WITH CANNELLINI BEANS

Prep: 20 minutes   Cook: 55 minutes   Serves: 8

2 tablespoons olive oil
6 large Walla Walla, Vidalia, or Spanish onions, cut in half and sliced
3 garlic cloves, minced
½ teaspoon dried thyme leaves
1 imported bay leaf

1 cup dry white wine
1 (10½-ounce) can cannellini beans, drained
4 cups Vegetable Stock (page 266) or canned broth
½ cup grated Parmesan cheese

1. In a large soup pot, heat oil over medium-high heat. Add onions and cook, stirring occasionally, until very soft, about 30 minutes.

2. Stir in garlic, thyme, bay leaf, and white wine and cook until wine is reduced by half, about 5 minutes.

3. Stir in beans and vegetable stock and simmer 20 minutes longer. Remove and discard bay leaf.

4. Ladle soup into bowls and sprinkle with cheese.

143   WHITE BEAN AND SAVOY CABBAGE SOUP

Prep: 20 minutes   Stand: 12 hours   Cook: 1 hour 15 minutes
Serves: 8

Remember to put the cannellini beans up to soak the night before.

1½ cups dried cannellini beans, rinsed and picked over
2 tablespoons unsalted butter
2 medium leeks (white and tender green), rinsed and thinly sliced
½ small Savoy cabbage, thinly sliced
1 imported bay leaf

6 cups Vegetable Stock (page 266) or canned broth
¼ cup heavy cream
¼ cup chopped parsley
1 teaspoon chopped fresh tarragon
½ teaspoon salt
½ teaspoon pepper

1. Place cannellini beans in a large bowl and add enough water to cover by at least 2 inches. Let stand 12 hours or overnight. Drain and rinse beans before using.

2. In a large soup pot, melt butter over medium-high heat. Add leeks and cook, stirring occasionally, until softened, about 2 minutes. Stir in cabbage and continue cooking until cabbage is wilted, about 8 minutes. Add beans, bay leaf, and vegetable stock. Reduce heat to low and simmer until beans are tender, about 1 hour.

3. Stir in cream, parsley, tarragon, salt, and pepper, simmer to heat through, 5 minutes longer, and serve.

144 GREEN SPLIT PEA SOUP WITH BACON AND ROSEMARY CROUTONS

Prep: 25 minutes   Cook: 1 hour 34 minutes   Serves: 6

This soup has a nice coarse texture. If you prefer, you can puree it in the food processor before adding the bacon.

¼ pound thickly sliced bacon, cut into ½-inch pieces
1 large onion, finely chopped
2 medium celery ribs with leaves, chopped
2 medium carrots, peeled and sliced
1 medium parsnip, peeled and sliced
1 medium turnip, peeled and diced

3 large garlic cloves, minced
2 bay leaves
⅛ teaspoon crushed hot red pepper
6 cups Chicken Stock (page 262) or reduced-sodium canned broth
1 cup green split peas, rinsed and picked over
Rosemary Croutons (recipe follows)

1. In a soup pot, cook bacon over medium-high heat until crisp, about 5 minutes. With slotted spoon, remove bacon to paper towels to drain. Add onion, celery, carrots, parsnip, and turnip to soup pot. Cook, stirring occasionally, until vegetables are softened, about 8 minutes. Add garlic, bay leaves, and hot red pepper and stir 1 minute longer.

2. Stir in chicken stock and split peas and bring to a boil. Reduce heat to low. Cook, partially covered, 1 hour 10 minutes, or until peas are tender. Stir in bacon and simmer 10 minutes longer. Remove and discard bay leaves.

3. Ladle soup into bowls and top with Rosemary Croutons.

145 ROSEMARY CROUTONS

Prep: 5 minutes   Cook: 2 minutes   Serves: 6

2 tablespoons olive oil
1 sprig of fresh rosemary
6 (½-inch-thick) slices of French bread

Pinch of salt

1. In a medium skillet, heat olive oil and rosemary over high heat. Add bread and cook until browned, about 1 minute on each side.

2. Remove to paper towels and sprinkle with salt. Cut into bite-size pieces.

146 TOMATO AND WHITE BEAN SOUP

Prep: 20 minutes   Stand: 12 hours
Cook: 1 hour 37 minutes to 1 hour 39 minutes   Serves: 8

Marrow beans are plump white beans with a mild flavor. If you can't find them, use navy or Great Northern beans. Remember to put the beans up to soak the night before.

2 cups marrow or other white beans, rinsed and picked over
6 garlic cloves
2 imported bay leaves
1½ teaspoons salt
¼ cup extra-virgin olive oil

4 large shallots, minced
6 large plum tomatoes, seeded and chopped
10 large basil leaves, chopped
¼ cup chopped parsley
½ teaspoon pepper

1. Place marrow beans in a large bowl and add enough water to cover by at least 2 inches. Let stand 12 hours or overnight. Drain and rinse beans before using.

2. In a large nonreactive soup pot, combine beans, garlic, bay leaves, and 8 cups water. Bring to a boil. Reduce heat to medium and cook, partially covered, 30 minutes. Stir in salt and continue cooking until beans are tender, about 30 minutes longer.

3. In a medium skillet, heat oil over medium-high heat. Add shallots and cook, stirring occasionally, until softened, 2 to 3 minutes. Add tomatoes and cook until softened, about 3 minutes. Stir into beans and simmer, uncovered, 30 minutes longer. Stir in basil, parsley, and pepper, simmer until heated through, 2 to 3 minutes, and serve.

147 TURKISH RED LENTIL SOUP WITH MINT

Prep: 10 minutes   Cook: 49 minutes   Serves: 6

Soups are an integral part of Turkish cuisine. Serve this one with warm, crusty bread for a satisfying lunch or light dinner.

1 cup red lentils, rinsed and picked over
2 tablespoons short-grain brown rice
6 cups Chicken Stock (page 262), Vegetable Stock (page 266), or reduced-sodium canned broth

3 tablespoons butter
1 large onion, finely chopped
⅓ cup dried mint
½ teaspoon crushed hot red pepper
3 egg yolks
½ cup milk
½ teaspoon salt

1. In a soup pot, combine lentils, rice, and chicken stock. Bring to a boil. Reduce heat to medium-low and simmer until rice is tender, about 40 minutes. Transfer solids to a food processor, puree until smooth, and return to pot.

2. In a medium skillet, melt butter over medium heat. Add onion and cook until golden, about 3 minutes. Add mint and hot red pepper and cook, stirring constantly, 1 minute. Add to soup pot and simmer 5 minutes.

3. In a small bowl, beat together egg yolks and milk and pour into soup, whisking constantly. Bring to a simmer and remove from heat. Stir in salt and serve immediately.

148 SICILIAN FOUR-BEAN SOUP WITH FENNEL

Prep: 15 minutes   Stand: 12 hours   Cook: 1 hour 35 minutes
Serves: 4

This full-bodied soup, which originated in Sicily, is a great source of protein. Remember to put the beans up to soak the night before.

1 cup dried shelled fava or
  large lima beans, rinsed
  and picked over
½ cup dried garbanzo beans,
  rinsed and picked over
¼ cup dried lentils, rinsed and
  picked over
¼ cup dried green split peas,
  rinsed and picked over
¼ cup extra-virgin olive oil

1 large onion, chopped
2 medium celery ribs,
  chopped
1 fennel bulb, chopped,
  fronds reserved
1 teaspoon crushed fennel
  seed
1 teaspoon salt
½ teaspoon pepper

1. Place beans in a large bowl and add enough water to cover by at least 2 inches. Let stand 12 hours or overnight. Drain and rinse beans before using. If using fava beans, peel off outer skins after soaking.

2. In a large saucepan, combine beans, lentils, and split peas with 8 cups water. Bring to a boil. Reduce heat to low and simmer 1 hour, or until beans are very soft and begin to break apart.

3. In a large skillet, heat 2 tablespoons oil over medium-high heat. Add onion, celery, chopped fennel, and fennel seed and cook, stirring occasionally, until vegetables are softened, about 5 minutes. Stir into saucepan with salt and pepper and continue cooking 30 minutes longer.

4. Chop enough fennel fronds to make ¼ cup and stir into soup. Ladle soup into bowls and drizzle remaining 2 tablespoons oil evenly over each serving.

149   JAMAICAN YELLOW SPLIT PEA SOUP

Prep: 20 minutes   Cook: 1 hour 38 minutes to 1 hour 39 minutes
Serves: 6

Allspice, which comes from ground allspice berries, is an aromatic West Indian spice integral to Caribbean cooking.

2 tablespoons vegetable oil	½ teaspoon dried thyme leaves
2 medium celery ribs with leaves, chopped	¼ teaspoon ground allspice
	½ teaspoon salt
1 large parsnip, peeled and chopped	¼ teaspoon crushed hot red pepper
1 small sweet potato, peeled and cut into ½-inch dice	1½ cups yellow split peas, rinsed and picked over
1 bunch of scallions, trimmed and sliced	6 cups Chicken Stock (page 262) or reduced-sodium canned broth
1 bay leaf	

1. In a soup pot, heat oil over medium-high heat. Add celery, parsnip, sweet potato, and scallions and cook until celery is softened, about 5 minutes. Add bay leaf, thyme, allspice, and salt and cook, stirring constantly, 1 minute. Add split peas and chicken stock and simmer, partially covered, until split peas are tender, 1½ hours.

2. Remove and discard bay leaf. Transfer half of the soup to a blender or food processor and puree until smooth. Return to pot and simmer until heated through, 2 to 3 minutes.

150   MEXICAN OATMEAL SOUP WITH ROASTED TOMATOES

Prep: 10 minutes   Cook: 46 to 47 minutes   Serves: 6 to 8

Toasting the oatmeal gives this soup a nice nutty flavor.

6 plum tomatoes	½ teaspoon dried oregano, preferably Mexican
2 cups old-fashioned oatmeal	
2 tablespoons vegetable oil	6 cups Vegetable Stock (page 266) or canned broth
1 medium onion, chopped	
4 large garlic cloves, chopped	½ teaspoon salt
1 small jalapeño pepper, seeded and minced	½ teaspoon black pepper
	¼ cup chopped cilantro

1. Preheat oven to 500°F. Place tomatoes in 15 × 10-inch jelly-roll pan and roast until blackened and shriveled, about 25 minutes. Transfer to a small bowl and let cool.

2. Meanwhile, in a soup pot, toast oatmeal over medium-high heat, stirring frequently, until dark golden brown, about 10 minutes. Transfer to a small bowl and let cool.

3. In same pot, heat oil over medium-high heat. Add onion and cook, stirring frequently, until golden, about 8 minutes. Add garlic, jalapeño pepper, and oregano and cook, stirring constantly, until garlic is fragrant, 1 minute longer. Reduce heat to low, stir in vegetable stock, oatmeal, salt, and black pepper and simmer 10 minutes.

4. Chop tomatoes and discard seeds. Stir tomatoes into soup along with cilantro, simmer until heated through, 2 to 3 minutes longer, and serve.

---

151 YELLOW SPLIT PEA SOUP WITH SUMMER SQUASH AND GARLIC-CHIVE OIL

Prep: 25 minutes   Cook: 1 hour 20 minutes   Serves: 6

This showstopping soup gets a nice jolt of flavor from a swirl of chive oil in each serving.

2 tablespoons olive oil
1 large onion, minced
1 medium celery rib with
    leaves, chopped
3 large garlic cloves, minced
⅛ teaspoon crushed hot red
    pepper
6 cups Vegetable Stock (page
    266), Chicken Stock (page
    262), or canned broth

1 cup yellow split peas, rinsed
    and picked over
½ teaspoon salt
2 small summer squash, cut
    into ½-inch pieces
    Garlic-Chive Oil (recipe
    follows)

1. In a soup pot, heat olive oil over medium-high heat. Add onion and celery and cook, stirring occasionally, until onion is softened, 4 to 5 minutes. Add garlic and hot red pepper and cook, stirring constantly, 1 minute longer.

2. Add vegetable stock, split peas, and salt to soup pot and bring to a boil. Reduce heat to low and simmer 1 hour. Stir in squash and simmer 15 minutes longer.

3. To serve, ladle soup into bowls and stir in a swirl of Garlic-Chive Oil.

GARLIC-CHIVE OIL
Makes: ⅓ cup

¼ cup olive oil
1 large garlic clove

1 bunch of chives, coarsely
    chopped

In a blender or food processor, combine oil, garlic, and chives and puree until smooth.

152 QUINOA SOUP WITH BEETS AND BEET GREENS

Prep: 25 minutes   Cook: 20 minutes   Serves: 6

Quinoa, an ancient grain from South America, is high in protein and low in fat.

3 medium beets with tops
½ cup quinoa, rinsed
½ teaspoon salt
6 cups Vegetable Stock (page 266) or canned broth
1 tablespoon vegetable oil
2 large shallots, minced
2 medium celery ribs, chopped

3 scallions, finely chopped
2 tablespoons chopped fresh dill
1 jalapeño pepper, seeded and minced
¼ teaspoon freshly ground black pepper
1 cup plain yogurt

1. Chop off beet tops and reserve. Scrub and peel beets and shred on large holes of grater. Rinse and chop beet greens.

2. In a large soup pot, place quinoa, salt, and vegetable stock. Bring to a boil. Reduce heat to low and simmer 10 minutes.

3. Meanwhile, heat oil in a large skillet over medium heat. Add shallots and celery and cook until vegetables are softened, about 2 minutes. Stir in shredded beets and chopped beet greens. Cover and cook 3 minutes.

4. Add contents of skillet to soup pot and simmer 5 minutes longer. Stir in scallions, dill, jalapeño pepper, and black pepper. Ladle soup into bowls and top each serving with a dollop of yogurt.

153 ASPARAGUS AND ITALIAN RICE SOUP

Prep: 10 minutes   Cook: 26 to 30 minutes   Serves: 6

6 cups Chicken Stock (page 262) or reduced-sodium canned broth
½ teaspoon salt
1 pound asparagus, cut into 1-inch pieces
2 tablespoons extra-virgin olive oil

3 garlic cloves, minced
Pinch of saffron threads
½ cup Arborio rice
2 egg yolks
½ teaspoon pepper

1. In a soup pot, bring chicken stock and salt to a boil over high heat. Add asparagus and cook until crisp-tender, 3 to 5 minutes. Drain, reserving stock.

2. In same pot, heat olive oil over medium heat. Add garlic and cook, stirring frequently, until soft and fragrant, 1 to 2 minutes. Stir in all but 1 cup reserved stock, saffron, and rice and cook until rice is tender, about 20 minutes. Stir in asparagus.

3. Whisk egg yolks together in medium mixing bowl and whisk in 1 cup of reserved stock. Pour back into soup, whisking constantly, and cook until thickened, 2 to 3 minutes. Stir in pepper just before serving.

154 RICE AND ESCAROLE SOUP
Prep: 10 minutes   Cook: 31 minutes   Serves: 4

2 tablespoons olive oil
1 medium onion, finely
   chopped
2 garlic cloves, minced
1 head of escarole, coarsely
   chopped
6 cups Chicken Stock (page
   262) or reduced-sodium
   canned broth

1 bay leaf
1 cup long-grain white rice
1 teaspoon salt
½ teaspoon pepper
   Fontina and Parmesan
   Toasts (recipe follows)

1. In a large saucepan, heat olive oil over medium heat. Add onion and garlic and cook, stirring frequently, until softened but not browned, about 3 minutes. Add escarole and cook, stirring frequently, until wilted, about 3 minutes. Add 3 cups of chicken stock and the bay leaf. Bring to a boil, reduce heat to low, and simmer 10 minutes.

2. Add remaining chicken stock, rice, salt, and pepper. Return to a boil. Reduce heat to low, cover, and simmer 15 minutes, or until rice is tender. Remove and discard bay leaf. Serve with Fontina and Parmesan Toasts.

155 FONTINA AND PARMESAN TOASTS
Prep: 15 minutes   Cook: 11 minutes   Makes: about 16 toasts

3 tablespoons butter
3 tablespoons olive oil
1 loaf of Italian semolina
   bread, cut into ½-inch-
   thick slices

⅔ cup grated fontina cheese
¼ cup grated Parmesan cheese

1. Preheat oven to 375°F. In a small saucepan, melt butter in oil over medium heat. Brush mixture onto one side of each bread slice. Arrange slices, buttered side up, on a baking sheet. Bake 10 minutes.

2. Preheat broiler. Sprinkle fontina and Parmesan cheeses evenly over toasts. Broil about 4 inches from heat 1 minute, or until fontina begins to melt.

156　WILD RICE AND MUSHROOM SOUP
Prep: 25 minutes　　Cook: 42 to 43 minutes　　Serves: 4

⅓　cup wild rice
2　tablespoons butter
4　shallots, minced
1　garlic clove, minced
½　pound mushrooms,
　　preferably cremini, sliced

⅓　cup tomato puree
4　cups Simple Beef Stock
　　(page 264) or reduced-
　　sodium canned broth
2　tablespoons heavy cream

1. In a small saucepan, bring 2 cups water to a boil. Add rice. Cover, reduce heat to low, and simmer until rice pops open, about 40 minutes. Drain rice.

2. In a large saucepan, melt butter over medium heat. Add shallots and garlic and cook, stirring occasionally, until softened, 2 to 3 minutes. Transfer to a bowl.

3. Add mushrooms to saucepan and stir in tomato puree, beef stock, and rice. Bring to a boil. Remove from heat, stir in cream, and serve.

157　LENTIL, TURKEY, AND WILD RICE SOUP
Prep: 15 minutes　　Cook: 57 to 58 minutes　　Serves: 6

This homey, yet elegant soup is a wonderful way to use up leftover roast turkey.

2　tablespoons butter
2　medium leeks (white and
　　tender green), well rinsed
　　and thinly sliced
1　medium carrot, peeled and
　　chopped
1　medium celery rib, chopped
1　imported bay leaf
2　large sprigs of fresh thyme
　　or 1 teaspoon dried thyme
　　leaves
½　cup wild rice, rinsed

6　cups Chicken Stock (page
　　262) or reduced-sodium
　　canned broth
¾　cup dried lentils, rinsed and
　　picked over
1½　cups chopped cooked
　　turkey or ½ pound turkey
　　sausage
2　tablespoons chopped
　　parsley
½　teaspoon pepper

1. In a soup pot, melt butter over medium-high heat. Add leeks, carrot, and celery and cook, stirring occasionally, until leeks have softened, 2 to 3 minutes. Stir in bay leaf, thyme, wild rice, and chicken stock. Cover and bring to a boil. Reduce heat to medium-low and simmer 30 minutes.

2. Stir in lentils and turkey, cover, and cook until rice is tender, 25 minutes longer. Remove and discard bay leaf and thyme sprigs. Stir in parsley and pepper just before serving.

158 TURKISH WHEAT BERRY SOUP WITH YOGURT

Prep: 20 minutes   Cook: 54 to 57 minutes   Serves: 4

Although this soup is served hot, it would be quite refreshing as a cold summer soup. Look for wheat berries in your health food store.

2 tablespoons butter
1 large onion, finely chopped
¾ cup wheat berries, rinsed
½ teaspoon salt
⅛ teaspoon cayenne
6 cups Vegetable Stock (page 266) or canned broth

2 cups plain yogurt
2 tablespoons flour
3 egg yolks
2 small zucchini, shredded
½ cup chopped cilantro
1 tablespoon chopped fresh mint or 1 teaspoon dried

1. In a large saucepan, melt butter over medium heat. Add onion and cook, stirring occasionally, until softened, 3 to 5 minutes. Add wheat berries, salt, cayenne, and vegetable stock and simmer until wheat berries are tender, about 45 minutes.

2. Meanwhile, in a large bowl, whisk together yogurt, flour, egg yolks, and ½ cup water.

3. When wheat berries are cooked, gradually whisk yogurt mixture into soup. Bring to a boil, reduce heat to low, and simmer 5 minutes. Stir in zucchini, cilantro, and mint and simmer until heated through, 1 to 2 minutes.

159 TOASTED RICE SOUP WITH SPINACH AND PARMESAN CHEESE

Prep: 15 minutes   Cook: 28 to 30 minutes   Serves: 4

1 cup long-grain white rice
2 tablespoons extra-virgin olive oil
1 large onion, chopped
4 garlic cloves, minced
½ teaspoon salt
½ teaspoon grated nutmeg

⅛ teaspoon cayenne
6 cups Vegetable Stock (page 266) or canned broth
2 cups chopped fresh spinach leaves
⅓ cup grated Parmesan cheese
1 teaspoon grated lemon zest

1. Preheat oven to 350°F. Place rice in a shallow baking pan and toast, stirring occasionally, until golden brown, 8 to 10 minutes.

2. In a large soup pot, heat olive oil over medium-high heat. Add onion and cook, stirring frequently, until golden, about 5 minutes. Stir in garlic, salt, nutmeg, cayenne, vegetable stock, and rice and bring to a boil. Reduce heat to low, cover, and simmer until rice is tender, about 12 minutes.

3. Stir in spinach, Parmesan cheese, and lemon zest, simmer until spinach is wilted, about 3 minutes longer, and serve.

160   THAI-STYLE RICE SOUP WITH SCALLOPS
Prep: 10 minutes   Cook: 7 minutes   Serves: 4

This is a quick, easy soup and a great way to use up any kind of leftover rice.

2 stalks of lemongrass or
   3 large strips of lemon
   zest (2 × 1 inch)
4 cups Chicken Stock (page
   262) or 2 cups reduced-
   sodium canned broth
   mixed with 2 cups water
1 cup cooked rice, preferably
   jasmine

1 tablespoon Thai fish sauce
   (nam pla) or soy sauce
1 tablespoon lime juice
1 teaspoon brown sugar
⅛ teaspoon cayenne
¼ pound bay scallops (or
   quartered sea scallops)
2 scallions, thinly sliced

1. Trim off tops of lemongrass stalks. Remove and discard outer leaves. Cut lemongrass into 2-inch pieces and crush lightly with flat side of a large knife.

2. In a large soup pot, bring chicken stock to a boil. Add lemongrass and rice. Reduce heat to low and simmer 5 minutes.

3. Stir in fish sauce, lime juice, brown sugar, cayenne, and scallops. Cook until scallops are just opaque throughout, about 2 minutes longer. Stir in scallions just before serving.

161   JAPANESE RICE SOUP WITH CRAB
Prep: 10 minutes   Cook: 7 minutes   Serves: 4

3 cups Chicken Stock (page
   262) or reduced-sodium
   canned broth
2 teaspoons soy sauce
4 thin slices of fresh ginger
6 fresh shiitake mushrooms,
   stems discarded, caps
   thinly sliced

1 cup thinly shredded fresh
   spinach leaves
2 cups cooked white rice,
   rinsed
1 egg, beaten
½ cup flaked cooked crabmeat
2 scallions, thinly sliced

1. In a large saucepan, combine chicken stock, soy sauce, and ginger. Bring to a boil, reduce heat to low, and simmer 5 minutes. Remove ginger slices and discard.

2. Add mushrooms, spinach, and rice to stock. Simmer until mushrooms are tender and spinach is wilted, 2 minutes. Bring to a boil; drizzle in egg, whisking constantly. Ladle into bowls and top with crab and scallions.

162 INDIAN-SPICED TOMATO SOUP WITH BASMATI RICE

Prep: 10 minutes   Cook: 33 to 35 minutes   Serves: 4

By roasting the tomatoes first, most of the water is cooked out, which results in a more concentrated tomato flavor.

8 plum tomatoes
1 teaspoon yellow mustard seed
¼ teaspoon ground cardamom
1 tablespoon vegetable oil
2 imported bay leaves
⅛ teaspoon crushed hot red pepper
2 teaspoons sugar

1 tablespoon grated fresh ginger
1 large onion, chopped
2 cups Vegetable Stock (page 266) or canned broth
1 cup cooked basmati or long-grain white rice
¼ teaspoon salt

1. Preheat oven to 500°F. Place tomatoes in 15 × 10-inch jelly-roll pan and roast 25 minutes, or until tomatoes are shriveled. Transfer tomatoes to a food processor and puree until smooth.

2. In a spice grinder or with a mortar and pestle, grind together mustard seed with cardamom. In a large saucepan, heat oil over medium-high heat. Add cardamom mixture, bay leaves, hot pepper, sugar, and ginger. Cook, stirring frequently, until spices darken, 1 to 2 minutes. Add onion and cook, stirring occasionally, until softened, 2 to 3 minutes.

3. Add tomato puree, vegetable stock, rice, and salt. Reduce heat to low and simmer 5 minutes, stirring occasionally. Remove and discard bay leaves and serve.

163 CELERY, RICE, AND PROSCIUTTO SOUP

Prep: 20 minutes   Cook: 29 to 31 minutes   Serves: 6

Celery is often a forgotten vegetable. Here it stars in a quick and satisfying soup.

1½ tablespoons extra-virgin
    olive oil
1 large onion, finely chopped
½ cup dry white wine
12 medium celery ribs with
    leaves, chopped
½ cup Arborio rice
6 cups Chicken Stock (page
    262) or reduced-sodium
    canned broth

¼ teaspoon salt
½ teaspoon pepper
¼ cup chopped parsley
4 thin slices of prosciutto,
    chopped

1. In a large nonreactive soup pot, heat olive oil over medium-high heat. Add onion and cook, stirring occasionally, until softened, 2 to 3 minutes. Stir in wine and simmer 5 minutes. Stir in celery, rice, chicken stock, salt, and pepper and bring to a boil.

2. Reduce heat to low, cover, and simmer until rice and vegetables are tender, about 20 minutes.

3. Stir in parsley and prosciutto and simmer until heated through, 2 to 3 minutes.

Chapter 7

Seafood Soups, Chowders, and Bisques

In this chapter, fish and shellfish star in every recipe. Whether it's as simple and American as New England Clam Chowder or as exotic as Spanish Chickpea and Cod Soup with Toasted Almond and Spinach Puree, they all rely on the sweet taste and light texture of seafood.

When buying fish, try to find the freshest possible. If purchasing fillets or steaks, look for moist, firm flesh. If the fish appears dry, don't buy it. Fresh fish should have a light subtle scent. If it has the clean smell of the ocean, you're on the right track.

When buying shellfish, the general rule is to make sure it's alive or very newly shelled. Mussels, clams, oysters, lobsters, and crabs are usually sold in the shell alive. Scallops and oysters are frequently sold shucked, packed in their own juice, and chilled. As a general rule, use shellfish the same day as purchasing. Fish and shellfish should both be kept very cold, preferably on ice.

When embarking on making a seafood soup, chowder, or bisque, remember that fish and shellfish are delicate, and they cook very quickly. In most of these recipes, the fish is added at the very end of the cooking time. This is terrific for entertaining purposes, since many of these recipes can be prepared just until the point of adding the fish. When ready to serve, reheat the soup base, stir in the fish, and in a few minutes, it's ready to eat.

164 SPANISH CHICKPEA AND COD SOUP WITH TOASTED ALMOND AND SPINACH PUREE

Prep: 20 minutes   Cook: 30 minutes   Serves: 6

The combination of cod, chickpeas, almonds, and spinach is commonly found in a Catalan soup usually served on Good Friday.

2 **tablespoons olive oil**	5 **cups Chicken Stock (page**
1 **large onion, chopped**	**262) or reduced-sodium**
2 **large garlic cloves, minced**	**canned broth**
4 **plum tomatoes, seeded and**	½ **pound cod or other firm**
chopped	**white fish, cut into 1-inch**
½ **teaspoon salt**	**chunks**
Pinch of cayenne	**Toasted Almond and**
⅛ **teaspoon cinnamon**	**Spinach Puree (recipe**
1 **(15½-ounce) can chickpeas,**	**follows)**
drained and rinsed	

1. In a large nonreactive soup pot, heat olive oil over medium heat. Add onion and cook, stirring occasionally, until golden, about 5 minutes. Add garlic, tomatoes, salt, cayenne, cinnamon, chickpeas, and chicken stock. Bring to a boil, reduce heat to medium, and cook 20 minutes.

2. Transfer 2 cups soup to a food processor or blender and puree until smooth. Return to soup pot. Stir in fish and spinach puree and simmer until fish flakes easily when tested with a fork, about 5 minutes longer.

165 TOASTED ALMOND AND SPINACH PUREE

Prep: 10 minutes   Cook: 12 to 14 minutes   Serves: 6

12 **blanched almonds**	2 **garlic cloves, minced**
3 **tablespoons butter**	½ **teaspoon salt**
1 **(½-inch-thick) slice of**	½ **teaspoon pepper**
French bread	
4 **cups chopped fresh spinach**	
leaves	

1. Preheat oven to 350°F. Place almonds in a shallow baking pan and bake, stirring occasionally, until toasted, 8 to 10 minutes.

2. In a medium skillet, melt 1 tablespoon butter over medium heat. Add bread and cook 1 minute on each side, or until browned on both sides. Transfer to paper towels and break into 1-inch chunks.

3. To the same skillet, add spinach and cook, stirring frequently, until wilted, about 2 minutes.

4. In a food processor or blender, process almonds and bread until fine crumbs form. Add spinach and puree until smooth. Add remaining 2 tablespoons butter, garlic, salt, and pepper and process until well blended.

166   CREAMY MUSSEL SOUP WITH SAFFRON AND WHITE WINE

Prep: 15 minutes   Cook: 35 to 40 minutes   Serves: 6

This is a perfect first-course soup. Saffron adds not only its subtle flavor but beautiful color.

3 pounds mussels, scrubbed and debearded	1 teaspoon dried thyme leaves
1 cup dry white wine	1 bay leaf
2 tablespoons butter	12 black peppercorns
1 large leek (white and tender green), well rinsed and minced	12 parsley stems
	1 teaspoon saffron threads
1 medium celery rib, minced	1 tablespoon cornstarch
2½ cups Quick Fish Stock (page 265) or clam juice	1 cup heavy cream
	¼ teaspoon salt
	¼ teaspoon pepper

1. In a nonreactive soup pot, combine mussels and wine. Bring to a boil over medium-high heat, cover, and cook until mussels have opened, 5 to 7 minutes. Remove mussels from shells, reserving 6 large mussels and 6 half-shells for garnish. Discard any mussels that don't open. Strain cooking liquid through a fine sieve into a large bowl.

2. In same soup pot, melt butter over medium heat. Add leek and celery and cook, stirring occasionally, until softened, about 5 minutes. Add fish stock, thyme, bay leaf, peppercorns, parsley, saffron, remaining cooked mussels, and reserved mussel liquid. Bring to a boil, reduce heat to low, and simmer 20 minutes. Remove and discard bay leaf.

3. In a food processor or blender, puree soup in batches until smooth and return to soup pot. Bring to a boil. In a small bowl, blend cornstarch with cream and stir into soup. Add salt and pepper and simmer, stirring constantly, until slightly thickened, 2 to 3 minutes.

4. Strain soup through a sieve into a large saucepan and simmer over medium heat until heated through, 3 to 5 minutes. Divide soup among 6 soup plates and garnish each serving with a mussel on the half-shell.

167   FINNAN HADDIE SOUP
Prep: 15 minutes   Cook: 47 minutes   Serves: 4

Finnan haddie—smoked haddock—makes a wonderful soup. It is especially good served with warm Cream Biscuits with Dill.

½ **pound finnan haddie
       (smoked haddock)**
2½ **cups milk**
3 **tablespoons butter**
2 **medium onions, minced**
1 **medium carrot, peeled and
       minced**
1 **medium celery rib, minced**
2 **tablespoons flour**
3 **cups Quick Fish Stock (page
       265) or reduced-sodium
       canned chicken broth**

1 **bay leaf**
¼ **teaspoon salt**
¼ **teaspoon white pepper**
½ **cup heavy cream**
1 **teaspoon lemon juice
       Cream Biscuits with Dill
       (recipe follows)**

1. In a medium saucepan, combine finnan haddie and milk. Bring to a boil, reduce heat to medium-low, and cook until fish flakes easily when tested with a fork, 15 minutes. With a slotted spoon, transfer fish to a plate and gently flake with a fork. Reserve milk.

2. In a large saucepan, melt butter over medium heat. Add onions, carrot, and celery and cook, stirring occasionally, until softened, 5 minutes. Add flour and cook, stirring constantly, 2 minutes without allowing to color. Add fish stock, reserved milk, bay leaf, salt, and white pepper. Bring to a boil, reduce heat to low, and simmer 20 minutes. Remove and discard bay leaf.

3. In a food processor or blender, puree soup in batches and return to saucepan. Add finnan haddie and cream. Bring to a boil, reduce heat to medium-low, and simmer to heat through, 5 minutes. Stir in lemon juice just before serving. Serve with Cream Biscuits with Dill.

168   CREAM BISCUITS WITH DILL

Prep: 5 minutes   Cook: 15 to 18 minutes   Makes: 8 biscuits

2 cups flour
1 tablespoon baking powder
1 teaspoon salt
¼ cup cold unsalted butter, cut into small pieces

3 tablespoons minced fresh dill
1 cup heavy cream

1. Preheat oven to 425°F. Into a medium bowl, sift flour, baking powder, and salt. Add butter and blend with pastry blender or 2 knives until mixture resembles coarse meal. Stir in dill and cream until well blended.

2. Form dough into a ball and place on lightly floured surface. Pat dough into an 8-inch circle and cut into 8 wedges. Arrange wedges on greased baking sheet and bake 15 to 18 minutes, or until golden brown. Serve warm.

169   CHINESE CRAB AND CORN SOUP

Prep: 15 minutes   Cook: 6½ minutes   Serves: 4

Here's a quick, satisfying soup. If you like, substitute cooked chopped clams for the crabmeat.

1 teaspoon vegetable oil
3 scallions, sliced
2 teaspoons grated fresh ginger
1 tablespoon dry sherry
3 cups Chicken Stock (page 262) or reduced-sodium canned broth
2 ears of corn, kernels cut off and cobs scraped (about 1 cup), or 1 (10-ounce) package frozen corn, thawed

2 tablespoons cornstarch
1 tablespoon soy sauce
¼ teaspoon salt
1 cup cooked crabmeat
1 egg, slightly beaten

1. In a large soup pot, heat oil over high heat. Add scallions and ginger and cook, stirring constantly, 1 minute. Add sherry and cook 30 seconds. Stir in chicken stock and corn and bring to a boil. Reduce heat to medium and cook until corn is tender, about 5 minutes. Transfer 1 cup soup to blender or food processor and puree until smooth. Return to pot.

2. In a small bowl, blend cornstarch with 3 tablespoons cold water. Whisk into soup and bring to a boil. Stir in soy sauce, salt, and crabmeat. Drizzle in egg, stirring in a figure-eight fashion. Serve immediately.

170   CREAMY CLAM SOUP WITH WHITE WINE, SHALLOTS, AND SAGE TOASTS

Prep: 10 minutes   Cook: 10 to 15 minutes   Serves: 4

2 cups dry white wine
¼ cup butter
4 shallots, minced
3 garlic cloves, minced
½ cup chopped parsley

2 dozen littleneck or 2 pounds manila clams, rinsed well
2 tablespoons heavy cream
Sage Toasts (recipe follows)

1. In a nonreactive soup pot, combine wine, butter, shallots, garlic, and parsley. Bring to a boil and cook until shallots are tender, about 5 minutes.

2. Add clams, cover, and return to a boil. Reduce heat to medium and cook until all clams open, 5 to 10 minutes. Remove and discard any clams that do not open. Stir in cream and ladle soup into bowls. Serve sprinkled with Sage Toasts.

171   SAGE TOASTS

Prep: 5 minutes   Cook: 2 minutes   Makes: 8 toasts

2 tablespoons butter
1 tablespoon olive oil
4 fresh sage leaves

8 (½-inch-thick) slices of French bread
Pinch of salt

In a medium skillet, heat butter, oil, and sage over high heat until butter is melted. Add bread and cook until browned, about 1 minute on each side. Remove to paper towels and sprinkle with salt.

172   VIETNAMESE CRAB AND PORK SOUP

Prep: 30 minutes   Stand: 15 minutes   Cook: 2 minutes   Serves: 4

This easy Vietnamese soup has definite Chinese influences.

5 dried shiitake mushrooms
1 tablespoon cornstarch
2 cups Chicken Stock (page 262) or reduced-sodium canned broth
1 tablespoon Thai fish sauce (*nam pla*) or soy sauce
1 tablespoon lime juice
¼ teaspoon cayenne

¼ pound boneless pork tenderloin, cut into thin strips
½ pound cooked crabmeat, picked over and shredded
1 teaspoon Asian sesame oil
2 scallions, thinly sliced
1 egg, lightly beaten

1. Place mushrooms in a medium heatproof bowl and cover with 1 cup boiling water. Let stand 15 minutes. Discard stems and chop mushrooms. In a small bowl, blend cornstarch with soaking liquid.

2. In a large saucepan, combine chicken stock, 2 cups cold water, mushroom liquid and cornstarch mixture, and mushrooms. Bring to a boil. Stir in fish sauce, lime juice, cayenne, and pork. Reduce heat to medium and cook until pork is no longer pink, about 2 minutes. Stir in crab, sesame oil, and scallions. Drizzle in egg, stirring constantly in a figure-eight pattern. (Do not boil.) Serve immediately.

---

173 HERBED MUSSEL AND TOMATO SOUP WITH GRUYÈRE TOASTS
Prep: 20 minutes   Cook: 10 minutes   Serves: 6

Cleaning and debearding the mussels make up the bulk of preparation for this soup.

2 **cups dry white wine**
3 **tablespoons butter**
1 **small onion, finely chopped**
3 **garlic cloves, minced**
3 **sprigs of fresh thyme or**
    1 teaspoon dried thyme
    leaves

½ **cup chopped parsley**
4 **plum tomatoes, seeded and**
    chopped
3 **dozen mussels, scrubbed**
    and debearded
    Gruyère Toasts (recipe
    follows)

1. In a large nonreactive soup pot, combine wine, butter, onion, garlic, thyme, parsley, and tomatoes. Bring to a boil, cover, and simmer 5 minutes. Add mussels and cook until mussels open, about 5 minutes longer. Discard any mussels that don't open.

2. Ladle mussels and liquid into soup bowls and serve with Gruyère Toasts.

---

174 GRUYÈRE TOASTS
Prep: 5 minutes   Cook: 3 minutes   Makes: 12 toasts

12 **(½-inch-thick) slices of**
     sourdough baguette
½ **cup shredded Gruyère or**
    Jarlsberg cheese

Pinch of cayenne

1. Preheat broiler. Arrange bread slices on cookie sheet. Place 3 to 4 inches from heat source and broil 2 minutes. Turn bread slices over.

2. In a small bowl, combine cheese and cayenne and sprinkle onto untoasted side of bread. Broil until cheese is melted, about 1 minute.

175   CLAM SOUP WITH ZUCCHINI AND CARTWHEELS

Prep: 20 minutes   Cook: 22 to 24 minutes   Serves: 4

This soup reminds me of pasta with white clam sauce.

1 dozen littleneck or 1 pound manila clams
1 cup dry white wine
2 tablespoons olive oil
1 small onion, finely chopped
3 garlic cloves, minced
3 tablespoons chopped parsley

4 cups Quick Fish Stock (page 265) or clam juice
1 cup cartwheel pasta or small shells
2 small zucchini, thinly sliced

1. Rinse clams well. In a nonreactive soup pot, combine clams and wine. Bring to a boil, cover, and cook until clams open, 6 to 8 minutes. Transfer clams to a bowl as they open. Strain liquid through a coffee filter or cheese-cloth-lined strainer. Remove clams from shells and coarsely chop.

2. In the same soup pot, heat olive oil over medium-high heat. Add onion, garlic, and parsley and cook, stirring occasionally, until vegetables are golden, about 5 minutes. Add fish stock and strained claim liquid and bring to a boil. Add pasta and cook until tender but still firm, about 6 minutes. Stir in zucchini and cook until softened, about 5 minutes longer. Stir in clams and serve hot.

176   MUSSEL AND CABBAGE SOUP

Prep: 20 minutes   Cook: 35 minutes   Serves: 4

In this hearty soup, the cabbage flavor becomes very mild and melds with the wonderful mussel flavor.

2 tablespoons extra-virgin olive oil
3 shallots, minced
3 garlic cloves, minced
½ teaspoon salt
¼ teaspoon crushed hot red pepper
1 small head of Savoy cabbage, cored and shredded

1 medium russet potato, peeled and cut into ½-inch dice
5 cups Quick Fish Stock (page 265) or clam juice
12 mussels, scrubbed and debearded
2 tablespoons chopped parsley

1. In a large heavy saucepan, heat olive oil over medium-high heat. Add shallots and cook, stirring constantly, until golden, about 2 minutes. Add garlic, salt, hot pepper, and cabbage, reduce heat to medium, and cook, stirring occasionally, until cabbage is wilted, about 5 minutes.

2. Add potato and fish stock and simmer until cabbage and potato are very tender, about 25 minutes. Stir in mussels and parsley and simmer until mussels open, about 3 minutes longer. Discard any mussels that don't open.

---

177 PORTUGUESE SHRIMP SOUP
Prep: 30 minutes   Cook: 41 minutes   Serves: 4

Here's an easy, elegant soup that is great for entertaining.

3 tablespoons olive oil
2 large onions, chopped
1 pound medium shrimp, shelled and deveined, shells reserved
3 garlic cloves, minced
¼ teaspoon cayenne
½ teaspoon black pepper
1 cup dry white wine
1 (14½-ounce) can diced tomatoes, juices reserved
1 bay leaf
4 cups Quick Fish Stock (page 265) or clam juice
½ teaspoon salt
3 tablespoons chopped cilantro

1. In a large nonreactive soup pot, heat olive oil over medium-high heat. Add onions and cook, stirring occasionally, until golden, about 5 minutes. Stir in half of the shrimp, the shrimp shells, and garlic and cook, stirring frequently, until shrimp turn pink, about 5 minutes. Stir in cayenne, black pepper, wine, tomatoes with their juices, bay leaf, and fish stock and bring to a boil. Reduce heat to medium-low and cook 30 minutes.

2. Remove and discard bay leaf. Strain soup through a fine sieve, pressing hard on solids, or force through a food mill. Discard solids. Return broth to soup pot and bring to a simmer over medium-high heat. Coarsely chop remaining shrimp and stir in along with salt and cilantro. Cook until shrimp turn pink, about 1 minute longer, and serve.

178 MANHATTAN CLAM CHOWDER
Prep: 25 minutes   Stand: 2 minutes   Cook: 40 minutes   Serves: 6

For just a touch of heat, this clam chowder uses poblano peppers instead of traditional green bell peppers.

3 tablespoons olive oil
1 medium onion, chopped
1 medium carrot, peeled and chopped
1 medium celery rib, chopped
1 to 2 poblano peppers, seeded and chopped
¾ pound red potatoes, cut into ½-inch dice
½ teaspoon dried thyme leaves
½ teaspoon dried oregano
½ teaspoon salt

¼ teaspoon black pepper
1 (28-ounce) can peeled tomatoes, chopped, juices reserved
2 cups Quick Fish Stock (page 265) or clam juice
24 littleneck or manila clams, shucked, coarsely chopped, liquor reserved
2 tablespoons chopped parsley

1. In a nonreactive soup pot, heat olive oil over medium-high heat. Add onion, carrot, celery, and poblano pepper. Cook, stirring occasionally, until vegetables are softened, about 10 minutes. Stir in potatoes, thyme, oregano, salt, pepper, tomatoes with their juices, fish stock, and clam liquid. Bring to a boil, reduce heat to medium, and cook until potatoes are softened, 30 minutes.

2. Stir in clams, cover, and let stand 2 minutes. Stir in parsley just before serving.

179 NEW ENGLAND CLAM CHOWDER
Prep: 15 minutes   Cook: 24 to 25 minutes   Serves: 6

Usually, this soup contains salt pork. Here, I've chosen to use bacon instead, which imparts a nice, smoky flavor.

4 slices of bacon, cut into ½-inch pieces
1 small onion, finely chopped
2 medium red potatoes, cut into ½-inch dice
½ cup Quick Fish Stock (page 265) or clam juice
2 dozen littleneck, razor, or manila clams, shucked, coarsely chopped, liquor reserved

2 cups milk
1 cup half-and-half
½ teaspoon salt
Pinch of cayenne

1. In a soup pot, cook bacon over medium heat, stirring occasionally, until crisp, about 5 minutes. With a slotted spoon, remove bacon to paper towels.

2. Add onion to pot and cook, stirring occasionally, until softened, about 2 minutes. Stir in potatoes, fish stock, and clam liquor. Bring to a boil, cover, and simmer until potatoes are softened, about 15 minutes.

3. Stir in milk, half-and-half, clams, bacon, salt, and cayenne. Cook until heated through, 2 to 3 minutes, and serve.

180   CARIBBEAN RED SNAPPER CHOWDER
Prep: 15 minutes   Stand: 3 minutes   Cook: 21 minutes   Serves: 4

1 tablespoon vegetable oil
1 medium red onion, chopped
3 garlic cloves, minced
½ teaspoon dried oregano
½ teaspoon dried thyme leaves
1 bay leaf
½ teaspoon ground allspice
½ teaspoon salt
¼ teaspoon crushed hot red pepper
1 (14½-ounce) can recipe-ready chopped tomatoes, juices reserved

2 cups Quick Fish Stock (page 265) or clam juice
1 large russet potato, peeled and cut into ½-inch dice
1 pound red snapper or other firm white fish, cut into 1-inch pieces
2 tablespoons chopped parsley

1. In a large saucepan, heat oil over medium-high heat. Add onion and cook, stirring frequently, until golden, about 8 minutes. Add garlic, oregano, thyme, bay leaf, allspice, salt, and hot pepper and cook, stirring constantly, until garlic is fragrant, 1 minute. Stir in tomatoes with their juices, fish stock, and potato. Bring to a boil, reduce heat to medium, and cook until potato is tender, 10 minutes.

2. Add fish and simmer 2 minutes. Remove from heat, cover, and let stand until fish flakes easily when tested with a fork, about 3 minutes. Serve at once, garnished with chopped parsley.

181   OYSTER AND HALIBUT CHOWDER

Prep: 15 minutes   Cook: 31 to 32 minutes   Serves: 6

Serve this hearty chowder with Buttermilk Corn Sticks and it's a meal in itself. If you prefer, substitute cod or haddock for the halibut.

¼ pound lean salt pork or
    bacon, diced
2 medium onions, minced
1 large celery rib, minced
2 tablespoons flour
1 pound red potatoes, peeled
    and cut into 1-inch dice
½ cup dry white wine
3 cups milk
1 teaspoon dried thyme leaves
⅛ teaspoon cayenne
⅛ teaspoon grated fresh
    nutmeg

½ teaspoon salt
2 dozen oysters, shucked,
    liquor reserved
1 cup heavy or light cream
2 pounds halibut, cod, or
    haddock, cut into 1½-inch
    pieces
2 tablespoons butter, softened
3 tablespoons minced fresh
    parsley
    Buttermilk Corn Sticks
    (recipe follows)

1. In a nonreactive soup pot, cook salt pork over medium heat, stirring occasionally, until crisp, about 5 minutes. Add onions and celery and cook, stirring occasionally, until softened, about 5 minutes. Add flour and cook, stirring constantly, 2 minutes without allowing to color. Stir in potatoes, wine, milk, thyme, cayenne, nutmeg, and salt. Bring to a boil. Reduce heat to low, cover, and simmer, stirring occasionally, until potatoes are softened, about 10 minutes.

2. Strain reserved oyster liquor through a fine sieve into a medium bowl; discard solids. Add liquor and cream to soup pot and bring to a boil. Reduce heat to medium, add halibut, and simmer, stirring occasionally, until fish is firm, about 8 minutes. Add oysters and simmer, stirring occasionally, until oysters begin to curl, 1 to 2 minutes. Stir in butter and parsley just before serving. Serve with Buttermilk Corn Sticks.

182   BUTTERMILK CORN STICKS

Prep: 10 minutes   Cook: 15 minutes   Makes: 10

1 cup cornmeal
1 cup flour
1½ teaspoons baking powder
1 teaspoon baking soda

1 teaspoon salt
1 cup buttermilk
2 eggs, lightly beaten
¼ cup unsalted butter, melted

Preheat oven to 400°F. Into a medium bowl, sift cornmeal, flour, baking powder, baking soda, and salt. In a small bowl, whisk together buttermilk, eggs, and butter. Add milk mixture to cornmeal mixture and stir just until moistened. Spoon batter into two (5-stick) corn stick molds and bake 15 minutes, or until golden. Invert onto racks to cool.

183   LOBSTER AND CORN CHOWDER
Prep: 30 minutes   Cook: 35 to 36 minutes   Serves: 6

This soup is also wonderful when made with cooked crab instead of lobster.

3 tablespoons butter
1 large onion, chopped
1 red bell pepper, stemmed,
    seeded, and chopped
½ teaspoon dried thyme leaves
¼ teaspoon dried marjoram
½ teaspoon salt
½ teaspoon black pepper
½ teaspoon sugar

½ pound red potatoes, cut into
    ½-inch dice
3 cups milk
2 to 3 cups fresh corn kernels
    or 2 (10-ounce) packages
    frozen corn kernels
2 cups chopped cooked
    lobster meat

1. In a soup pot, melt butter over medium-high heat. Add onion and bell pepper and cook until onion is golden, about 8 minutes. Add thyme, marjoram, salt, pepper, sugar, potatoes, and milk and bring to a boil. Reduce heat to medium and cook, uncovered, until potatoes are softened, about 15 minutes.

2. Stir in corn and cook until tender, about 10 minutes longer. Stir in lobster and cook until heated through, 2 to 3 minutes.

184   SALT COD CHOWDER
Prep: 10 minutes   Stand: 6 hours   Cook: 17 to 18 minutes
Serves: 4

Look for salt cod in Latin American markets. Buy fish that is still supple, with as little skin as possible.

1 pound salt cod
3 tablespoons butter
1 large onion, chopped
1 pound red potatoes, cut into
    ½-inch dice

1 cup Quick Fish Stock (page
    265) or water
1½ cups milk
½ cup heavy cream
3 to 4 drops hot sauce

1. Rinse salt cod under cold running water. Place in a large bowl and fill with cold water. Refrigerate 6 hours or overnight, changing water several times. Drain into a colander and rinse well.

2. In a soup pot, melt butter over medium-high heat. Add onion and cook, stirring occasionally, until golden, about 5 minutes. Stir in potatoes, cod, and fish stock and simmer until potatoes are softened, about 10 minutes.

3. Stir in milk, cream, and hot sauce. Cook, stirring occasionally, until mixture is heated through, 2 to 3 minutes.

185 SALMON CHOWDER WITH RED PEPPER AND SCALLIONS

Prep: 10 minutes   Cook: 20 minutes   Serves: 4

Here's a tasty chowder inspired by the flavors of the great Northwest.

3 tablespoons butter
1 large onion, chopped
½ medium red bell pepper, chopped
3 medium red potatoes, peeled and cut into ½-inch dice
1 cup Quick Fish Stock (page 265) or water

1 pound skinless salmon fillet, cut into 1-inch pieces
1½ cups milk
½ cup heavy cream
½ teaspoon salt
Pinch of cayenne
3 scallions, minced

1. In a soup pot, melt butter over medium-high heat. Add onion and bell pepper and cook, stirring occasionally, until softened, about 5 minutes. Stir in potatoes and fish stock and simmer until potatoes are softened, about 10 minutes.

2. Stir in salmon, milk, cream, salt, and cayenne. Simmer until salmon flakes easily when tested with a fork, about 5 minutes. Serve sprinkled with scallions.

186 THAI SHRIMP SOUP WITH LEMONGRASS AND STRAW MUSHROOMS

Prep: 20 minutes   Cook: 2 minutes   Serves: 4

2 stalks of lemongrass or 2 large (2 x 1-inch) strips of lemon zest
2 cups Chicken Stock (page 262) or reduced-sodium canned broth
2 (2 x 1-inch) strips of lime zest
1 tablespoon Thai fish sauce *(nam pla)* or soy sauce
1 tablespoon lime juice

1 teaspoon brown sugar
¼ teaspoon cayenne
½ pound medium shrimp, peeled and deveined
½ cup canned straw mushrooms or 1 (4-ounce) can sliced mushrooms, drained
2 scallions, thinly sliced

1. Trim tops from lemongrass; remove and discard outer leaves. Cut lemongrass into 2-inch lengths, crush with flat side of knife, and set aside.

2. In a soup pot, bring chicken stock and 2 cups water to a boil. Add lemongrass and lime zest. Stir in fish sauce, lime juice, brown sugar, cayenne, shrimp, and mushrooms. Cook until shrimp turn pink, 2 minutes. Stir in scallions just before serving.

187 FRENCH SEAFOOD SOUP WITH BASIL OIL
Prep: 15 minutes   Cook: 46 to 48 minutes   Serves: 6

Vary the seafood in this soup to your personal taste. Serve the soup with warm crusty rolls.

¼ cup olive oil
2 large leeks (white and tender green), well rinsed and minced
1 large celery rib, minced
3 large garlic cloves, minced
1 cup dry white wine
8 cups Quick Fish Stock (page 265) or reduced-sodium canned chicken broth
3 large tomatoes, peeled, seeded, and chopped
1 tablespoon tomato paste

1 teaspoon dried thyme leaves
1 teaspoon dried basil
1 bay leaf
1 teaspoon salt
½ teaspoon pepper
1 dozen mussels, scrubbed and debearded
6 clams, scrubbed
1 pound red snapper fillet, cut into 2-inch pieces
1 pound large shrimp, shelled and deveined
Basil Oil (recipe follows)

1. In a nonreactive soup pot, heat oil over medium heat. Add leeks, celery, and garlic and cook, stirring occasionally, until softened, about 5 minutes. Stir in wine, fish stock, tomatoes, tomato paste, thyme, basil, bay leaf, salt, and pepper. Bring to a boil, reduce heat to medium-low, and cook, stirring and skimming surface occasionally, 30 minutes.

2. Add mussels and clams, cover, and cook over medium-high heat until shells have opened, 6 to 8 minutes. With a slotted spoon, transfer mussels and clams to a tureen or serving dish and keep warm. Discard any mussels and clams that have not opened.

3. Add snapper and shrimp. Bring to a boil, reduce heat to medium-low, and cook, stirring occasionally, until fish flakes easily when tested with a fork and shrimp turn pink, about 5 minutes. Transfer soup to tureen and stir in Basil Oil to taste.

BASIL OIL
Makes: about 1 cup

This oil is a flavorful enrichment to sauces, soups, and stews.

3 cups fresh basil leaves, rinsed

1 cup extra-virgin olive oil

1. In a medium saucepan of boiling water, blanch basil leaves for 30 seconds. Drain and rinse under cold water.

2. Squeeze leaves dry and transfer to a blender. With machine running, add oil in a stream and blend until combined well. Strain oil through a fine-mesh sieve into a small bowl. Discard solids.

188 ROASTED CORN AND SHRIMP SOUP WITH RED PEPPER PUREE

Prep: 25 minutes   Cook: 42 minutes   Serves: 4

Even though this soup contains no cream, it is wonderfully thick and rich.

4 **ears of corn**	½ **teaspoon salt**
2 **tablespoons butter**	**Pinch of cayenne**
1 **large onion, chopped**	½ **pound medium shrimp,**
1 **sprig of fresh rosemary or**	**shelled, deveined, and**
½ teaspoon dried	**cut in half lengthwise**
2 **sprigs of fresh thyme or**	2 **tablespoons chopped**
½ teaspoon dried thyme	**cilantro**
leaves	**Red Pepper Puree (recipe**
4 **cups milk**	**follows)**
1 **teaspoon sugar**	

1. Preheat broiler. Broil corn 2 to 3 inches from heat source until blackened on all sides, about 15 minutes. Remove corn from broiler and let cool. Scrape kernels from cobs, reserving cobs.

2. In a large soup pot, melt butter over medium-high heat. Add onion and cook, stirring occasionally, until golden, about 5 minutes. Add rosemary, thyme, milk, sugar, salt, cayenne, and corn cobs. Bring to a boil. Reduce heat to medium, cover, and cook 10 minutes.

3. Remove cobs, stir in corn kernels, and cook until corn is tender, 10 minutes. Transfer 2 cups of the soup to a food processor or blender and puree until smooth. Return puree to soup pot. Add shrimp and cilantro and cook until shrimp turn pink, 2 minutes. Ladle into soup bowls, swirl in Red Pepper Puree, and serve.

189 RED PEPPER PUREE

Prep: 15 minutes   Cook: 12 minutes   Serves: 4

2 **red bell peppers or 2 jarred**	1 **shallot, minced**
roasted red bell peppers,	1 **garlic clove, minced**
drained	⅛ **teaspoon salt**
2 **tablespoons butter**	⅛ **teaspoon cayenne**

1. Place fresh bell peppers over gas burners set on high and roast, turning occasionally, until blackened on all sides, about 10 minutes. Place peppers in a paper bag and set aside to cool, about 10 minutes. (Alternately, if you have an electric stove, place bell peppers on a cookie sheet and broil 2 to 3 inches from heat source, turning occasionally, until blackened all over, about 15 minutes. Place peppers in a paper bag to cool as directed.)

2. When peppers are cool, scrape off blackened skin with back of a paring knife or with fingers. Seed and chop peppers.

3. In a small skillet, melt butter over medium-high heat. Add shallot and garlic and cook, stirring frequently, until softened, about 2 minutes. Transfer shallot mixture to a food processor or blender, add roasted peppers, salt, and cayenne. Puree until smooth.

190 CREAM OF SCALLOP AND LEEK SOUP WITH HERBED PITA TOASTS

Prep: 15 minutes   Cook: 37 to 40 minutes   Serves: 6

This is another lovely first-course soup. The soup may be prepared several hours ahead of time and reheated just before serving.

3 tablespoons butter
2 large leeks (white and tender green), well rinsed and minced
½ cup minced fresh fennel or celery
1½ pounds sea scallops
1 teaspoon salt
¼ teaspoon pepper
½ cup dry white wine
6 cups Quick Fish Stock (page 265) or reduced-sodium canned chicken broth

1 bay leaf
1 tablespoon cornstarch
½ cup heavy or light cream
1 teaspoon lemon juice
1 tablespoon minced fresh dill
Herbed Pita Toasts (recipe follows)

1. In a large nonreactive saucepan, melt butter over medium heat. Add leeks, fennel, half of the scallops, salt, and pepper. Cover and cook, stirring occasionally, until scallops turn opaque, about 5 minutes. Add wine, fish stock, and bay leaf and bring to a boil. Reduce heat to low, cover, and simmer, skimming surface and stirring occasionally, 20 minutes. Remove and discard bay leaf.

2. In a food processor or blender, puree soup in batches until smooth. Strain soup through a fine sieve into a large soup pot. Bring to a boil, reduce heat to medium, and cook until soup is reduced to 6 cups, about 5 minutes.

3. In a small bowl, blend cornstarch with cream and add to soup. Cook, stirring, until slightly thickened, 2 to 3 minutes. Add remaining scallops and simmer over medium heat, stirring frequently, until scallops are opaque throughout, about 5 minutes. Stir in lemon juice and dill just before serving. Serve with Herbed Pita Toasts.

191 HERBED PITA TOASTS
Prep: 10 minutes   Cook: 5 minutes   Serves: 6

6 tablespoons softened butter
1 tablespoon minced fresh
    parsley
1 tablespoon minced fresh
    dill
1 tablespoon minced fresh
    chives

1 large garlic clove, minced
½ teaspoon grated lemon zest
½ teaspoon salt
¼ teaspoon pepper
6 pita breads

1. Preheat oven to 450°F.

2. In a small bowl, combine butter, parsley, dill, chives, garlic, lemon zest, salt, and pepper.

3. Split pita breads horizontally in half to form 2 rounds each. Spread butter mixture onto rough side of each piece of pita. Cut each round into 4 wedges. Arrange bread in single layer on baking sheet.

4. Bake 5 minutes, or until pita wedges are golden brown around edges.

192 JAPANESE BROTH WITH OYSTERS, SHRIMP, AND SHIITAKE MUSHROOMS
Prep: 20 minutes   Stand: 18 minutes   Cook: 2 minutes   Serves: 4

Dashi, a soup stock made with dried tuna flakes, dried kelp, and water, is commonly used in Japanese cooking. If dashi is unavailable, you may substitute fish stock, clam juice, or even chicken stock.

4 dried shiitake mushrooms
2 cups dashi, Quick Fish
    Stock (page 265), or
    canned clam juice
1 tablespoon soy sauce
2 tablespoons mirin or dry
    sherry
1½ cups cooked rice

1 cup shredded collard, kale,
    or mustard greens
2½ teaspoons grated fresh
    ginger
¼ pound medium shrimp,
    shelled, deveined, and
    cut in half lengthwise
4 medium oysters, shucked

1. Place mushrooms in a small heatproof bowl and cover with 1 cup boiling water. Let stand 15 minutes. Discard stems, slice mushrooms, and reserve soaking liquid.

2. In a large saucepan, combine dashi, mushroom soaking liquid, soy sauce, mirin, rice, collard greens, and ginger and bring to a boil. Simmer until greens are wilted, 2 minutes.

3. Stir in shrimp and oysters, cover, and let stand until shrimp turn pink, about 3 minutes.

193   SHRIMP BISQUE

Prep: 15 minutes   Cook: 1 hour 2½ minutes to 1 hour 6½ minutes
Serves: 4

The addition of cayenne gives this soup a slightly spicy flavor. Adjust the amount to suit your taste.

1 **pound large shrimp, shelled and deveined, shells reserved**
5 **tablespoons unsalted butter**
1 **large leek (white and tender green), well rinsed and chopped, or 1 onion, chopped**
2 **medium celery ribs, minced**
2 **garlic cloves, minced**
½ **cup dry white wine**
4 **cups Quick Fish Stock (page 265) or reduced-sodium canned chicken broth**

½ **teaspoon dried thyme leaves**
½ **teaspoon salt**
½ **teaspoon ground paprika**
¼ **teaspoon cayenne, or to taste**
1 **bay leaf**
3 **tablespoons long-grain white rice**
2 **tablespoons cognac or brandy**
1 **cup light cream or half-and-half**
2 **teaspoons lemon juice**

1. Coarsely chop shrimp. In a large nonreactive saucepan, melt 3 table-spoons butter over medium heat. Add leek, celery, and garlic. Cook, stir-ring occasionally, until softened, 3 to 5 minutes. Add wine, fish stock, thyme, salt, paprika, cayenne, bay leaf, and reserved shrimp shells. Bring to a boil, reduce heat to medium-low, and cook, skimming and stirring occasionally, 30 minutes.

2. Strain broth through a fine sieve and return to saucepan. Add rice, cover, and simmer 20 minutes.

3. Add half of shrimp and simmer, covered, 5 minutes longer. In a food processor or blender, puree soup in batches until smooth and return to saucepan.

4. In a medium skillet, melt remaining 2 tablespoons butter over medium heat. Add remaining shrimp and cook, stirring frequently, until shrimp turn pink, 2 to 3 minutes. Add cognac and boil 30 seconds. Add shrimp mixture to soup along with cream. Cook over medium heat, stirring, until heated through, 2 to 3 minutes. Stir in lemon juice and serve.

194   OYSTER BISQUE
Prep: 15 minutes   Cook: 39 to 40 minutes   Serves: 6

For optimum flavor, buy the freshest oysters you can find.

¼ cup long-grain white rice
3 tablespoons butter
1 garlic clove, minced
2 shallots, minced
½ fennel bulb, finely chopped
2 tablespoons dry sherry
1 tablespoon tomato paste
18 oysters, shucked, liquor
    reserved

5 cups Quick Fish Stock (page
    265) or clam juice
2 tablespoons heavy cream
¼ teaspoon lemon juice
    Pinch of cayenne
2 tablespoons minced fresh
    chives

1. In a small covered saucepan, bring ½ cup water to a boil. Stir in rice, reduce heat to medium, and cook until rice is tender, about 15 minutes.

2. In a soup pot, melt butter over medium-high heat. Add garlic, shallots, and fennel and cook, stirring occasionally, until golden, 4 to 5 minutes. Add sherry and simmer 5 minutes.

3. Stir in tomato paste, 12 of the oysters, oyster liquor, fish stock, and rice, cover, and simmer 15 minutes. Transfer to a food processor or blender and puree until smooth.

4. Return puree to soup pot, bring to a simmer, and stir in cream, lemon juice, cayenne, and remaining oysters. Ladle into bowls, floating 1 oyster in each bowl. Serve sprinkled with chives.

195   SCALLOP BISQUE
Prep: 15 minutes   Cook: 39 to 40 minutes   Serves: 6

Cooked rice helps thicken this wonderfully rich soup. Make sure to cook the rice completely, so the bisque will become a smooth puree.

¼ cup long-grain white rice
3 tablespoons butter
1 garlic clove, minced
2 shallots, minced
1 ripe plum tomato, seeded
    and diced
½ fennel bulb, finely chopped
2 tablespoons dry sherry

½ pound scallops
5 cups Quick Fish Stock (page
    265) or clam juice
2 tablespoons heavy cream
¼ teaspoon lemon juice
    Pinch of cayenne
    Parsleyed Croutons
    (page 159)

1. In a small, covered saucepan, bring ½ cup water to a boil. Stir in rice, reduce heat to medium, and cook until rice is tender, about 15 minutes.

2. In a nonreactive soup pot, melt butter over medium-high heat. Add garlic, shallots, tomato, and fennel and cook until shallots are golden, stirring occasionally, 4 to 5 minutes. Add sherry and simmer 5 minutes.

3. Stir in scallops, fish stock, and rice, cover, and simmer until scallops are tender and opaque, about 15 minutes. Transfer solids plus 1 cup broth to a food processor or blender and puree until smooth.

4. Return puree to pot, bring to a simmer, and stir in cream, lemon juice, and cayenne. Serve sprinkled with Parsleyed Croutons.

---

196 LOBSTER BISQUE
Prep: 15 minutes   Cook: 35½ to 36½ minutes   Serves: 4

2 lobster tails	3 tablespoons minced fresh
5 tablespoons unsalted butter	parsley
1 medium onion, minced	½ teaspoon dried thyme leaves
1 cup minced fennel	½ teaspoon salt
1 medium carrot, peeled and	¼ teaspoon cayenne, or to taste
chopped	1 bay leaf
3 garlic cloves, minced	1 tablespoon Pernod
½ cup dry white wine	(optional)
4 cups Quick Fish Stock (page	1 cup light cream or half-and-
265) or reduced-sodium	half
canned chicken broth	1 to 2 teaspoons lemon juice
1 (14½-ounce) can plum	
tomatoes, drained and	
chopped	

1. Remove shells from lobster tails, reserving shells. Cut lobster meat into ½-inch pieces

2. In a large saucepan, melt 3 tablespoons butter over medium heat. Add onion, fennel, carrot, and garlic. Cook, stirring occasionally, 5 minutes. Add wine, fish stock, tomatoes, parsley, thyme, salt, cayenne, bay leaf, and reserved lobster shells. Bring to a boil, reduce heat to low, cover, and simmer, skimming occasionally, 20 minutes. Add half of lobster meat and simmer, covered, 5 minutes. Remove and discard bay leaf.

3. In a food processor or blender, puree soup and reserved lobster shells in batches until smooth. Strain back into saucepan.

4. In a medium skillet, melt the remaining 2 tablespoons butter over medium heat. Add remaining lobster meat and cook, stirring frequently, until firm and opaque throughout, about 3 minutes. Add Pernod and cook 30 seconds. Add lobster mixture to soup along with cream. Cook until heated through, 2 to 3 minutes. Stir in lemon juice and serve.

197   CRAB BISQUE

Prep: 15 minutes   Stand: 30 minutes   Cook: 41 to 42 minutes
Serves: 6

¼ cup long-grain white rice
3 tablespoons butter
1 garlic clove, minced
2 shallots, minced
1 carrot, peeled and finely
    chopped
¼ cup dry white wine
1 tablespoon tomato paste
½ pound chopped cooked
    crabmeat, picked over

5 cups Quick Fish Stock (page
    265) or clam juice
2 tablespoons heavy cream
¼ teaspoon lemon juice
    Pinch of cayenne
    Thyme Croutons (recipe
    follows)

1. In a small covered saucepan, bring ½ cup water to a boil. Stir in rice, reduce heat to medium, and cook until rice is tender, about 15 minutes.

2. In a nonreactive soup pot, melt butter over medium-high heat. Add garlic, shallots, and carrot and cook until golden, stirring occasionally, 4 to 5 minutes. Add wine and simmer 5 minutes.

3. Stir in tomato paste, crabmeat, fish stock, and rice, cover, and simmer 15 minutes. Remove from heat and let stand, covered, 30 minutes. Transfer solids plus 1 cup stock to a food processor or blender and puree until smooth.

4. Return soup to pot, bring to a simmer, and stir in cream, lemon juice and cayenne. Serve hot with Thyme Croutons.

THYME CROUTONS
Makes: about 1½ cups

3 tablespoons butter
½ teaspoon dried thyme leaves

6 (½-inch-thick) slices of
    French bread, cut into
    ½-inch cubes

In a large skillet, melt butter over medium heat. Add thyme and bread and cook, stirring occasionally, until bread is browned and crisp, about 2 minutes.

198   SWEET-AND-SOUR THAI FISH SOUP

Prep: 25 minutes   Cook: 2 minutes   Serves: 4

Tamarind gives this soup a mild sour taste. If you can't find it in your market, substitute lime juice.

4 shallots, peeled and coarsely chopped
1 garlic clove, minced
½ cup chopped cilantro plus ¼ cup cilantro leaves
1 tablespoon grated fresh ginger
1 tablespoon tamarind paste, softened with 2 tablespoons hot water or 1 tablespoon lime juice
1 teaspoon fish paste or 1 anchovy fillet

2 teaspoons brown sugar
⅛ teaspoon cayenne
1 teaspoon fish sauce
3 cups Quick Fish Stock (page 265) or clam juice
1 pound white fish fillets (cod, halibut, snapper), cut into 1-inch pieces
2 cups shredded lettuce
2 scallions, sliced
½ small cucumber, peeled, trimmed, seeded, and cut into thin julienne strips

1. In a food processor or blender, combine shallots, garlic, chopped cilantro, ginger, tamarind paste, fish paste, and brown sugar and puree until smooth.

2. In a soup pot, combine puree, cayenne, fish sauce, and fish stock and bring to a boil. Add fish and lettuce and simmer 2 minutes. Ladle soup into bowls and serve sprinkled with scallions, cilantro leaves, and cucumber.

Chapter 8

Chilis, Gumbos, and Curries

Here are all those zesty dishes that bridge the gap between soups and stews while they satisfy everyone's craving for more spice. This is wonderful, down-home comfort food, derived largely from three cuisines: Southwestern American, Cajun, and Indian.

These one-pot dishes also make great party food. Most taste even better the next day, and they freeze well. All that's needed to create a complete menu are rice and an assortment of condiments. For the rice, serve a large mound of steamed white rice (try one of the more aromatic rices, such as basmati or jasmine rice); or sample one of the seasoned rices that accompany these recipes, such as Lemon Pilaf or Saffron Rice.

Letting guests choose their own toppings is half the fun of eating these stews. Most of the chilis here, from Beef and Black Bean Chili to White Chicken Chili, would be delightful accompanied by a basket of crisp tortilla chips and bowls of shredded Cheddar or Monterey Jack cheese, chopped scallions, sliced black olives, pickled jalapeño peppers, and sour cream.

Even with their amazing variety of flavors, from Gingery Chicken Curry to Ground Beef Curry with Peas, chilis can be garnished with toasted almonds or roasted peanuts, grated coconut, raisins, and diced sweet onion. Gumbos takes less doctoring up, but a bottle of hot sauce on the table is absolutely authentic with any one, and squares of corn bread would not be amiss.

There are seven chilis, including a Vegetarian Black Bean Chili, nine curries, and four gumbos—something for everyone. Make big pots of these stews so that you have plenty of leftovers.

Chilis are the most versatile. They can be accompanied by shredded cheese, finely diced onion, taco chips, or whatever suits your fancy. Similarly, curries can be garnished with toasted nuts, grated coconut, and dried fruit. All lend themselves to informal entertaining.

199   WHITE CHICKEN CHILI
Prep: 5 minutes   Cook: 21½ to 22½ minutes   Serves: 4

Here's a super-quick dinner. Serve it with warmed tortillas and crisp tossed salad.

2 tablespoons vegetable oil
2 skinless, boneless chicken
   breasts, cut into 1-inch
   pieces
1 large onion, chopped
4 garlic cloves, minced
1 teaspoon ground cumin
1 teaspoon chili powder
½ teaspoon dried thyme leaves

½ teaspoon dried marjoram
½ teaspoon pepper
2 (15-ounce) cans white beans,
   rinsed and drained
1 cup Chicken Stock (page
   262) or reduced-sodium
   canned broth
¼ cup chopped cilantro

1. In a large saucepan, heat oil over high heat. Add chicken and cook, stirring frequently, until browned on all sides, 4 to 5 minutes. Remove chicken to a plate.

2. Add onion to saucepan and cook, stirring constantly, until golden, 2 minutes. Add garlic, cumin, chili powder, thyme, marjoram, and pepper and stir 30 seconds. Add beans, chicken stock, and chicken and simmer until chicken is no longer pink in center, about 15 minutes. Sprinkle with cilantro just before serving.

200   SOUTHWESTERN BEEF CHILI
Prep: 15 minutes   Cook: 2 hours 24 minutes to 3 hours 3 minutes
Serves: 6

This is an authentic chili made with small cubes of beef chuck simmered with toasted chiles and spices. Serve cooked pinto or black beans, finely diced onion, and shredded Cheddar cheese as accompaniments, along with plain tortilla chips.

1 tablespoon cumin seed
¼ cup vegetable oil
3 pounds boneless lean beef
   chuck, cut into ¼-inch
   dice
2 medium onions, finely
   chopped
1 garlic clove, minced
2 tablespoons chili powder
1 teaspoon dried oregano

1 (14½-ounce) can peeled
   tomatoes, juices reserved
3 to 4 cups Simple Beef Stock
   (page 264) or reduced-
   sodium canned broth
1 bay leaf
1 to 2 jalapeño peppers,
   seeded and minced
1 teaspoon salt
½ teaspoon pepper

1. Place cumin seed in a small skillet. Cook over medium heat, stirring and shaking pan frequently, until lightly toasted and fragrant, 2 to 3 minutes. Transfer to a small bowl.

2. In a large nonreactive flameproof casserole, heat 2 tablespoons oil over medium-high heat. Add beef in 3 batches, adding remaining 2 tablespoons oil as needed, and cook, stirring occasionally, until beef is browned, 6 to 8 minutes per batch. Transfer beef to a plate.

3. Add onions to casserole and cook, stirring occasionally, until softened, 3 to 5 minutes. Add garlic, toasted cumin seed, chili powder, and oregano. Cook, stirring, 1 minute. Return beef to casserole along with tomatoes with their juices, enough beef stock to cover meat, bay leaf, jalapeño peppers, salt, and pepper.

4. Bring to a boil, reduce heat to medium-low, and simmer, partially covered and stirring occasionally, until meat is tender, 2 to 2½ hours; add additional beef stock or water if too much liquid evaporates. Remove and discard bay leaf before serving.

201   BEEF AND BLACK BEAN CHILI

Prep: 20 minutes   Cook: 21 to 22 minutes   Serves: 4

This quickly made chili is also low in fat.

1 large onion, peeled and quartered
3 garlic cloves, peeled and left whole
1 red bell pepper, stemmed and quartered
  Vegetable cooking spray
2 (14½-ounce) cans Mexican-style stewed tomatoes, juices reserved

2 (15-ounce) cans black beans, rinsed and drained
1 (4-ounce) can chopped mild chiles, juices reserved
1 tablespoon chili powder
¾ teaspoon ground cumin
¾ teaspoon salt
¾ teaspoon black pepper
½ pound flank steak, trimmed

1. With food processor running, feed onion, garlic, and bell pepper through feed tube and process until finely chopped. Spray a large nonstick skillet with cooking spray and place over high heat. Add onion mixture and cook, stirring occasionally, until golden, 3 minutes. Stir in tomatoes with their juices, beans, chiles with their juices, chili powder, ½ teaspoon cumin, ½ teaspoon salt, and ½ teaspoon black pepper. Break up tomatoes with a spoon and simmer 15 minutes.

2. Meanwhile, preheat broiler or grill. In a small bowl, combine remaining ¼ teaspoon cumin, ¼ teaspoon salt, and ¼ teaspoon black pepper. Rub seasoning mixture onto both sides of steak. Broil 3 to 4 inches from heat source 3 to 4 minutes for medium-rare, or to desired doneness, turning steak over halfway through cooking time. Transfer steak to a cutting board and let stand 5 minutes before cutting into ½-inch pieces.

3. To serve, spoon chili into soup bowls and top evenly with meat.

202   TURKEY AND RED BEAN CHILI

Prep: 20 minutes   Stand: 12 hours   Cook: 1 hour 40 minutes
Serves: 4

Chipotle chiles packed in adobo sauce can be found in specialty stores. Remember to put the beans up to soak the night before.

1½ **cups dried red beans, rinsed and picked over**
1 **large onion, chopped**
2 **bay leaves**
1 **teaspoon salt**
1 **tablespoon vegetable oil**
½ **pound skinless, boneless turkey breast, cut into 1½-inch cubes**
½ **teaspoon black pepper**
6 **garlic cloves, chopped**
½ **teaspoon dried thyme leaves**

½ **teaspoon dried oregano**
1 **teaspoon ground cumin**
½ **teaspoon sugar**
1 **bunch of scallions, trimmed and cut into 1-inch lengths**
1 **(28-ounce) can crushed tomatoes, juices reserved**
1 **to 2 canned chipotle chiles in adobo sauce, chopped**
¼ **cup chopped cilantro**

1. Place red beans in a large bowl and add enough water to cover by at least 2 inches. Let stand at least 12 hours or overnight. Drain and rinse before using.

2. In a large saucepan, combine beans, onion, bay leaves, and 5 cups water. Bring to a boil, reduce heat to medium-low, and simmer 30 minutes. Add ½ teaspoon salt and simmer until beans are tender, about 10 minutes longer. Drain bean mixture, reserving ½ cup cooking liquid.

3. Meanwhile, heat oil in a large nonreactive skillet over high heat. Season turkey with remaining ½ teaspoon salt and ¼ teaspoon black pepper. Add turkey to skillet and cook, turning occasionally, until turkey is no longer pink, about 5 minutes. Remove turkey to a plate. Add garlic, thyme, oregano, cumin, sugar, and scallions to skillet and cook, stirring constantly, until scallions are softened, 2 minutes. Return turkey to skillet along with tomatoes with their juices and chiles. Simmer until heated through, about 5 minutes.

4. When beans are cooked, return drained beans to saucepan along with ½ cup reserved bean liquid. Add contents of skillet and bring to a boil. Reduce heat to medium-low and simmer, partially covered, 1 hour. Stir in cilantro just before serving.

203   DUCK AND PINTO BEAN CHILI

Prep: 30 minutes   Stand: 12 hours   Cook: 1 hour 50 minutes
Serves: 4

Remember to put the beans up to soak the night before.

1½ **cups dried red pinto beans, rinsed and picked over**
1 **large onion, chopped**
2 **bay leaves**
1 **teaspoon salt**
1 **pound duck legs and thighs**
1 **teaspoon black pepper**
6 **garlic cloves, minced**
½ **teaspoon dried thyme leaves**
½ **teaspoon dried oregano**
1 **teaspoon ground cumin**

½ **teaspoon sugar**
1 **red bell pepper, stemmed and chopped**
1 **yellow bell pepper, stemmed and chopped**
2 **poblano peppers, stemmed, seeded, and chopped**
1 **(14½-ounce) can crushed tomatoes, juices reserved**
2 **tablespoons chopped cilantro**

1. Place pinto beans in a large bowl and add enough water to cover by at least 2 inches. Let stand at least 12 hours or overnight. Drain and rinse before using.

2. In a large saucepan, place beans, onion, bay leaves, and 5 cups water and bring to a boil. Reduce heat to medium-low and simmer 20 minutes. Add ½ teaspoon salt and simmer until beans are tender, about 10 minutes longer. Drain. Remove and discard bay leaves.

3. Meanwhile, heat a large flameproof casserole over high heat. Season duck with remaining ½ teaspoon salt and ½ teaspoon black pepper. Add duck to casserole and cook, stirring frequently, until browned on all sides, about 5 minutes. Remove duck to a plate.

4. Add remaining ½ teaspoon black pepper, garlic, thyme, oregano, cumin, sugar, bell peppers, poblano peppers, and 2 tablespoons water to nonreactive saucepan. Cook, stirring frequently, until bell peppers are softened, 5 minutes. Add tomatoes with their juices and add duck. Reduce heat to medium-low, cover, and simmer 1 hour. When beans are cooked, add to saucepan and simmer 10 minutes longer. Stir in cilantro just before serving.

204   GREEN TOMATO AND PORK CHILI
Prep: 20 minutes   Cook: 23 to 25 minutes   Serves: 4

This is a perfect way to use up those green tomatoes and usher in the cool weather.

1   pound pork tenderloin, cut into 1-inch chunks
½   teaspoon salt
½   teaspoon pepper
3   tablespoons flour
2   tablespoons vegetable oil
1   large onion, chopped
4   garlic cloves, minced
1   jalapeño pepper with seeds, minced
4   large green tomatoes, chopped

2   (15-ounce) cans pink or pinto beans, rinsed and drained
1   cup Chicken Stock (page 262) or reduced-sodium canned broth
½   cup chopped cilantro
1   avocado, peeled and cut into chunks

1. Season pork with salt and pepper. Dredge to coat lightly with flour; shake off excess flour. In a large nonreactive saucepan, heat oil over high heat. Add pork and cook, stirring frequently, until browned on all sides, 4 to 5 minutes. With a slotted spoon, remove pork to a plate.

2. Add onion to saucepan and cook, stirring constantly, until golden, 2 minutes. Stir in garlic, jalapeño pepper, and tomatoes. Add beans and chicken stock and stir, scraping up any browned bits on bottom of pan. Reduce heat to low and simmer 15 minutes. Stir in pork and cilantro and cook until pork is no longer pink in center, 2 to 3 minutes longer. Serve sprinkled with avocado.

205   CHICKEN AND SAUSAGE GUMBO
Prep: 15 minutes   Cook: 43 to 44 minutes   Serves: 6

3   pounds chicken parts
4   cups Chicken Stock (page 262) or reduced-sodium canned broth
3   large garlic cloves, minced
1   bay leaf
1   teaspoon dried thyme leaves
½   teaspoon salt
¼   teaspoon cayenne
½   pound smoked sausage, such as andouille, kielbasa, or chorizo

1   (28-ounce) can Italian plum tomatoes, chopped, juices reserved
2   medium onions, chopped
1   medium green bell pepper, chopped
1   (10-ounce) package frozen cut okra, thawed
1   cup frozen corn kernels
¼   cup minced fresh parsley
½   cup minced scallions

1. In a nonreactive soup pot, combine chicken, chicken stock, garlic, bay leaf, thyme, salt, and cayenne. Bring to a boil. Reduce heat to low, cover, and simmer until chicken is no longer pink in center, 20 minutes.

2. Remove chicken from stock. When cool enough to handle, remove skin and bones from chicken and discard. Cut meat into large pieces and set aside.

3. Heat a large skillet over medium heat. Add sausage and cook, turning occasionally, until browned on all sides, 3 to 4 minutes. Cut into slices.

4. Add tomatoes with their juices, onions, bell pepper, and sausage to stock in soup pot. Bring to a boil, reduce heat to medium-low, and simmer 10 minutes. Add okra, corn, and reserved chicken. Cover and simmer until okra is tender, 10 minutes longer. Remove and discard bay leaf. Stir in parsley and sprinkle with scallions just before serving.

---

206   CHICKEN WING GUMBO
Prep: 10 minutes   Cook: 35 to 42 minutes   Serves: 4

Chicken wings are often overlooked, yet they are tremendously flavorful and economical.

2 **pounds chicken wings, wing tips removed**	1 **large tomato, seeded and chopped**
1½ **cups flour**	½ **teaspoon dried thyme leaves**
1 **teaspoon salt**	½ **teaspoon dried oregano**
½ **teaspoon black pepper**	1 **bay leaf**
3 **tablespoons vegetable oil**	¼ **teaspoon cayenne**
2 **medium onions, chopped**	1 **(10-ounce) package frozen cut okra, thawed and drained**
1 **small green bell pepper, chopped**	
1 **medium celery rib, chopped**	
3 **garlic cloves, minced**	
4 **cups Chicken Stock (page 262) or reduced-sodium canned broth**	

1. Dredge wings to coat lightly with flour; shake off excess flour. Season wings with ½ teaspoon salt and ¼ teaspoon black pepper.

2. In a large flameproof casserole, heat oil over medium-high heat. Add chicken wings and cook until browned on both sides, 5 to 7 minutes. Transfer to a platter.

3. Add onions, green pepper, celery, and garlic to casserole. Reduce heat to medium and cook, stirring occasionally, until golden, 5 minutes. Add chicken stock, tomato, thyme, oregano, bay leaf, cayenne, and remaining ½ teaspoon salt and ¼ teaspoon black pepper. Return wings to casserole. Bring to a boil. Reduce heat to medium-low, cover, and simmer until chicken is no longer pink in center, 15 minutes. Add okra and simmer until soup is slightly thickened, 10 to 15 minutes. Remove and discard bay leaf and serve.

207 CHICKEN CREOLE
Prep: 15 minutes   Cook: 30 minutes   Serves: 4

2 tablespoons olive oil
1 medium onion, minced
1 medium green bell pepper, chopped
1 medium celery rib, diced
3 garlic cloves, minced
1 (14½-ounce) can plum tomatoes, chopped, juices reserved
5 cups Chicken Stock (page 262) or reduced-sodium canned broth
½ teaspoon dried thyme leaves
½ teaspoon dried basil
½ teaspoon salt
¼ teaspoon black pepper
4 carrots, peeled and thinly sliced
1½ pounds skinless, boneless chicken breasts, cut into 1-inch pieces
1 (10-ounce) package frozen cut okra, thawed
3 tablespoons minced fresh parsley

1. In a large nonreactive saucepan, heat olive oil over medium heat. Add onion, bell pepper, celery, and garlic and cook, stirring frequently, until vegetables are softened but not browned, about 5 minutes. Add tomatoes with their juices, chicken stock, thyme, basil, salt, and black pepper. Bring to a boil. Reduce heat to medium-low, cover, and simmer 10 minutes.

2. Add carrots, cover, and simmer 5 minutes. Add chicken and simmer, covered, 5 minutes longer. Add okra and simmer, uncovered, until chicken is no longer pink in center and vegetables are just cooked through, about 5 minutes. Stir in parsley just before serving.

208 VEGETARIAN BLACK BEAN CHILI
Prep: 20 minutes   Stand: 12 hours   Cook: 1 hour 50 minutes
Serves: 6

Serve this chili with chopped scallions, diced tomatoes, avocado, and sour cream. Remember to put the beans up to soak the night before.

2 cups dried black beans, rinsed and picked over
2 bay leaves
1 small onion, chopped
1 teaspoon salt
2 tablespoons vegetable oil
1 large red onion, chopped
4 garlic cloves, chopped
1 teaspoon ground cumin
2 teaspoons chili powder
½ teaspoon dried oregano
1 (14½-ounce) can chopped peeled tomatoes, juices reserved
½ teaspoon chopped canned chipotle chile in adobo sauce or ¼ to ½ teaspoon cayenne
½ cup chopped cilantro

1. Place the beans in a large bowl and add enough water to cover by at least 2 inches. Let stand at least 12 hours or overnight. Drain and rinse before using.

2. In a large nonreactive soup pot, place beans, bay leaves, onion, and 6 cups water. Bring to a boil. Reduce heat to medium-low and cook 30 minutes. Add salt and continue cooking until beans are tender, about 15 minutes longer.

3. Meanwhile, in a large nonreactive skillet, heat oil over medium-high heat. Add red onion and cook, stirring frequently, until softened, about 5 minutes. Add garlic, cumin, chili powder, and oregano and stir 1 minute. Stir in tomatoes with their juices and chile and simmer 10 minutes.

4. When beans are tender, stir tomato mixture into beans. Reduce heat to low and simmer 1 hour. Remove and discard bay leaves. Place half of soup mixture in a food processor, puree until smooth, and return to pot. Simmer until heated through, about 5 minutes. Stir in cilantro just before serving.

---

209   SCALLOP GUMBO

Prep: 15 minutes   Cook: 1 hour 12 minutes   Serves: 6

This gumbo uses filé powder, which is ground dried sassafras leaves. It is available at specialty food shops. Serve this gumbo with rice.

4 tablespoons butter	1 (28-ounce) can crushed
¼ cup flour	tomatoes, juices reserved
2 medium onions, chopped	1 teaspoon dried thyme leaves
1 large green bell pepper,	1 teaspoon dried oregano
chopped	½ teaspoon ground cayenne
2 medium celery ribs,	1 bay leaf
chopped	1 teaspoon salt
3 garlic cloves, minced	1½ pounds sea scallops,
6 cups Quick Fish Stock (page	trimmed
265) or reduced-sodium	2 teaspoons gumbo filé
canned chicken broth	powder

1. In a large saucepan, melt butter over medium-low heat. Add flour and cook, stirring constantly with a whisk, until roux is golden brown, about 5 minutes. Add onions, green pepper, and celery, increase heat to medium, and cook, stirring occasionally, until softened but not browned, 5 minutes. Add garlic and cook, stirring constantly, until fragrant, 1 minute. Add fish stock, tomatoes with their juices, thyme, oregano, cayenne, bay leaf, and salt. Bring to a boil, reduce heat to medium-low, and cook, stirring occasionally, 1 hour. Remove and discard bay leaf.

2. Increase heat to high and return soup to a boil. Add scallops and simmer, stirring constantly, until scallops are opaque, 1 minute. Remove pan from heat and stir in filé powder. Let stand, covered, until thickened, about 10 minutes, and serve.

210   SHRIMP AND OKRA GUMBO WITH SAVORY RICE

Prep: 25 minutes   Cook: 1 hour 7 minutes   Serves: 6

The combination of a medium roux and lots of okra thickens this gumbo.

¼ cup vegetable oil
½ cup flour
1 large onion
1 medium green bell pepper, chopped
1½ teaspoons salt
½ teaspoon black pepper
¼ teaspoon cayenne
½ teaspoon dried thyme leaves
2 large tomatoes, seeded and chopped
1 pound okra, thickly sliced
6 cups Quick Fish Stock (page 265) or water
1½ pounds medium shrimp, peeled and deveined
2 garlic cloves, minced
4 scallions (green part only), finely chopped
2 tablespoons chopped parsley
Savory Rice (recipe follows)

1. In a large, heavy nonreactive soup pot, heat oil over high heat. Gradually stir in flour with a whisk or wooden spoon. Cook, stirring constantly, until roux is medium brown, about 5 minutes.

2. Remove from heat and add onion and green pepper. Stir 2 minutes and return pot to heat. Stir in salt, black pepper, cayenne, thyme, tomatoes, okra, and fish stock and bring to a boil. Reduce heat to low and simmer 1 hour.

3. Stir in shrimp, garlic, scallions, and parsley and turn off heat. Let stand until shrimp turn pink, 5 minutes. Serve with Savory Rice.

211   SAVORY RICE

Prep: 10 minutes   Cook: 19 minutes   Serves: 4 to 6

2 tablespoons butter
3 scallions (white part only), finely chopped
1 medium celery rib, finely chopped
1 garlic clove, minced
¾ teaspoon salt
½ teaspoon pepper
Pinch of cayenne
1½ cups long-grain white rice
3 cups Quick Fish Stock (page 265) or reduced-sodium canned chicken broth

In a medium saucepan, melt butter over medium heat. Add scallions, celery, and garlic and cook, stirring occasionally until vegetables are softened, 4 minutes. Add salt, pepper, cayenne, rice, and fish stock and bring to a boil. Reduce heat to low, cover, and simmer until rice is tender, about 15 minutes.

212 CHICKEN CURRY WITH BROCCOLI

Prep: 20 minutes   Cook: 52 to 53 minutes   Serves: 4

1 pound ground chicken or
    turkey
1 egg, lightly beaten
6 garlic cloves, minced
5 tablespoons minced cilantro
2 teaspoons finely minced
    fresh ginger
1 teaspoon salt
½ teaspoon black pepper
3 tablespoons vegetable oil
1 medium onion, minced
1 tablespoon imported curry
    powder

1 teaspoon ground turmeric
⅛ teaspoon cayenne
2 tablespoons flour
1 (14½-ounce) can peeled
    tomatoes, juices reserved
1 cup Chicken Stock (page
    262) or reduced-sodium
    canned broth
1 bay leaf
2 tablespoons sliced almonds
1 (10-ounce) package frozen
    chopped broccoli, thawed
½ cup plain yogurt

1. In a medium bowl, combine chicken, egg, half of garlic, 3 tablespoons cilantro, ginger, ¼ teaspoon salt, and ¼ teaspoon black pepper. Mix well with hands and form into 1½-inch meatballs.

2. In a large nonreactive flameproof casserole, heat oil over medium-high heat. Add meatballs in 2 batches, if necessary, and cook, turning occasionally, until browned all over, about 5 minutes per batch. Transfer meatballs to a plate.

3. Add onion to casserole and cook, stirring occasionally, until golden, about 5 minutes. Add remaining garlic, curry powder, turmeric, and cayenne, reduce heat to medium-low, and cook, stirring constantly, 1 minute. Add flour and cook, stirring, 1 to 2 minutes without allowing to color. Add tomatoes with their juices, chicken stock, bay leaf, and remaining ¾ teaspoon salt and ¼ teaspoon black pepper. Return meatballs to pan and bring to a boil. Reduce heat to low, cover, and simmer, stirring occasionally, until meatballs are no longer pink in center, 30 minutes.

4. Meanwhile, place almonds in a small dry skillet and cook over medium heat, stirring frequently, until lightly toasted, 3 to 5 minutes.

5. Add broccoli and yogurt to casserole and cook, stirring occasionally, until heated through, about 5 minutes. Remove and discard bay leaf. Stir in remaining cilantro and sprinkle with toasted almonds just before serving.

213   INDONESIAN PORK CURRY

Prep: 20 minutes   Cook: 1 hour 49 minutes to 1 hour 55 minutes
Serves: 6

This is a wonderful dish for entertaining.

3 tablespoons vegetable oil
3 pounds boneless pork
   shoulder, cut into 2-inch
   pieces
1 teaspoon salt
½ teaspoon pepper
2 medium onions, sliced
6 garlic cloves, minced
1 tablespoon minced fresh
   ginger
3 tablespoons soy sauce
1 teaspoon crushed hot red
   pepper
1 tablespoon ground
   coriander

1 tablespoon dried lemon-
   grass or 1 small strip of
   lemon zest
1 teaspoon ground cumin
1 teaspoon grated nutmeg
1 teaspoon grated lemon zest
½ teaspoon ground turmeric
¼ teaspoon ground mace
¼ teaspoon ground cloves
1 (13½-ounce) can
   unsweetened coconut
   milk
2 bay leaves
   Saffron Rice (recipe follows)

1. In a large flameproof casserole, heat 2 tablespoons oil over medium-high heat. Season pork with salt and pepper. Add to casserole in 2 batches and cook, adding remaining 1 tablespoon oil as needed, stirring frequently until browned on all sides, 6 to 8 minutes per batch. Transfer pork to a platter.

2. Add onions to casserole, reduce heat to medium, and cook, stirring frequently, until golden, 6 to 8 minutes. Add garlic and cook, stirring constantly, until fragrant, about 1 minute. Add ginger, soy sauce, hot red pepper, coriander, lemongrass, cumin, nutmeg, lemon zest, turmeric, mace, cloves, coconut milk, and bay leaves.

3. Return pork to casserole and bring to a boil. Reduce heat to low, cover, and simmer until pork is tender, about 1½ hours. Remove and discard bay leaves. Serve with Saffron Rice.

214   SAFFRON RICE

Prep: 10 minutes   Stand: 10 minutes   Cook: 28 minutes   Serves: 6

1½ cups basmati rice or other
   long-grain white rice
¼ teaspoon saffron threads
2½ cups Chicken Stock (page
   262) or reduced-sodium
   canned broth, heated
½ teaspoon salt
3 tablespoons butter

1 cinnamon stick, broken in
   half
4 whole cloves
½ teaspoon cumin seed
1 bay leaf
1 teaspoon ground cardamom
1 medium onion, chopped

1. In a large bowl, wash rice in several changes of water until water runs clear. Drain.

2. In a medium bowl, combine saffron, chicken stock, and salt and let stand 5 minutes. In a large saucepan, melt butter over medium heat. Add cinnamon, cloves, cumin seed, bay leaf, and cardamom and cook, stirring constantly, 1 minute. Add onion and cook, stirring frequently, until softened, about 5 minutes.

3. Add rice and cook, stirring constantly until golden, 2 minutes. Stir in stock mixture. Bring to a boil. Reduce heat to medium-low, cover, and simmer until rice is tender, 20 minutes. Remove and discard bay leaf and cinnamon stick. Let stand 5 minutes before serving.

---

215 CURRIED CHICKEN WITH CAULIFLOWER AND RICE

Prep: 15 minutes   Cook: 37 to 41 minutes   Serves: 4

1½ pounds skinless, boneless chicken breasts, cut into 1-inch pieces
½ teaspoon salt
¼ teaspoon black pepper
2 tablespoons vegetable oil
2 medium onions, chopped
3 garlic cloves, minced
1 tablespoon curry powder
1 teaspoon ground coriander
1 teaspoon ground ginger
1 teaspoon ground cumin
1 cinnamon stick, broken in half

1 cup long-grain white rice
2 cups Chicken Stock (page 262) or reduced-sodium canned broth
1 (14½-ounce) can chopped tomatoes, drained
½ teaspoon grated lemon zest
1 (10-ounce) package frozen cauliflower florets, thawed
1 cup frozen peas
2 tablespoons minced cilantro

1. Season chicken with salt and pepper. In a large nonreactive flameproof casserole, heat oil over medium-high heat. Add chicken to casserole in batches, if necessary, and cook, stirring occasionally, until chicken is no longer pink in center, 3 to 5 minutes per batch. Transfer chicken to a plate.

2. Add onions and garlic to casserole and cook, stirring frequently, until golden, about 5 minutes. Add curry powder, coriander, ginger, cumin, and cinnamon stick and cook, stirring constantly, 1 minute. Add rice, chicken stock, tomatoes, lemon zest, cauliflower, and peas, cover, and simmer until rice is tender, about 15 minutes.

3. Return chicken to casserole, cover, and simmer until heated through, 10 minutes. Remove and discard cinnamon stick. Stir in cilantro just before serving.

216   CURRIED BEEF WITH SPINACH AND YOGURT

Prep: 10 minutes   Cook: 1 hour 52 minutes to 2 hours 27 minutes
Serves: 6

Serve this stew with Saffron Rice (page 146), assorted Indian chutneys, and a refreshing yogurt and cucumber salad.

¼ cup vegetable oil
2½ pounds boneless beef chuck, cut into 2-inch pieces
½ teaspoon salt
2 medium onions, chopped
4 garlic cloves, minced
1 tablespoon imported curry powder
1 teaspoon ground coriander
1½ teaspoons ground cumin
2 teaspoons grated fresh ginger
¼ teaspoon cayenne, or to taste

3 tablespoons flour
1 (14½-ounce) can peeled tomatoes, juices reserved
2 cups Simple Beef Stock (page 264) or reduced-sodium canned broth
1½ teaspoons grated lemon zest
2 teaspoons lemon juice
1 pound fresh spinach leaves, stemmed and trimmed
½ cup plain yogurt
2 tablespoons chopped cilantro

1. In a large nonreactive flameproof casserole, heat 1 tablespoon oil over medium-high heat. Season beef with salt. Add beef to casserole in 2 batches and cook, adding additional 1 tablespoon oil as needed, turning occasionally, until browned on all sides, 5 to 7 minutes per batch. Transfer beef to a plate.

2. Heat remaining 2 tablespoons oil in casserole over medium heat. Add onions and cook, stirring frequently, until golden, about 5 minutes. Reduce heat to medium-low. Add garlic, curry powder, coriander, cumin, ginger, and cayenne and cook, stirring constantly, 1 minute. Add flour and cook, stirring constantly, 1 to 2 minutes without allowing to color. Stir in tomatoes with their juices, beef stock, lemon zest, and lemon juice.

3. Return beef to casserole and bring to a boil. Reduce heat to low, cover, and simmer until beef is tender, 1½ to 2 hours.

4. Meanwhile, place spinach and ½ cup water in a large saucepan and cook over medium heat, stirring occasionally, until spinach is wilted, 4 to 5 minutes. Drain spinach, rinse under cold water, and squeeze dry.

5. When beef is cooked, add spinach and yogurt to casserole and simmer until heated through, about 5 minutes. Stir in cilantro just before serving.

217 GINGERY CHICKEN CURRY

Prep: 15 minutes   Cook: 43 to 44 minutes   Serves: 4

Serve this curry with Lemon Pilaf and assorted condiments, such as mango chutney, onion relish, and toasted coconut.

1 (3-pound) chicken, cut into serving pieces
½ cup flour
½ teaspoon salt
¼ teaspoon black pepper
3 tablespoons vegetable oil
2 medium onions, chopped
4 garlic cloves, minced
1 tablespoon imported curry powder
1 tablespoon grated fresh ginger
1 teaspoon ground coriander
1 teaspoon cumin seed
⅛ teaspoon cayenne, or to taste

1 (14½-ounce) can peeled tomatoes, juices reserved
1½ cups Chicken Stock (page 262) or reduced-sodium canned broth
1½ teaspoons grated lemon zest
2 teaspoons lemon juice
1 bay leaf
1 Granny Smith or other tart apple, peeled, cored, and cubed
2 tablespoons sliced almonds
2 tablespoons minced cilantro
Lemon Pilaf (recipe follows)

1. Dredge chicken to coat lightly with flour; shake off excess flour. Season chicken with salt and black pepper.

2. In a large nonreactive flameproof casserole, heat 2 tablespoons oil over medium-high heat. Add chicken and cook, turning occasionally, until browned on both sides, 7 to 8 minutes. Transfer chicken to a platter.

3. Heat remaining 1 tablespoon oil in casserole over medium heat. Add onions and cook, stirring frequently, until golden, about 5 minutes. Add garlic, curry powder, ginger, coriander, cumin seed, and cayenne. Reduce heat to medium-low and cook, stirring constantly, 1 minute. Add tomatoes with their juices, chicken stock, lemon zest, lemon juice, and bay leaf.

4. Return chicken to casserole and bring to a boil. Reduce heat to low, cover, and simmer 20 minutes. Add apple and simmer until chicken is no longer pink in center, about 10 minutes longer.

5. Meanwhile, place almonds in a small skillet. Cook, stirring frequently, over medium heat until lightly toasted, 3 to 5 minutes.

6. When chicken is cooked, remove and discard bay leaf. Stir in cilantro, sprinkle with toasted almonds, and serve with Lemon Pilaf.

218   LEMON PILAF
Prep: 5 minutes   Cook: 30 to 32 minutes   Serves: 4

3 tablespoons butter
1 medium onion, chopped
2 cups long-grain white rice
2¾ cups Chicken Stock (page
  262) or reduced-sodium
  canned broth

2 tablespoons lemon juice
1 bay leaf
2 (3-inch) strips of lemon zest
½ teaspoon salt
¼ teaspoon pepper
3 tablespoons sliced almonds

1. Preheat oven to 350°F. In a large flameproof casserole with a lid, melt butter over medium heat. Add onion and cook, stirring occasionally, until softened, about 5 minutes. Add rice and cook, stirring constantly, until golden, 2 minutes. Add chicken stock, lemon juice, bay leaf, lemon zest, salt, and pepper. Bring to a boil. Cover with an oiled round of wax paper or foil and the lid. Place in oven and bake 20 minutes, or until liquid is absorbed and rice is tender.

2. Meanwhile, place almonds in a small skillet. Cook, stirring frequently, over medium heat until lightly toasted, 3 to 5 minutes. Remove and discard bay leaf and lemon zest from rice mixture. Fluff rice with fork and sprinkle with toasted almonds.

219   LAMB VINDALOO
Prep: 15 minutes   Marinate: 4 hours
Cook: 1 hour 26 minutes to 1 hour 48 minutes   Serves: 6

A vindaloo is a very spicy curry. The seasoning we have given here is hot, although not searingly so. Adjust the "heat" according to taste. Serve with hot cooked rice.

2½ pounds boneless lamb
  shoulder, cut into 2-inch
  pieces
1 tablespoon ground
  coriander
2 teaspoons ground cumin
2 teaspoons ground turmeric
1 teaspoon ground cardamom
1 teaspoon cinnamon
1 teaspoon ground fenugreek
  (optional)
¼ teaspoon ground black
  pepper

¼ teaspoon cayenne
½ teaspoon salt
3 tablespoons cider vinegar
3 tablespoons vegetable oil
2 large onions, minced
6 large garlic cloves, minced
1 tablespoon minced fresh
  ginger
1½ cups Lamb Stock (page 265)
  or reduced-sodium
  canned beef broth
1 bay leaf
1 tablespoon tomato paste

1. In a large bowl, toss lamb with coriander, cumin, turmeric, cardamom, cinnamon, fenugreek, black pepper, cayenne, salt, and cider vinegar. Cover and refrigerate at least 4 hours or overnight.

2. In a large flameproof casserole, heat 2 tablespoons oil over medium-high heat. Add lamb in 2 batches and cook, adding remaining 1 tablespoon oil as needed, until browned on all sides, 7 to 8 minutes per batch. Transfer lamb to a platter. Add onions to casserole, reduce heat to medium, and cook, stirring occasionally, until golden, 7 to 10 minutes. Add garlic and ginger and cook, stirring constantly, until fragrant, 2 minutes.

3. Return lamb to casserole and stir in lamb stock, bay leaf, and tomato paste. Bring to a boil. Reduce heat to low, cover, and simmer until lamb is tender, 1 to 1¼ hours. Skim fat from surface, increase heat to high, and boil until lamb mixture is slightly thickened, 3 to 5 minutes. Remove and discard bay leaf before serving.

220 CURRIED LAMB WITH RAISINS AND APPLE

Prep: 10 minutes   Cook: 2 hours 11 minutes to 2 hours 14 minutes
Serves: 6

3 tablespoons vegetable oil
2½ pounds boneless lamb
    shoulder, cut into 2-inch
    pieces
1 teaspoon salt
¼ teaspoon black pepper
2 medium onions, chopped
3 garlic cloves, minced
1 tablespoon imported curry
    powder
1½ teaspoons cumin seed
1 teaspoon ground ginger
¼ teaspoon cayenne

2 tablespoons flour
1 (14½-ounce) can peeled
    tomatoes, juices reserved
1½ cups Lamb Stock (page 265)
    or reduced-sodium
    canned beef broth
½ cup raisins
2 teaspoons grated lemon zest
1 tablespoon lemon juice
1 large McIntosh apple,
    peeled, cored, and cubed
2 tablespoons minced cilantro

1. In a large nonreactive flameproof casserole, heat 1 tablespoon oil over medium-high heat. Season lamb with salt and black pepper. Add lamb to casserole in 2 batches and cook, adding 1 tablespoon oil as needed, turning occasionally until browned on all sides, 7 to 8 minutes per batch. Transfer lamb to a plate.

2. Heat remaining 1 tablespoon oil in casserole over medium heat. Add onions and cook, stirring occasionally, until golden, about 5 minutes. Add garlic, curry powder, cumin seed, ginger, and cayenne. Reduce heat to medium-low and cook, stirring constantly, 1 minute. Add flour and cook, stirring constantly, 1 to 2 minutes without allowing to color. Add tomatoes with their juices, lamb stock, raisins, lemon zest, and lemon juice. Return lamb to casserole and bring to a boil. Reduce heat to medium-low, cover, and simmer until lamb is tender, 1½ hours.

3. Add apple, cover, and simmer about 20 minutes longer. Stir in cilantro just before serving.

221   GROUND BEEF CURRY WITH PEAS

Prep: 20 minutes   Cook: 48 to 50 minutes   Serves: 4

This is a quick version of classic curry using ground beef instead of cubes.

1 **pound ground beef**	½ **teaspoon ground cardamom**
1 **egg, lightly beaten**	2 **tablespoons flour**
2½ **teaspoons ground cumin**	1 **(14½-ounce) can peeled**
1½ **teaspoons ground coriander**	**tomatoes, cut up, juices**
1 **teaspoon ground ginger**	**reserved**
6 **garlic cloves, minced**	1 **cup Simple Beef Stock (page**
5 **tablespoons minced cilantro**	**264) or reduced-sodium**
or fresh parsley	**canned broth**
1 **teaspoon salt**	1 **bay leaf**
½ **teaspoon pepper**	2 **teaspoons grated lemon zest**
3 **tablespoons vegetable oil**	1 **cup frozen peas**
1 **medium onion, minced**	½ **cup plain yogurt**
1 **tablespoon imported curry**	
powder	

1. In a medium bowl, combine ground beef, egg, 1½ teaspoons cumin, ground coriander, ginger, half of garlic, 3 tablespoons cilantro, ½ teaspoon salt, and ¼ teaspoon pepper. Mix with your hands to blend well and form into 1½-inch meatballs.

2. In a large nonreactive flameproof casserole, heat oil over medium-high heat. Add meatballs and cook, turning occasionally, until browned on all sides, 5 to 7 minutes. Transfer meatballs to a plate.

3. Add onion to casserole, reduce heat to medium, and cook, stirring occasionally, until golden, about 5 minutes. Add curry powder, cardamom, and remaining garlic and 1 teaspoon cumin. Cook, stirring constantly, 1 minute. Add flour and cook, stirring constantly, 2 minutes without allowing to color. Add tomatoes with their juices, beef stock, bay leaf, lemon zest, and remaining ½ teaspoon salt and ¼ teaspoon pepper. Return meatballs to casserole and bring to a boil. Reduce heat to medium-low, cover, and simmer, stirring occasionally until meatballs are no longer pink in center, 30 minutes. Remove and discard bay leaf

4. Stir in peas and yogurt and simmer, stirring occasionally, until heated through, about 5 minutes. Stir in remaining 2 tablespoons cilantro just before serving.

222   CURRIED BEEF WITH GREEN BEANS
Prep: 10 minutes   Cook: 1 hour 55 minutes to 2 hours   Serves: 6

3 tablespoons vegetable oil
2½ pounds boneless beef chuck, cut into 2-inch pieces
1 teaspoon salt
¼ teaspoon black pepper
2 medium onions, minced
3 garlic cloves, minced
1 tablespoon imported curry powder
2 teaspoons grated fresh ginger
1 teaspoon cinnamon

¼ teaspoon crushed hot red pepper
⅛ teaspoon ground cloves
2 tablespoons flour
1 (14½-ounce) can peeled tomatoes, juices reserved
1½ cups Simple Beef Stock (page 264) or reduced-sodium canned broth
1 bay leaf
1 (10-ounce) package frozen cut green beans
2 tablespoons minced cilantro

1. In a nonreactive soup pot, heat 1 tablespoon oil over medium-high heat. Season beef with salt and pepper. Add to soup pot in 2 batches, adding 1 tablespoon oil as needed, and cook, turning occasionally, until browned on all sides, 5 to 7 minutes per batch. Transfer beef to a plate.

2. Add remaining 1 tablespoon oil to soup pot and heat over medium heat. Add onions and cook, stirring frequently, until golden, about 5 minutes. Add garlic, curry powder, ginger, cinnamon, hot pepper, and cloves. Cook, stirring constantly, 1 minute. Add flour and cook, stirring, 1 to 2 minutes without allowing to color. Stir in tomatoes with their juices, beef stock, and bay leaf. Return beef to soup pot and bring to a boil. Reduce heat to low, cover, and simmer until beef is tender, about 1½ hours.

3. Add green beans, cover, and simmer until beans are tender, about 8 minutes. Remove and discard bay leaf. Stir in cilantro just before serving.

223 CURRIED PORK WITH POTATO AND CABBAGE

Prep: 20 minutes
Cook: 2 hours 12 minutes to 2 hours 16 minutes   Serves: 4

2 tablespoons vegetable oil
1½ pounds boneless pork shoulder, cut into 1-inch pieces
½ teaspoon salt
¼ teaspoon black pepper
2 medium onions, sliced
3 garlic cloves, minced
1 tablespoon minced fresh ginger

1 tablespoon curry powder
1 tablespoon flour
1 cup apple cider
2 cups Chicken Stock (page 262) or reduced-sodium canned broth
1 bay leaf
1 pound red potatoes, cut into 1-inch dice
2 cups thinly sliced cabbage

1. In a large saucepan, heat 1 tablespoon oil over medium heat. Season pork with salt and pepper. Add to saucepan in 2 batches and cook, adding remaining 1 tablespoon oil as needed, until browned on all sides, 3 to 5 minutes per batch. Transfer pork to a plate.

2. Add onions, garlic, and ginger to saucepan and cook, stirring occasionally, until golden, about 5 minutes. Add curry powder and flour and cook, stirring constantly, without allowing to color, 1 minute. Add cider, chicken stock, and bay leaf. Return pork to saucepan and bring to a boil. Reduce heat to medium-low, cover, and simmer until pork is tender, about 1½ hours.

3. Add potatoes and simmer, covered, until potatoes are softened, about 15 minutes. Add cabbage and simmer, covered, until cabbage is tender, about 15 minutes longer. Remove and discard bay leaf before serving.

Chapter 9

Chicken (and Duck) Stews

Chicken is probably one of the most versatile foods available. While it can be prepared in many different ways, it lends itself beautifully to stewing. The recipes that follow feature chicken in its many guises: whole, as in Chicken in a Pot; cut into serving pieces, as in Chicken Marengo; and chicken parts (wings, thighs, or breasts) as in Chicken Wing Stew with Tomatoes and Black Olives.

Unlike red meat, chicken does not require a very long cooking time. Most chicken stews cook in about 45 minutes. Using only the breast meat reduces the cooking time by half.

Also included here are several recipes that use duck. Braised duck is one of the most delicious ways to eat this succulent bird. The long, slow moist cooking tenderizes the meat, while the liquid keeps it juicy. Best of all, the duck can be prepared the day before, allowed to cool, and chilled overnight. Before reheating, all the fat can be removed from the surface of the liquid. The flavors only intensify when left to sit overnight.

224   CHICKEN IN A POT

Prep: 15 minutes   Cook: 43 to 46 minutes   Serves: 4

1 (3-pound) chicken, cut into
   serving pieces
½ cup flour
1 teaspoon salt
½ teaspoon pepper
3 tablespoons olive oil
1 large onion, chopped
2 medium carrots, peeled and
   chopped
1 medium celery rib, sliced
3 garlic cloves, minced
½ pound mushrooms, sliced

1 cup dry white wine
1 (14½-ounce) can peeled
   tomatoes, drained and
   chopped
1½ cups Chicken Stock (page
   262) or reduced-sodium
   canned broth
½ teaspoon dried thyme leaves
½ teaspoon dried tarragon
1 bay leaf
2 tablespoons chopped
   parsley

1. Dredge chicken to coat lightly with flour; shake off excess flour. Season chicken with ½ teaspoon salt and ¼ teaspoon pepper.

2. In a large nonreactive flameproof casserole, heat 2 tablespoons olive oil over medium-high heat. Add chicken and cook, turning occasionally, until browned on both sides, 6 to 8 minutes. Transfer chicken to a platter.

3. Heat remaining 1 tablespoon olive oil in casserole. Add onion, carrots, and celery, reduce heat to medium, and cook, stirring occasionally, until softened but not browned, 5 minutes. Add garlic and mushrooms and cook, stirring occasionally, until vegetables are softened, about 5 minutes longer. Stir in wine, tomatoes, chicken stock, thyme, tarragon, bay leaf, and remaining ½ teaspoon salt and ¼ teaspoon pepper.

4. Return chicken to casserole and bring to a boil. Reduce heat to medium-low, cover, and simmer until chicken is no longer pink in center, about 25 minutes. Remove and discard bay leaf.

5. With a slotted spoon, transfer chicken to a serving dish. Skim fat from cooking liquid in casserole. Bring cooking liquid to a boil over medium-high heat and boil until slightly thickened, 2 to 3 minutes. Pour sauce over chicken and sprinkle with parsley.

225   COQ AU VIN

Prep: 20 minutes   Cook: 49 to 59 minutes   Serves: 4

Serve this classic chicken and red wine stew with buttered boiled potatoes and green beans.

¼ **pound bacon, cut into 1-inch pieces**	1 **tablespoon tomato paste**
1 **(3-pound) chicken, cut into serving pieces**	½ **teaspoon dried thyme leaves**
1 **teaspoon salt**	½ **teaspoon dried rosemary**
½ **teaspoon pepper**	3 **whole cloves**
1 **medium onion, chopped**	6 **black peppercorns**
1 **small carrot, peeled and chopped**	1 **large bay leaf**
4 **garlic cloves, minced**	12 **small white onions, peeled**
1½ **cups dry red wine**	2 **tablespoons butter**
2 **cups Chicken Stock (page 262) or reduced-sodium canned broth**	½ **pound mushrooms, quartered**
	2 **tablespoons cornstarch**

1. In a large nonreactive flameproof casserole, cook bacon over medium heat, stirring occasionally, until crisp, about 5 minutes. With a slotted spoon, transfer bacon to a paper towel-lined plate to drain.

2. Add chicken, ½ teaspoon salt, and ¼ teaspoon pepper to casserole and cook, turning, until chicken is browned on both sides, 6 to 8 minutes. With a slotted spoon, transfer chicken to a platter.

3. Add chopped onion and carrot to casserole. Cook, stirring occasionally, until onion is golden, about 5 minutes. Add garlic and cook, stirring constantly, until fragrant, about 1 minute. Add wine, chicken stock, tomato paste, thyme, rosemary, cloves, peppercorns, bay leaf, and remaining ½ teaspoon salt and ¼ teaspoon pepper. Return chicken to casserole and bring liquid to a boil. Reduce heat to medium-low, cover, and cook 10 minutes.

4. Add whole onions and continue to cook, covered, until chicken and onions are tender and there is no trace of pink near thigh bone of chicken, 15 to 20 minutes longer. With a slotted spoon, transfer chicken and onions to a platter. Strain cooking liquid through a sieve; return to casserole and skim fat from surface.

5. In a large skillet, melt butter over medium-high heat. Add mushrooms and cook, stirring frequently, until lightly browned, 5 to 7 minutes. Add to casserole with reserved bacon and bring cooking liquid to a boil.

6. In a small bowl, blend cornstarch with ¼ cup cold water. Gradually add to simmering stock in casserole and cook, stirring constantly, until slightly thickened, 2 to 3 minutes. Serve over chicken and onions.

226 CHICKEN MARENGO

Prep: 20 minutes   Cook: 42 to 46 minutes   Serves: 4 to 6

This dish is said to have been created by the cook on one of Napoleon's expeditions. The classic version is garnished with crayfish, deep-fried eggs, and parsley croutons. We have eliminated crayfish and eggs but have kept the crispy topping of Parsleyed Croutons, which are delicious with any of the stews in this chapter.

1 (3-pound) chicken, cut into
  serving pieces
½ cup flour
1 teaspoon salt
½ teaspoon pepper
¼ cup olive oil
2 tablespoons butter
1 medium onion, chopped
1 medium celery rib, chopped
1 small carrot, peeled and
  chopped
1 pound mushrooms, sliced
3 garlic cloves, minced

½ cup dry white wine
1½ cups Chicken Stock (page
  262) or reduced-sodium
  canned broth
1 (14½-ounce) can peeled
  tomatoes, chopped,
  juices reserved
½ teaspoon dried thyme leaves
½ teaspoon dried oregano
1 bay leaf
1 tablespoon tomato paste
  Parsleyed Croutons (recipe
  follows)

1. Dredge chicken to coat lightly with flour; shake off excess flour. Season chicken with ½ teaspoon salt and ¼ teaspoon pepper.

2. In a large nonreactive flameproof casserole, heat 3 tablespoons oil over medium-high heat. Add chicken and cook, turning, until browned on both sides, 6 to 8 minutes. Transfer chicken to a platter.

3. Melt butter in remaining 1 tablespoon oil in casserole over medium heat. Add onion, celery, and carrot and cook, stirring occasionally, until softened, about 3 minutes. Add mushrooms and garlic and cook, stirring occasionally, until mushrooms are softened, 5 minutes. Stir in wine, chicken stock, tomatoes with their juices, thyme, oregano, bay leaf, tomato paste, and remaining ½ teaspoon salt and ¼ teaspoon pepper. Return chicken to casserole and bring to a boil. Reduce heat to medium-low, cover, and cook until chicken is no longer pink in center, about 25 minutes. Remove and discard bay leaf.

4. Transfer chicken to a serving dish. Bring cooking liquid in casserole to a boil, reduce heat to medium-low, and cook until slightly thickened, 3 to 5 minutes. Pour sauce over chicken and top with Parsleyed Croutons.

227   PARSLEYED CROUTONS
Prep: 10 minutes   Cook: 2 minutes   Serves: 6

2 tablespoons butter
1 tablespoon olive oil
6 (½-inch-thick) slices of
    French bread

1 tablespoon minced fresh
    parsley

In a large skillet, melt butter in olive oil over medium heat. Add bread and cook 1 minute on each side, or until browned and crisp on both sides. Sprinkle with the parsley and transfer to a plate.

228   CHICKEN CACCIATORE
Prep: 15 minutes   Cook: 37 to 43 minutes   Serves: 4

This is a perfect dish for company since it can be prepared completely ahead and reheated before serving.

1 (3-pound) chicken, cut into
    serving pieces
½ cup flour
1 teaspoon salt
½ teaspoon pepper
3 tablespoons olive oil
1 large onion, chopped
1 large green bell pepper, cut
    into strips

3 garlic cloves, minced
½ cup dry white wine
1 (28-ounce) can tomatoes,
    drained and chopped
1 teaspoon dried basil
½ teaspoon dried oregano
1 bay leaf
1 tablespoon chopped fresh
    basil or parsley

1. Dredge chicken to coat lightly with flour; shake off excess flour. Season chicken with ½ teaspoon salt and ¼ teaspoon black pepper.

2. In a large nonreactive flameproof casserole, heat oil over medium-high heat. Add chicken and cook, turning, until browned on both sides, 6 to 8 minutes. With a slotted spoon, transfer chicken to a platter.

3. Add onion and bell pepper to casserole, reduce heat to medium, and cook, stirring occasionally, until softened, 3 to 5 minutes. Add garlic and cook, stirring constantly, until fragrant, 1 to 2 minutes. Add wine, tomatoes, basil, oregano, bay leaf, and remaining ½ teaspoon salt and ¼ teaspoon black pepper. Return chicken to casserole and bring to a boil. Reduce heat to medium-low, cover, and simmer, stirring occasionally, until chicken is no longer pink in center, about 25 minutes. Remove and discard bay leaf.

4. Transfer chicken to a serving dish. Bring cooking liquid in casserole to a boil and cook, stirring frequently, until slightly thickened, 2 to 3 minutes. Pour sauce over chicken and garnish with basil.

229   CHICKEN STEW WITH BUTTERMILK DUMPLINGS

Prep: 15 minutes   Cook: 1 hour 4 minutes to 1 hour 7 minutes
Serves: 4

4   tablespoons butter
1   (3-pound) chicken, cut into serving pieces, skinned
1   teaspoon salt
½   teaspoon pepper
1   medium onion, chopped
2   celery ribs, chopped
1   small carrot, peeled and chopped
2   garlic cloves, minced
5   cups Chicken Stock (page 262) or reduced-sodium canned broth

½   teaspoon dried marjoram
½   teaspoon dried thyme leaves
1   bay leaf
6   whole cloves
2   tablespoons cornstarch
½   cup heavy or light cream
     Buttermilk Dumplings (recipe follows)

1. In a large flameproof casserole, melt 3 tablespoons butter over medium heat. Season chicken with ½ teaspoon salt and ¼ teaspoon pepper. Add to casserole and cook, turning, until browned on both sides, 6 to 8 minutes. Transfer chicken to a platter and set aside.

2. Melt remaining 1 tablespoon butter in casserole over medium heat. Add onion, celery, and carrot and cook, stirring occasionally, until softened, about 5 minutes. Add garlic and cook, stirring constantly, until fragrant, 1 minute. Add chicken stock, marjoram, thyme, bay leaf, cloves, and remaining ½ teaspoon salt and ¼ teaspoon pepper. Return chicken to casserole and bring to a boil. Reduce heat to low, cover, and simmer, stirring occasionally, 30 minutes.

3. Remove chicken from casserole and place on cutting board. When cool enough to handle, remove bones from chicken and discard. Cut chicken into 1-inch pieces. Strain cooking liquid through a sieve into a large saucepan and bring to a boil.

4. In a small bowl, blend cornstarch with cream, stir into boiling stock, and cook until slightly thickened, 2 to 3 minutes. Transfer chicken to casserole, return stock to simmer, and top with Buttermilk Dumplings, spacing them evenly. Cover, reduce heat to medium, and cook until dumplings are firm to the touch and cooked through, about 20 minutes.

230 BUTTERMILK DUMPLINGS

Prep: 8 minutes   Cook: 20 minutes   Serves: 4

These tasty dumplings make a great addition to any soup or stew.

1 cup sifted flour
1 teaspoon baking powder
½ teaspoon baking soda
½ teaspoon salt
¼ teaspoon pepper

2 tablespoons minced fresh
   parsley
2 tablespoons cold butter
⅓ to ½ cup buttermilk

1. In a medium bowl, combine flour, baking powder, baking soda, salt, pepper, and parsley. Mix well. Cut in butter with pastry blender or 2 knives until mixture resembles coarse meal. Stir in just enough buttermilk to form a soft dough.

2. Shape dough into 12 balls. Add to simmering stock, cover, and cook until dumplings are firm to the touch and cooked through, about 20 minutes.

231 CHICKEN WITH 40 CLOVES OF GARLIC

Prep: 15 minutes   Cook: 43 to 46 minutes   Serves: 4

When garlic is slowly simmered, it mellows and becomes almost sweet in flavor. Serve this stew with crusty bread onto which the softened garlic may be spread.

2 heads of garlic
4 tablespoons butter
1 tablespoon olive oil
1 (3-pound) chicken, cut into
   serving pieces
1 teaspoon salt
½ teaspoon pepper

½ cup dry white wine
1 cup Chicken Stock (page
   262) or reduced-sodium
   canned broth
½ teaspoon dried thyme leaves
½ teaspoon dried rosemary
1 bay leaf

1. Separate garlic into cloves and peel. Add to a small pan of boiling water, reduce heat to low, and simmer 10 minutes. Drain and let cool.

2. In a large nonreactive flameproof casserole, melt 2 tablespoons butter in olive oil over medium-high heat. Season chicken with ½ teaspoon salt and ¼ teaspoon pepper. Add chicken to casserole and cook, turning, until browned on all sides, 6 to 8 minutes.

3. Separate garlic cloves and add to casserole. Stir in wine, chicken stock, thyme, rosemary, bay leaf, and remaining ½ teaspoon salt and ¼ teaspoon pepper. Bring to a boil. Reduce heat to medium-low, cover, and cook until chicken is no longer pink in center, about 25 minutes. Remove and discard bay leaf. Transfer chicken and garlic to a serving dish.

4. Skim fat from cooking liquid and discard. Bring cooking liquid to a boil and cook until liquid is reduced to 1 cup, 2 to 3 minutes. Stir in remaining 2 tablespoons butter and pour over chicken.

232 POZOLE WITH CHICKEN

Prep: 20 minutes   Cook: 1 hour 41 minutes to 1 hour 46 minutes
Serves: 4

Pozole is also known as hominy. You'll find it on many supermarket shelves, either in the Mexican food section or near canned beans and vegetables.

2 ancho chiles, stemmed,
    seeded, and deveined
1 tablespoon vegetable oil
4 bone-in chicken thighs
    (about 1 pound), skinned
1 medium onion, chopped
6 garlic cloves, chopped
½ teaspoon dried oregano,
    preferably Mexican
1 teaspoon ground cumin

1 tablespoon flour
2 (16-ounce) cans hominy,
    drained and rinsed
½ teaspoon salt
¼ head of iceberg lettuce,
    shredded
1 avocado, cubed
4 radishes, thinly sliced
4 lime wedges

1. Open chiles into large flat pieces. Place chiles in a large skillet, preferably cast iron. Cook over medium heat while holding down with a spatula until blistered, 2 to 3 minutes. Transfer chiles to a coffee grinder or small food processor and process until finely ground.

2. In a large flameproof casserole, heat oil over medium-high heat. Add chicken and cook, turning occasionally, until browned on both sides, 6 to 8 minutes. Transfer chicken to a plate.

3. Add onion to casserole and cook, stirring occasionally, until softened, 3 to 5 minutes. Stir in garlic, oregano, cumin, and flour. Add chicken, hominy, salt, and 3 cups water. Bring to a boil, reduce heat to low, and simmer 1½ hours.

4. Serve topped with lettuce, avocado, and radishes. Garnish with lime wedges.

233 CHICKEN POT PIE

Prep: 15 minutes   Cook: 1½ hours   Serves: 4

This is a very easy-to-prepare dish. Serve it directly from the casserole in which it was cooked.

¼ cup vegetable oil
1 (3-pound) chicken, cut into serving pieces
1½ teaspoons salt
¾ teaspoon pepper
¼ pound small white onions, peeled
2 medium carrots, peeled and sliced
1 medium celery rib, sliced
2 tablespoons flour
½ cup dry white wine
2 cups Chicken Stock (page 262) or reduced-sodium canned broth

½ teaspoon dried oregano
¼ teaspoon dried sage
1 bay leaf
½ cup heavy or light cream
4 baking potatoes (about 1½ pounds), peeled and diced
2 tablespoons butter
¼ cup sour cream
⅛ teaspoon paprika

1. In a large nonreactive flameproof casserole, heat 3 tablespoons oil over medium heat. Season chicken with ½ teaspoon salt and ¼ teaspoon pepper. Add chicken to casserole and cook, turning, until chicken is browned on both sides, 6 to 8 minutes. Transfer chicken to a platter.

2. Heat remaining 1 tablespoon oil in casserole. Add onions, carrots, and celery. Cook, stirring occasionally, until vegetables are softened, 5 minutes. Add wine, chicken stock, oregano, sage, bay leaf, ½ teaspoon salt, and ¼ teaspoon pepper. Return chicken to casserole and bring to a boil. Reduce heat to medium-low, cover, and cook, skimming surface and stirring occasionally, 30 minutes. Remove cover and boil until stock is slightly thickened, 3 to 5 minutes. Stir in heavy cream.

3. Meanwhile, in a large saucepan, cook potatoes in boiling salted water until potatoes are tender, 20 to 25 minutes. Drain potatoes and mash. Beat in butter, sour cream, and remaining ½ teaspoon salt and ¼ teaspoon pepper.

4. Preheat oven to 400°F. Place spoonfuls of mashed potatoes over chicken stew in casserole. Dust top with paprika. Bake, uncovered, 20 minutes, or until hot and bubbly.

234   THAI GREEN CHICKEN CURRY

Prep: 40 minutes   Cook: 16 minutes   Serves: 6

Serve this rich curry over lots of steamed jasmine rice or rice noodles.

1 (13½-ounce) can
  unsweetened coconut
  milk
2 tablespoons canned Thai
  green curry
4 chicken thighs (about 1
  pound), skinned, boned,
  and cut into 1-inch dice
½ small eggplant, cut into
  ½-inch dice

½ red bell pepper, cut into ½-
  inch dice
1 tablespoon Thai fish sauce
  (*nam pla*) or soy sauce
1 tablespoon brown sugar
¼ teaspoon salt
2 teaspoons lime juice
¼ cup fresh basil leaves,
  shredded
¼ cup cilantro leaves

1. Carefully pour off cream from top of coconut milk. Reserve coconut milk; pour cream into large saucepan. Cook, stirring frequently, over medium heat until slightly thickened, about 5 minutes. Stir in green curry and cook 1 minute longer.

2. Add chicken and cook, stirring frequently, 2 minutes. Add reserved coconut milk, eggplant, bell pepper, fish sauce, brown sugar, salt, and lime juice. Simmer until chicken is no longer pink in center and eggplant is softened, about 8 minutes. Transfer chicken mixture to a serving dish and garnish with basil and cilantro.

235   COUNTRY CAPTAIN

Prep: 10 minutes   Cook: 42 to 44 minutes   Serves: 4

This classic stew is the South's version of curried chicken.

3 tablespoons vegetable oil
1 (3-pound) chicken, cut into
  serving pieces
1 teaspoon salt
½ teaspoon black pepper
1 medium onion, chopped
1 small green bell pepper,
  chopped

2 garlic cloves, minced
1 tablespoon curry powder
1 (14½-ounce) can crushed
  tomatoes, juices reserved
½ teaspoon dried thyme leaves
1 bay leaf
¼ cup slivered almonds
½ cup raisins

1. In a large nonreactive flameproof casserole, heat oil over medium-high heat. Season chicken with ½ teaspoon salt and ¼ teaspoon black pepper. Add chicken to casserole and cook, turning, until browned on both sides, 6 to 8 minutes. Transfer chicken to a platter.

2. Add onion and bell pepper to casserole, reduce heat to medium, and cook, stirring occasionally, until softened, about 5 minutes. Add garlic and curry powder and cook, stirring constantly, 1 minute. Add tomatoes with their juices, thyme, bay leaf, and remaining ½ teaspoon salt and ¼ teaspoon pepper.

3. Return chicken to casserole and bring to a boil. Reduce heat to medium-low, cover, and cook, stirring occasionally, until chicken is no longer pink in center, about 25 minutes.

4. Meanwhile, preheat oven to 350°F. Place almonds in shallow baking pan and bake, stirring occasionally, 15 minutes, or until lightly toasted.

5. When chicken is cooked, stir raisins into casserole and simmer 5 minutes longer. Remove and discard bay leaf, garnish with almonds, and serve.

---

236 CHICKEN BOUILLABAISSE
Prep: 25 minutes   Cook: 1 hour 44 minutes to 1 hour 46 minutes
Serves: 6

Here's a stew with bouillabaisse flavors—made with chicken rather than the traditional seafood.

3 tablespoons extra-virgin olive oil	½ cup dry white wine
6 bone-in chicken thighs, skinned (about 1½ pounds)	½ teaspoon ground saffron
	2 (2 x 1-inch) strips of orange zest
1¼ teaspoons salt	2 bay leaves
½ teaspoon pepper	1 pound small red potatoes, cut in half
1 large red onion, sliced	1 (28-ounce) can peeled Italian tomatoes, drained and chopped
2 large fennel bulbs, thickly sliced, fronds reserved	
4 large garlic cloves, minced	3 cups Chicken Stock (page 262) or reduced-sodium canned broth
1 teaspoon fennel seed, crushed	
1 teaspoon chopped fresh rosemary or ½ teaspoon dried	2 tablespoons chopped parsley

1. In a large nonreactive flameproof casserole, heat oil over medium-high heat. Season chicken with ½ teaspoon salt and pepper. Add chicken to casserole and cook, turning occasionally, until browned on both sides, 6 to 8 minutes. Transfer chicken to a plate.

2. Add onion and sliced fennel to pot and cook, stirring frequently, until onion is softened, about 5 minutes. Stir in garlic, fennel seed, and rosemary and cook, stirring constantly, 1 minute. Stir in wine and cook 2 minutes. Add saffron, orange zest, bay leaves, potatoes, tomatoes, chicken, and chicken stock and bring to a boil. Reduce heat to low and simmer until potatoes are softened and chicken is no longer pink in the center, 1½ hours.

3. Chop 2 tablespoons reserved fennel fronds, stir into soup pot along with parsley and remaining ¾ teaspoon salt, and serve.

237   CHICKEN, CORN, AND POTATO STEW
Prep: 30 minutes   Cook: 28 to 29 minutes   Serves: 4 to 6

2   tablespoons butter
2   medium onions, minced
1   medium celery rib, minced
1   small carrot, peeled and
     diced
2   garlic cloves, minced
2   tablespoons flour
3   large red potatoes, peeled
     and cut into ½-inch dice
5   cups Chicken Stock (page
     262) or reduced-sodium
     canned broth

½   teaspoon salt
1   bay leaf
1   (10-ounce) package frozen
     corn kernels, thawed
1½ pounds skinless, boneless
     chicken breasts, cut into
     1-inch pieces
1   cup light cream or milk
¼   teaspoon paprika

1. In a large flameproof casserole, melt butter over medium heat. Add onions, celery, carrot, and garlic, cover, and cook, stirring frequently, until softened, about 5 minutes. Add flour and cook, stirring constantly, 1 minute without allowing to color. Add potatoes, chicken stock, salt, and bay leaf and bring to a boil. Reduce heat to medium-low, cover, and cook, stirring occasionally, 10 minutes.

2. Add corn and chicken to pot and simmer until chicken is no longer pink in center, about 10 minutes. Stir in cream and simmer until heated through, 2 to 3 minutes. Remove and discard bay leaf. Sprinkle with paprika just before serving.

238   QUICK CHICKEN MOLE
Prep: 10 minutes   Cook: 36 to 42 minutes   Serves: 4

Black beans and rice would make a lovely accompaniment to this dish.

2   tablespoons blanched
     almonds
4   skinless, boneless chicken
     breast halves (about 1
     pound)
3   tablespoons flour
¼   teaspoon salt
¼   teaspoon black pepper
2   tablespoons vegetable oil

2   large shallots, minced
2   garlic cloves, minced
2   teaspoons unsweetened
     cocoa powder
2   teaspoons chili powder
1   teaspoon ground cumin
1   (14½-ounce) can crushed
     tomatoes, juices reserved
2   tablespoons minced cilantro

1. Place almonds in a small skillet. Cook over medium heat, stirring frequently, until lightly toasted, about 3 minutes. Transfer almonds to a coffee grinder or small food processor and process until finely ground.

2. Dredge chicken to coat lightly with flour; shake off excess flour. Season chicken with salt and black pepper.

3. In a large nonreactive flameproof casserole, heat oil over medium-high heat. Add chicken and cook 3 minutes on each side, or until golden brown. Transfer chicken to a plate.

4. Reduce heat to medium. Add shallots and garlic to casserole and cook, stirring frequently, until softened, 1 to 2 minutes. Add cocoa powder, chili powder, and cumin and cook, stirring constantly, 1 minute. Stir in tomatoes with their juices and the almonds and bring to a boil. Reduce heat to medium-low, cover, and cook, stirring occasionally, until chicken is tender with no trace of pink near bone, 20 to 25 minutes.

5. Transfer sauce to a blender or food processor and blend until smooth. Return to casserole with chicken and add cilantro. Cover and simmer 5 minutes to blend flavors before serving.

239 CHICKEN JAMBALAYA STEW

Prep: 20 minutes   Cook: 1 hour 24 minutes to 1 hour 28 minutes
Serves: 6

1 tablespoon vegetable oil	1 teaspoon salt
½ pound smoked sausage (andouille or kielbasa)	½ teaspoon black pepper
	¼ teaspoon cayenne
1 (3-pound) chicken, cut into serving pieces	½ teaspoon chili powder
	½ teaspoon dried thyme leaves
2 tablespoons butter	3 cups Chicken Stock (page 262) or reduced-sodium canned broth
1 large onion, chopped	
1 medium green bell pepper, chopped	
2 scallions, chopped	1 cup long-grain white rice
3 garlic cloves, minced	2 tablespoons chopped parsley
4 cups shredded cabbage	

1. In a large flameproof casserole, heat oil over medium-high heat. Add sausage and cook, turning occasionally, until browned on both sides, 8 to 10 minutes. Remove sausage to a cutting board and cut into slices ½ inch thick.

2. Add chicken to pot and cook, turning, until browned on both sides, 6 to 8 minutes. Transfer chicken to a plate and discard all but 1 tablespoon drippings from pot.

3. Add butter to pot and melt over medium heat. Stir in onion, green pepper, scallions, and garlic. Cook, stirring frequently, until vegetables are softened, about 5 minutes. Add cabbage and stir until wilted, about 5 minutes. Add salt, black pepper, cayenne, chili powder, thyme, sausage, and chicken. Pour in chicken stock and bring to a boil. Reduce heat to low, cover, and simmer 45 minutes.

4. Stir in rice and simmer, covered, until rice is tender, about 15 minutes longer. Stir in parsley just before serving.

240   QUICK TEX-MEX CHICKEN STEW
Prep: 20 minutes   Cook: 17 to 19 minutes   Serves: 4

2 tablespoons vegetable oil
2 tablespoons flour
½ teaspoon salt
½ teaspoon black pepper
4 skinless, boneless chicken
    breasts (about 1 pound),
    cut into 1-inch pieces
1 medium onion, thinly sliced
1 poblano pepper, seeded and
    thinly sliced
1 red bell pepper, thinly
    sliced
2 garlic cloves, minced

½ teaspoon dried oregano
½ teaspoon ground cumin
¼ teaspoon cinnamon
1 cup Chicken Stock (page
    262) or reduced-sodium
    canned broth
½ cup heavy cream
2 medium zucchini, cut into
    ½-inch pieces
2 plum tomatoes, seeded and
    chopped
1 cup frozen corn kernels

1. In a large nonreactive saucepan, heat oil over medium-high heat. In a shallow dish, combine flour, salt, and black pepper. Add chicken and toss lightly to coat. Add chicken to saucepan and cook, turning occasionally, until browned on all sides, 2 to 3 minutes. Transfer chicken to a bowl.

2. Add onion, poblano pepper, bell pepper, and garlic to saucepan and cook, stirring occasionally, until softened, 7 to 8 minutes. Stir in oregano, cumin, cinnamon, chicken stock, cream, zucchini, tomatoes, corn, and chicken. Reduce heat to low and simmer, stirring occasionally, until chicken is tender and no longer pink near bone, about 8 minutes.

241   QUICK CHICKEN, POTATO, AND CAPER STEW
Prep: 15 minutes   Cook: 29 minutes   Serves: 4

4 skinless, boneless chicken
    breast halves (about
    1 pound)
3 tablespoons flour
½ teaspoon paprika
¼ teaspoon salt
¼ teaspoon pepper
2 tablespoons olive oil
1 large onion, sliced
3 garlic cloves, minced
1½ cups Chicken Stock (page
    262) or reduced-sodium
    canned broth

1 medium tomato, peeled,
    seeded, and chopped
½ teaspoon dried oregano
1 bay leaf
3 medium red potatoes, cubed
½ cup small pimiento-stuffed
    olives
1 tablespoon drained
    chopped capers
2 tablespoons chopped
    parsley

1. Dredge chicken to coat lightly with flour; shake off excess flour. Season chicken with paprika, salt, and pepper.

2. In a large nonreactive flameproof casserole, heat oil over medium-high heat. Add chicken and cook 3 minutes on each side, or until golden brown. Transfer chicken to a plate.

3. Add onion and garlic to casserole and cook, stirring occasionally, until softened, about 5 minutes. Add chicken stock, tomato, oregano, bay leaf, and potatoes and bring to a boil. Reduce heat to medium-low, cover, and cook 10 minutes.

4. Add chicken, olives, and capers to casserole, cover, and simmer until chicken is no longer pink in center and potatoes are softened, about 8 minutes longer. Remove and discard bay leaf. Serve sprinkled with parsley.

242 CHICKEN WING STEW WITH TOMATOES AND BLACK OLIVES

Prep: 10 minutes   Cook: 38 to 42 minutes   Serves: 4

This quick-to-fix dish reflects the flavors of Southern France. If possible, use kalamata olives for a more robust taste.

2 **tablespoons olive oil**	1 **medium tomato, peeled,**
2 **pounds chicken wings,**	**seeded, and chopped**
wing tips removed	½ **teaspoon dried thyme leaves**
1 **teaspoon salt**	½ **teaspoon fennel seed,**
½ **teaspoon pepper**	**crushed**
1 **medium onion, chopped**	1 **bay leaf**
3 **garlic cloves, minced**	12 **pitted kalamata olives**
½ **cup dry white wine**	3 **tablespoons minced fresh**
1 **cup Chicken Stock (page**	**parsley**
262) or reduced-sodium	
canned broth	

1. In a large nonreactive flameproof casserole, heat oil over medium-high heat. Season chicken with ½ teaspoon salt and ¼ teaspoon pepper. Add chicken to casserole and cook, turning, until wings are browned on both sides, 6 to 8 minutes. Transfer wings to a platter.

2. Add onion to casserole, reduce heat to medium, and cook, stirring occasionally, until softened, 3 to 5 minutes. Add garlic and cook, stirring constantly, until fragrant, about 1 minute. Stir in wine, chicken stock, tomato, thyme, fennel seed, bay leaf, and remaining ½ teaspoon salt and ¼ teaspoon pepper.

3. Return chicken to casserole and bring to a boil. Reduce heat to medium-low, cover, and cook until chicken is no longer pink in center, 20 minutes. Add olives and cook 5 minutes longer. Remove and discard bay leaf.

4. Transfer chicken to a serving dish. Bring cooking liquid in casserole to a boil and boil, stirring occasionally, until liquid is reduced to 1 cup, about 3 minutes. Pour sauce over chicken and sprinkle with parsley.

243   QUICK JAMAICAN SWEET POTATO AND CHICKEN STEW

Prep: 20 minutes   Cook: 39 minutes   Serves: 4

2 tablespoons vegetable oil
4 skinless, boneless chicken
   thighs (about 1 pound)
½ teaspoon salt
½ teaspoon pepper
1 large onion, chopped
2 garlic cloves, minced
4 thin slices of fresh ginger

2 teaspoons curry powder
½ teaspoon ground allspice
1 pound sweet potato, peeled
   and cut into ½-inch dice
2 cups Chicken Stock (page
   262) or reduced-sodium
   canned broth
2 tablespoons heavy cream

1. In a large flameproof casserole, heat oil over high heat. Sprinkle chicken with salt and pepper and add to casserole. Cook until browned on both sides, about 5 minutes. Transfer chicken to a bowl.

2. Add onion to casserole and cook, stirring occasionally, until softened, about 4 minutes. Stir in garlic, ginger, curry powder, allspice, sweet potato, and chicken stock. Bring to a boil. Reduce heat to low and simmer 20 minutes. Stir in chicken and cook until chicken is no longer pink in center, about 10 minutes. Remove ginger slices, stir in cream, and serve.

244   CHICKEN STEW WITH WILD MUSHROOMS AND ROOT VEGETABLES

Prep: 30 minutes   Cook: 55 minutes   Serves: 6

The vegetables in the initial cooking of this stew are pureed. They add lots of flavor while acting as a thickening for the broth.

1 (3-pound) chicken, cut up,
   excess fat removed
4 cups Chicken Stock (page
   262) or reduced-sodium
   canned broth
6 garlic cloves
1 large carrot, peeled and
   thinly sliced
1 large parsnip, peeled and
   thinly sliced
1 medium red potato, thinly
   sliced
1 large onion, thinly sliced

½ teaspoon salt
2 bay leaves
2 tablespoons butter
2 large leeks (white and
   tender green), trimmed
   and thinly sliced
½ pound shiitake or cremini
   mushrooms, sliced
3 large white turnips, peeled
   and cut into 1-inch
   chunks
½ teaspoon dried tarragon
½ teaspoon pepper

1. In a large flameproof casserole, place chicken, chicken stock, garlic, carrot, parsnip, potato, onion, salt, and bay leaves. Bring to a boil, occasionally skimming foam from surface. Reduce heat to low and simmer, partially covered, 35 minutes. Remove chicken and let cool. Remove and discard bay leaves.

2. Strain broth, reserving vegetables. Skim surface of broth to remove fat. (Or prepare broth a day ahead, refrigerate, and discard any fat from surface.)

3. Shred chicken, discarding skin and bones. Set chicken aside. Place reserved cooked vegetables in blender or food processor with 1 cup reserved broth and puree until smooth. Set aside.

4. In same casserole, melt butter over medium-high heat. Add leeks and cook, stirring frequently, 2 minutes. Add mushrooms and stir until tender, about 5 minutes. Add turnips, tarragon, pepper, and remaining reserved broth. Bring to a boil. Reduce heat to low, cover, and simmer 10 minutes. Stir in vegetable puree and shredded chicken and simmer 3 minutes longer.

---

245   CHICKEN FRICASSEE
Prep: 15 minutes   Cook: 37 to 42 minutes   Serves: 4

Serve this stew with parsleyed egg noodles or a rice pilaf and accompany it with a crisp salad.

1 **(3-pound) chicken, cut into serving pieces**	½ **cup dry white wine**
½ **cup flour**	1 **cup Chicken Stock (page 262) or reduced-sodium canned broth**
1 **teaspoon salt**	
½ **teaspoon pepper**	
¼ **cup vegetable oil**	1 **teaspoon dried tarragon**
12 **small white onions, peeled**	½ **teaspoon dried rosemary**
½ **pound mushrooms, quartered**	1 **bay leaf**
	½ **cup heavy or light cream**
3 **garlic cloves, minced**	2 **teaspoons lemon juice**

1. Dredge chicken to coat lightly with flour; shake off excess flour. Season chicken with ½ teaspoon salt and ¼ teaspoon pepper.

2. In a large nonreactive flameproof casserole, heat 3 tablespoons oil over medium-high heat. Add chicken and cook, turning, until browned on both sides, 6 to 8 minutes. Transfer chicken to a platter.

3. Heat remaining 1 tablespoon oil in casserole over medium heat. Add onions and cook, stirring occasionally, until softened, 3 to 5 minutes longer. Add mushrooms and cook, stirring frequently, until lightly browned, about 5 minutes. Add garlic and cook, stirring constantly, until fragrant, about 1 minute. Stir in wine, chicken stock, tarragon, rosemary, bay leaf, and remaining ½ teaspoon salt and ¼ teaspoon pepper.

4. Return chicken to casserole and bring to a boil. Reduce heat to medium-low, cover, and cook, stirring occasionally, until chicken is tender with no trace of pink near bone, about 20 minutes. Remove and discard bay leaf. Stir in cream and lemon juice, heat through, 2 to 3 minutes, and serve.

246 MOROCCAN CHICKEN STEW WITH LEMON AND OLIVES

Prep: 15 minutes   Cook: 1 hour   Serves: 6

2 tablespoons butter
2 small onions—1 minced,
      1 sliced
¼ teaspoon ground saffron
1 teaspoon ground ginger
¼ teaspoon cayenne
1 teaspoon ground cumin
½ teaspoon black pepper

1 (3-pound) chicken, cut up
1 cup pitted oil-cured black
      olives, chopped
3 tablespoons lemon juice
2 tablespoons chopped
      cilantro
¼ teaspoon salt

1. In a large flameproof casserole, melt butter over medium heat. Stir in minced onion, saffron, ginger, cayenne, cumin, and black pepper. Add chicken and stir until evenly coated with spice mixture. Stir in 2 cups water and bring to a boil. Reduce heat to low, cover, and simmer 30 minutes.

2. Stir in sliced onion and simmer 30 minutes longer. Stir in olives, lemon juice, cilantro, and salt just before serving.

247 CHICKEN STEW WITH POTATOES AND ARTICHOKES

Prep: 30 minutes   Cook: 1 hour   Serves: 6

1 (3-pound) chicken, cut up,
      excess fat removed
4 cups Chicken Stock (page
      262) or reduced-sodium
      canned broth
6 garlic cloves
4 medium red potatoes—
      1 thinly sliced, 3 cut into
      ½-inch dice

1 large onion, thinly sliced
½ teaspoon salt
2 bay leaves
2 tablespoons butter
2 large shallots, minced
1 (10-ounce) package frozen
      artichoke hearts
½ teaspoon dried thyme leaves
½ teaspoon pepper

1. In a large flameproof casserole, place chicken, chicken stock, garlic, sliced potato, onion, salt, and bay leaves. Bring to a boil, occasionally skimming foam from surface. Reduce heat to medium-low and cook partially covered, 35 minutes. Remove chicken and let cool. Remove and discard bay leaves.

2. Strain broth, reserving vegetables. Skim surface of broth to remove fat. (Or prepare broth a day ahead, refrigerate, and discard any fat from surface.)

3. Shred chicken, discarding skin and bones. Set chicken aside. Place reserved cooked vegetables in blender or food processor with 1 cup reserved broth and puree until smooth. Set aside.

4. In same pot, melt butter over medium-high heat. Add shallots and cook, stirring frequently, 2 minutes. Add artichokes, remaining potatoes, thyme, pepper, and remaining broth and bring to a boil. Reduce heat to low, cover, and simmer 20 minutes. Stir in vegetable puree and shredded chicken, simmer 3 minutes longer, and serve.

---

248 ORANGE-FLAVORED DUCK STEW

Prep: 15 minutes   Cook: 1 hour 6 minutes to 1 hour 7 minutes
Serves: 4

1 (4- to 5-pound) duck, cut into serving pieces	1 tablespoon tomato paste
1 teaspoon salt	1 teaspoon dried thyme leaves
½ teaspoon pepper	1 teaspoon dried rosemary
1 tablespoon vegetable oil	4 whole cloves
2 tablespoons butter	6 peppercorns
1 medium onion, chopped	2 (3-inch) strips of orange zest plus 1 teaspoon grated orange zest
1 medium carrot, peeled and sliced	
1 medium celery rib, sliced	1 tablespoon cornstarch
3 garlic cloves, minced	2 tablespoons orange-flavored liqueur
½ cup dry white wine	
2 cups Simple Beef Stock (page 264) or reduced-sodium canned broth	

1. With the point of a sharp knife, prick duck to release fat. Season duck with ½ teaspoon salt and ¼ teaspoon pepper. In a large nonreactive flame-proof casserole, heat oil over medium-high heat. Add duck and cook, turning occasionally, until browned on both sides, about 8 minutes. Transfer duck to a platter and drain off fat from casserole.

2. Melt butter in same casserole over medium heat. Add onion, carrot, and celery and cook, stirring occasionally until softened but not browned, 5 minutes. Add garlic and cook, stirring constantly, until fragrant, about 1 minute. Stir in wine, beef stock, tomato paste, thyme, rosemary, cloves, peppercorns, strips of orange zest, and remaining ½ teaspoon salt and ¼ teaspoon pepper. Return duck to casserole and bring to a boil. Reduce heat to low, cover, and simmer until duck is no longer pink in center, about 45 minutes. Transfer duck to a serving dish. Skim fat from cooking liquid and strain liquid into a large saucepan. Stir in grated orange zest. Bring to a boil and cook until liquid is reduced to 2 cups, about 5 minutes.

3. In a small bowl, blend cornstarch and liqueur and stir into simmering liquid. Cook, stirring constantly, until slightly thickened, 2 to 3 minutes. Pour sauce over duck and serve.

249 DUCK CASSOULET

Prep: 1 hour   Stand: 12 hours   Cook: 4 hours 5 minutes
Serves: 12

This is a wonderful, classic French party dish. Break up the preparation by cooking the beans and duck a day before serving, then assemble and bake the dish the next day. Remember to put the beans up to soak the night before you're going to use them.

1½ pounds Great Northern or navy beans, rinsed and picked over
3 medium carrots, peeled—1 cut into 1-inch pieces, 2 thickly sliced
2 onions—1 whole, stuck with 4 whole cloves, 1 chopped
2 bay leaves
2 sprigs of fresh thyme or 1 teaspoon dried thyme leaves
2 sprigs of fresh parsley
8 garlic cloves—4 whole, 4 chopped

1 pork hock
1 (5-pound) duck, excess fat removed and meat cut into 8 pieces, giblets saved, liver discarded
1¾ teaspoons salt
¾ teaspoon freshly ground pepper
1 (28-ounce) can whole tomatoes, juices reserved
1 pound garlic sausage (kielbasa or Cotechino), thickly sliced
1 cup fresh bread crumbs

1. Place beans in a large bowl and add enough water to cover by at least 2 inches. Let stand 12 hours or overnight. Drain and rinse beans.

2. In a Dutch oven, combine beans, 1-inch carrot pieces, whole onion with cloves, 1 bay leaf, 1 sprig of thyme (or ½ teaspoon dried), 1 sprig of parsley, 4 whole garlic cloves, pork hock, and duck giblets. Pour in water to cover by 2 inches and bring to a boil. Reduce heat to low, cover, and simmer 45 minutes. Add 1 teaspoon salt and continue cooking until beans are very tender, about 20 minutes longer.

3. Drain beans, reserving liquid, pork hock, and giblets. Discard bay leaf, herbs, and vegetables.

4. Meanwhile, place duck in a large nonreactive skillet and cook, turning occasionally, over medium-high heat until browned on all sides, about 10 minutes. Remove duck to a plate. Pour off all but 1 tablespoon fat.

5. Add chopped onion and sliced carrots to reserved 1 tablespoon duck fat in skillet and cook, stirring frequently, until onion is softened, about 5 minutes. Add chopped garlic and cook until fragrant, 1 minute longer. Stir in tomatoes with their juices and break up tomatoes with a wooden spoon. Return duck to skillet along with the remaining sprig of parsley, bay leaf, and thyme and ½ cup of the reserved bean liquid. Reduce heat to low, cover, and simmer until duck is cooked, about 1 hour. Remove and discard bay leaf and as much fat as possible from the skillet.

6. Preheat oven to 350°F. Cut 1 garlic clove in half and rub the inside of the Dutch oven with it. Place one third of the beans in bottom and top with pork hock, duck giblets, ¼ teaspoon salt, and ¼ teaspoon pepper. Top with another one third of the beans, the duck and sauce, and ¼ teaspoon salt and pepper. Top with sausage, remaining beans, and remaining ¼ teaspoon salt and pepper. Add enough bean liquid to come to top of beans. Sprinkle with bread crumbs and drizzle with 2 tablespoons reserved duck fat. Bake 1 hour. Break crust and drizzle crust with juices. Bake 1 hour longer and serve.

250   QUICK HUNGARIAN CHICKEN STEW
Prep: 10 minutes   Cook: 35 to 39 minutes   Serves: 6

Make sure to buy good, sweet Hungarian paprika for this dish and serve it with hot buttered noodles and a mixed green salad.

2 tablespoons vegetable oil
4 skinless, boneless chicken breast halves (about 1 pound)
1 teaspoon salt
1 teaspoon pepper
¼ cup dry white wine
2 Spanish onions, cut in half lengthwise and thinly sliced
1 (14½-ounce) can peeled, chopped tomatoes, juices reserved

5 teaspoons sweet Hungarian paprika
1 pound red potatoes, peeled and cut into ½-inch dice
½ cup sour cream or nonfat sour cream
2 tablespoons chopped parsley

1. In a large nonreactive flameproof casserole, heat oil over high heat. Sprinkle chicken with ½ teaspoon salt and ½ teaspoon pepper. Add to pot and cook, turning occasionally, until browned on both sides, 4 to 5 minutes. Transfer chicken to a bowl. Stir wine into casserole and simmer 2 minutes, scraping browned bits off bottom of pot.

2. Add onions to pot and cook, stirring occasionally, until softened, 6 to 8 minutes. Stir in tomatoes with their juices, paprika, ¼ cup water, and potatoes. Bring to a boil. Reduce heat to low, cover, and simmer until potatoes are softened, about 20 minutes.

3. Cut chicken into 1-inch chunks and return to pot. Simmer until chicken is no longer pink in center, 3 to 4 minutes longer. Season with remaining ½ teaspoon salt and pepper, remove from heat, stir in sour cream, and serve sprinkled with parsley.

251   DUCK STEWED WITH TURNIPS
Prep: 15 minutes   Cook: 1 hour 4 minutes to 1 hour 9 minutes
Serves: 4

This dish is perfect for Sunday dinner. Serve it with sautéed spinach and warm crusty bread or biscuits.

1 (4- to 5-pound) duck, cut into serving pieces
1 teaspoon salt
½ teaspoon pepper
1 tablespoon olive oil
1 large onion, chopped
1 medium carrot, peeled and sliced
1 small celery rib, sliced
4 garlic cloves, minced
2 tablespoons flour
½ cup dry white wine
2 cups Simple Beef Stock (page 264) or reduced-sodium canned broth

1 teaspoon dried thyme leaves
1 bay leaf
1 tablespoon tomato paste
4 allspice berries or ¼ teaspoon ground allspice
3 whole cloves
3 tablespoons butter
12 small white onions, peeled
4 medium white turnips, peeled and quartered
¼ teaspoon sugar
¼ cup Madeira
1 tablespoon minced fresh parsley

1. Preheat oven to 350°F. With the point of a sharp knife, prick duck around legs and lower breast to release fat. Season duck with ½ teaspoon salt and ¼ teaspoon pepper.

2. In a large nonreactive flameproof casserole, heat oil over medium-high heat. Add duck and cook, turning occasionally, until browned on all sides, 10 to 15 minutes. Transfer duck to a platter.

3. Pour off all but 2 tablespoons fat from casserole. Reduce heat to medium, add chopped onion, carrot, and celery, and cook, stirring occasionally, until softened but not browned, 5 minutes. Add garlic and cook, stirring constantly, until fragrant, about 1 minute. Add flour and cook, stirring constantly, 1 minute without allowing to color. Stir in wine, beef stock, thyme, bay leaf, tomato paste, allspice berries, cloves, and remaining ½ teaspoon salt and ¼ teaspoon pepper. Return duck to casserole and heat to simmering. Place casserole in oven, cover, and bake 25 minutes.

4. In a medium skillet, melt butter over medium heat. Add whole onions and cook, stirring frequently, until golden, 5 to 7 minutes. With a slotted spoon, transfer onions to a plate. Add turnips to skillet, sprinkle with sugar, and sauté until golden brown on all sides, 5 minutes. With a slotted spoon, transfer turnips to a plate.

5. Transfer duck to a platter. Strain cooking liquid into a large bowl and set aside. Add onions and turnips to casserole and top with duck. Bake, uncovered, 20 minutes, or until vegetables are softened and skin of duck is crisp.

6. Transfer duck and vegetables to a serving dish. Skim fat from sauce, return to casserole, and bring to a boil. Stir in Madeira and boil 2 minutes. Pour sauce over duck and vegetables and sprinkle with parsley.

252 DUCK STEW WITH PRUNES, ONIONS, AND MUSHROOMS

Prep: 20 minutes   Cook: 1 hour 14 minutes to 1 hour 17 minutes
Serves: 4

We happen to love prunes. However, if you don't share our sentiments, dried apricots as well as dried apples may be substituted for the prunes.

½ pound pitted prunes
2 cups dry red wine
1 pound small white onions, peeled
2 tablespoons butter
¼ teaspoon sugar
¼ pound bacon, cut into 1-inch pieces
1 (4- to 5-pound) duck, cut into serving pieces
1 teaspoon salt
½ teaspoon pepper

1 medium onion, chopped
3 garlic cloves, minced
1 cup Simple Beef Stock (page 264) or reduced-sodium canned broth
1 teaspoon dried thyme leaves
1 teaspoon dried marjoram
1 bay leaf
1 tablespoon cornstarch
2 tablespoons port

1. In a medium nonreactive saucepan, place prunes and wine. Bring to a boil over medium heat, reduce heat to low, and simmer, stirring occasionally, until plump, 5 minutes. Drain prunes, reserving liquid.

2. In a large skillet, place small white onions and add enough water to cover. Add butter and sugar and bring to a boil. Reduce heat to medium, cover, and cook 8 minutes. Uncover, increase heat to medium-high, and boil, stirring frequently, until onions are golden brown, 3 to 5 minutes.

3. In a large flameproof casserole, cook bacon over medium-high heat, stirring occasionally, until crisp, about 5 minutes. With a slotted spoon, transfer bacon to paper towels to drain. Season duck with ½ teaspoon salt and ¼ teaspoon pepper. Add to casserole and cook, turning occasionally, until browned on both sides, about 8 minutes. Transfer duck to a plate. Pour off all but 1 tablespoon fat from pan.

4. Add chopped onion to casserole, reduce heat to medium, and cook, stirring occasionally, until softened, 5 minutes. Add garlic and cook, stirring constantly, until fragrant, about 1 minute. Stir in beef stock, thyme, marjoram, bay leaf, reserved prune cooking liquid, and remaining ½ teaspoon salt and ¼ teaspoon pepper. Return duck to casserole and bring liquid to a boil. Reduce heat to medium-low, cover, and cook until duck is tender, about 30 minutes.

5. Transfer duck to a platter. Strain cooking liquid into a medium saucepan. Skim fat from surface and bring cooking liquid to a boil. In a small bowl, blend cornstarch with port. Add to simmering liquid and bring to a boil, stirring constantly, until slightly thickened, 1 to 2 minutes.

6. Add reserved prunes, bacon, and small white onions to saucepan and simmer until heated through, about 8 minutes. Pour sauce over duck.

Chapter 10

Beef and Veal Stews

There is nothing more inviting than the smell of savory beef stew simmering away on the back burner, its aromas perfuming the entire house with the expectation of a wonderful meal to come. Most of us have on hand a favorite recipe we've used for years, but this chapter proves that one beef stew is just not enough.

If you enjoy a traditional French Beef Stew with Onions and Mushrooms in Red Wine, alias *boeuf bourguignon*, or a classic American Beef Stew with Biscuit Topping, imagine how much you might like tucking into a spicy Cajun Beef Stew or tangy Sauerbraten Beef Stew. In this chapter you'll find a dozen and a half varied ways of turning chunks of economical beef into excellent one-pot dinners. Here you'll also find a dozen tasty ways to turn veal, beef's younger, lighter self, into a succulent stew. Veal, Tomato, and Green Olive Stew and Braised Veal Shanks, otherwise known as *osso bucco*, are just a couple of the enticing options.

What makes all these hearty stews even more appealing to prepare is that the best cuts of meat to use for stews are the least expensive. Our favorite—beef chuck—is a flavorful cut from the forequarter or shoulder. Short ribs are also good. Veal shoulder and shank are ideal for stewing. Keep in mind that all these cuts require long, slow cooking with moist heat, which means some advance planning, but not much attention once they've begun cooking.

You'll notice that there is a general pattern working in most of these stews. First of all, the meat is browned to seal in the juices and enhance the flavor. (To maximize this flavor, whenever any browned meat is returned to the stew pot, be sure to include any juices that have accumulated around it.) Chopped vegetables, along with herbs and spices, and sometimes tomatoes or wine, are added to flavor the cooking liquid, which is based on stock. All are left to simmer slowly until the flavors blend and the meat is tender. During the last hour or so of cooking, other substantial ingredients are added to round out the stew: vegetables and sometimes dried fruit, nuts, or olives. A bright green herb for garnish is the final fillip.

Many of these dishes need little more than a hunk of good bread, some warm biscuits, or crusty rolls to soak up the sauce, with perhaps a green salad on the side. Some of the lighter recipes are good served over rice, noodles, or mashed potatoes. All are virtually meals unto themselves, cooked to perfection all in one pot.

253   BEEF STEW WITH ONIONS AND MUSHROOMS IN RED WINE

Prep: 15 minutes   Marinate: 6 hours
Cook: 2½ hours to 2 hours 42 minutes   Serves: 8

The secret to a robust and flavorful *boeuf bourguignon* like this is to marinate the meat in wine and spices for hours, or overnight if you have the time. Serve the stew with steamed potatoes, pasta, or rice.

5 pounds lean beef chuck, cut into 2-inch pieces
3 cups dry red wine
2 medium onions, chopped
1 large carrot, peeled and sliced
8 garlic cloves, chopped
1 teaspoon dried thyme leaves
1 teaspoon dried rosemary
6 whole cloves
6 black peppercorns
1 large bay leaf

4 cups Simple Beef Stock (page 264) or reduced-sodium canned broth
¼ pound slab bacon, cut into 1-inch pieces
1 tablespoon tomato paste
1 teaspoon salt
24 small white onions
2 tablespoons vegetable oil
1 pound button mushrooms
2 tablespoons cornstarch

1. In a large bowl, combine beef, wine, onions, carrot, garlic, thyme, rosemary, cloves, peppercorns, bay leaf, and enough beef stock to cover. Cover with plastic wrap and refrigerate at least 6 hours, or overnight. Drain beef, reserving marinade and vegetables. Tie cloves, peppercorns, and bay leaf in a cheesecloth bag.

2. In a nonreactive flameproof casserole, cook bacon over medium heat, stirring frequently, until crisp, about 5 minutes. With a slotted spoon, transfer bacon to paper towels to drain. Reheat bacon fat in pan over medium-high heat. Add beef in 3 batches and cook, turning frequently, until browned on all sides, 6 to 8 minutes per batch. Transfer beef to a plate.

3. Add reserved marinated vegetables to casserole and cook over medium heat, stirring occasionally, until softened, about 5 minutes. Return beef to pan along wih reserved marinade, spice bag, remaining beef stock, tomato paste, and salt. Bring to a boil. Reduce heat to low, cover, and simmer 1¾ hours.

4. Add pearl onions and simmer, covered, until beef and onions are tender, 15 to 20 minutes longer. Remove and discard spice bag.

5. Meanwhile, in a large skillet, heat oil over medium-high heat. Add mushrooms and cook, stirring frequently, until lightly browned, 5 to 7 minutes. Add mushrooms and reserved bacon to stew and simmer until slightly thickened, 2 to 3 minutes.

6. In a small bowl, blend cornstarch with 3 tablespoons cold water. Bring stew to a boil over medium-high heat. Gradually stir in cornstarch mixture and bring to a boil. Simmer, stirring constantly, until slightly thickened, 2 to 3 minutes, and serve.

254 BEEF STEW WITH ORANGE AND WALNUTS

Prep: 10 minutes   Cook: 2 hours 26 minutes to 2 hours 32 minutes
Serves: 6

The combination of a rich beef stock, tomatoes, and orange is magnificent. Add to that a garnish of toasted walnuts, and an ordinary stew becomes a dish fit for company. To obtain large strips of orange zest (the colored part of the peel) called for here, use a swivel-bladed vegetable peeler.

3 pounds lean beef chuck, cut
   into 2-inch pieces
½ cup flour
1 teaspoon salt
½ teaspoon pepper
3 tablespoons vegetable oil
2 medium onions, chopped
1 large celery rib, sliced
6 garlic cloves, chopped
1 cup dry wine
1 (14½-ounce) can peeled
   tomatoes, juices reserved
3 cups Brown Beef Stock
   (page 264) or reduced-
   sodium canned broth

3 (3 x 1-inch) strips of orange
   zest plus 2 teaspoons
   grated orange zest
12 sprigs of fresh parsley plus
   2 tablespoons minced
   fresh parsley
1 teaspoon dried thyme leaves
½ teaspoon dried basil
1 large bay leaf
⅔ cup walnut halves

1. Dredge beef to coat lightly with flour; shake off excess flour. Season beef with ½ teaspoon salt and ¼ teaspoon pepper.

2. In a large nonreactive flameproof casserole, heat oil over medium-high heat. Add meat in 3 batches without crowding and cook, turning occasionally, until browned all over, 7 to 8 minutes per batch. Transfer beef to a plate.

3. Add onions, celery, and garlic to casserole, reduce heat to medium, and cook, stirring occasionally, until softened but not browned, 3 to 5 minutes. Add wine, tomatoes with their juices, beef stock, strips of orange zest, parsley sprigs, thyme, basil, bay leaf, and remaining ½ teaspoon salt and ¼ teaspoon pepper. Return beef to casserole and bring to a boil. Reduce heat to low, cover, and simmer until beef is tender, about 2 hours.

4. Meanwhile, preheat oven to 350°F. Place walnuts in a shallow baking pan and bake, stirring occasionally, until lightly toasted, 8 to 10 minutes. Set aside to cool.

5. When beef is tender, remove beef to a bowl and set aside. Skim fat from top of cooking liquid. Remove and discard bay leaf, parsley sprigs, and strips of orange zest.

6. In a food processor, puree cooking liquid and vegetables until smooth. Return to casserole. Add meat with any liquid in bowl. Stir in grated orange zest and boil until slightly thickened, 2 to 3 minutes. Sprinkle with toasted walnuts and minced parsley just before serving.

255   TANGIER BEEF AND SWEET POTATO STEW
Prep: 15 minutes   Cook: 2 hours 10 minutes   Serves: 8

This stew combines beef, North African spices, and sweet potatoes in a rich and unusual combination. If you don't have cilantro, also called fresh coriander, increase the chopped parsley to 3 tablespoons.

3 pounds beef chuck, cut into
   1½-inch pieces
½ teaspoon salt
½ teaspoon pepper
3 tablespoons olive oil
1 large onion, chopped
½ teaspoon ground turmeric
½ teaspoon ground cumin
½ teaspoon paprika
3 plum tomatoes, peeled,
   seeded, and chopped

½ cup Simple Beef Stock (page
   264) or reduced-sodium
   canned broth
1½ pounds sweet potatoes,
   peeled and cut into
   1-inch dice
2 tablespoons chopped
   cilantro
2 tablespoons chopped
   parsley

1. Season beef with salt and pepper. In a large flameproof casserole, heat olive oil over high heat. Add beef in 2 batches without crowding and cook, turning occasionally, until browned all over, about 5 minutes per batch. Return beef to pan and add onion, spices, tomatoes, and beef stock. Bring to a boil. Reduce heat to low, cover, and simmer until beef is very tender, about 1½ hours.

2. Stir in sweet potatoes and simmer until softened, about 30 minutes longer. Stir in cilantro and parsley just before serving.

256   BEEF AND ONION BEER STEW
*Prep: 10 minutes   Cook: 1 hour 59 minutes to 2 hours 6 minutes
Serves: 8*

4 pounds boneless beef
   chuck, cut into 1½-inch
   pieces
1 teaspoon salt
½ teaspoon pepper
3 tablespoons vegetable oil
2 tablespoons butter
2 large onions, sliced
4 large garlic cloves, minced
2 tablespoons flour
2 tablespoons brown sugar

¼ cup cider vinegar
1 cup Brown Beef Stock (page
   264) or reduced-sodium
   canned broth
3 cups lager beer
1 teaspoon dried thyme leaves
1 teaspoon dried rosemary
1 large bay leaf
3 tablespoons minced fresh
   parsley

1. Season beef with salt and pepper. In a large flameproof casserole, heat oil over medium-high heat. Add beef in 3 batches and cook, turning occasionally, until browned on all sides, 6 to 8 minutes per batch. Transfer beef to a platter and pour off fat from casserole.

2. Reduce heat to medium. Add butter to pot and heat until melted. Add onions and garlic and cook, stirring occasionally, until golden, 7 to 8 minutes. Add flour and cook, stirring constantly, 2 minutes. Add brown sugar and vinegar and cook, stirring constantly, 2 minutes. Add beef stock, beer, thyme, rosemary, and bay leaf. Return beef to pan and bring to a boil. Reduce heat to medium-low, cover, and cook until beef is tender, about 1½ hours. Skim fat from surface of cooking liquid. Remove and discard bay leaf. Sprinkle with parsley just before serving.

---

257   INDONESIAN BEEF STEW WITH PEANUT SAUCE

Prep: 15 minutes   Cook: 1 hour 50 minutes to 2 hours 11 minutes
Serves: 4 to 6

2 pounds beef round, cut into 2-inch pieces	2½ teaspoons minced fresh ginger
½ teaspoon salt	¼ teaspoon crushed hot red pepper
¼ teaspoon pepper	1 teaspoon ground coriander
3 tablespoons vegetable oil	1 teaspoon ground cumin
1 large and 1 small onion, minced	⅛ teaspoon ground cloves
4 garlic cloves, minced	3 tablespoons smooth peanut butter
1½ cups Simple Beef Stock (page 264) or reduced-sodium canned broth	2 tablespoons chopped dry-roasted peanuts
2 tablespoons soy sauce	1 tablespoon minced cilantro or fresh parsley
1 tablespoon dark brown sugar	

1. Season beef with salt and pepper. In a large flameproof casserole, heat oil over medium-high heat. Add beef in 2 batches without crowding and cook, turning occasionally, until browned all over, 6 to 8 minutes per batch. Transfer beef to a platter.

2. Add large onion and 1 tablespoon garlic to casserole and cook, stirring occasionally, until softened, 3 to 5 minutes. Add beef stock, soy sauce, brown sugar, 2 teaspoons ginger, hot pepper, coriander, cumin, and cloves. Return beef to pan and bring to a boil. Reduce heat to medium-low, cover, and simmer until beef is tender, 1½ to 1¾ hours. Transfer beef to a serving dish, cover, and keep warm. Strain cooking liquid through a fine sieve, discard solids, and return to pan.

3. Transfer ½ cup liquid to a small bowl, add peanut butter, and whisk until well blended. Return to remaining liquid in pan. Add small onion and remaining garlic and ½ teaspoon ginger. Bring to a boil, reduce heat to medium, and cook, stirring occasionally, until onion is softened, about 5 minutes. Pour sauce over meat, sprinkle with peanuts and cilantro, and serve.

258   BEEF STEW WITH BISCUIT TOPPING

Prep: 15 minutes   Cook: 1 hour 47 minutes to 1 hour 51 minutes
Serves: 6

2 pounds boneless beef
   chuck, cut into 1-inch
   pieces
½ cup flour
½ teaspoon salt
¼ teaspoon pepper
2 tablespoons vegetable oil
2 tablespoons butter
1 medium onion, minced
1 medium celery rib, sliced
2 garlic cloves, minced
3 cups Simple Beef Stock
   (page 264) or reduced-
   sodium canned broth

1 tablespoon tomato paste
1 teaspoon dried thyme leaves
1 bay leaf
5 large carrots, peeled and
   sliced
2 large red potatoes, cut into
   ½-inch dice
1 (10-ounce) package frozen
   peas, thawed
1 (10-ounce) package
   buttermilk biscuits

1. Preheat oven to 350° F. Dredge beef to coat lightly with flour; shake off excess flour. Season beef with salt and pepper. In a large flameproof casserole, heat oil over medium-high heat. Add beef in 2 batches and cook, turning occasionally, until browned all over, 6 to 8 minutes per batch. Transfer beef to a platter.

2. Reduce heat to medium. Melt butter in casserole over medium heat. Add onion, celery, and garlic and cook, stirring occasionally, until softened, about 5 minutes. Stir in beef stock, tomato paste, thyme, and bay leaf. Return beef to casserole. Bring to a boil. Transfer casserole to oven, cover, and bake 45 minutes. Stir in carrots and potatoes and continue to bake, covered, until meat is tender, about 30 minutes longer. Stir in peas.

3. Separate biscuits and place on top of stew. Bake, uncovered, 15 minutes, or until biscuits are golden brown. Remove and discard bay leaf before serving.

259   SAUERBRATEN BEEF STEW

Prep: 10 minutes   Marinate: 3 hours
Cook: 2 hours 1 minute to 2 hours 36 minutes   Serves: 6

Serve this German-accented stew with potato dumplings and braised red cabbage.

1½ cups dry red wine	½ teaspoon pepper
1 tablespoon lemon juice	2 tablesspoons vegetable oil
8 black peppercorns	1 tablespoon butter
1 bay leaf	1 medium carrot, peeled and
4 whole cloves	minced
2 large onions, minced	1 tablespoon tomato paste
2 pounds beef round, cut into	1 tablespoon sugar
2-inch pieces	½ cup raisins
½ cup plus 2 tablespoons flour	2 tablespoons chopped
1 teaspoon salt	parsley

1. In a medium nonreactive saucepan, combine wine, ¾ cup water, lemon juice, peppercorns, bay leaf, cloves, and half of the onion. Bring to a boil, reduce heat to medium, and cook 5 minutes. Transfer to a large bowl, add beef, and mix lightly to coat. Cool to room temperature, cover, and marinate in refrigerator at least 3 hours or overnight.

2. Remove beef from marinade, reserving marinade. Pat meat dry. Strain marinade, reserving liquid.

3. Dredge beef in ½ cup flour to coat lightly; shake off excess flour. Season beef with salt and pepper. In a large nonreactive flameproof casserole, heat oil over medium-high heat. Add beef in 2 batches without crowding and cook, turning occasionally, until browned all over, 6 to 8 minutes per batch. Transfer beef to a platter.

4. Pour off drippings from pan and discard. Add butter to casserole and heat until melted. Add remaining onion, carrot, and reserved marinade solids and cook over medium heat, stirring occasionally, until softened, about 5 minutes. Return beef to pan and stir in reserved marinade and tomato paste. Bring to a boil. Reduce heat to low, cover, and simmer 1½ to 2 hours. Skim fat from cooking liquid. Stir in sugar and raisins and simmer 5 minutes.

5. In a small bowl, blend remaining 2 tablespoons flour with ¼ cup cold water. Whisk into simmering liquid and bring to a boil, stirring until slightly thickened, 1 to 2 minutes. Reduce heat and simmer 3 minutes longer. Serve, garnished with chopped parsley.

260 HEARTY BEEF STEW WITH PAPRIKA

Prep: 10 minutes   Cook: 1 hour 52 minutes to 1 hour 56 minutes
Serves: 4 to 6

This stew may be prepared 1 to 2 days ahead and reheated before serving.

3 tablespoons vegetable oil
1½ pounds boneless beef
    chuck, cut into 1-inch
    pieces
1 teaspoon salt
2 medium onions, minced
2 medium celery ribs, minced
4 garlic cloves, minced
3 tablespoons flour
2 tablespoons ground paprika
5 cups Simple Beef Stock
    (page 264) or reduced-
    sodium canned broth

2 tablespoons tomato paste
2 tablespoons red wine
    vinegar
1 bay leaf
½ teaspoon salt
1 medium green bell pepper,
    minced
1 pound red potatoes, diced

1. In a large flameproof casserole, heat oil over medium-high heat. Season beef with salt. Add to pan in 2 batches and cook, turning occasionally, until browned on all sides, 5 to 7 minutes per batch. Transfer beef to a platter.

2. Reduce heat to medium. Add onions, celery, and garlic to casserole and cook, stirring occasionally, until softened, about 5 minutes. Add flour and paprika and cook, stirring constantly, 2 minutes.

3. Add beef stock, tomato paste, red wine vinegar, bay leaf, and salt. Return beef to casserole and bring to a boil. Reduce heat to low, cover, and simmer, stirring occasionally, until meat is tender, about 1¼ hours. Add green pepper and potatoes, cover, and simmer, stirring occasionally, until potatoes are tender, about 20 minutes. Remove and discard bay leaf before serving.

261   BEEF STEW MEXICAN STYLE

Prep: 10 minutes   Cook: 1 hour 47 minutes to 1 hour 51 minutes
Serves: 6

Accompany this stew with warmed flour tortillas.

2 pounds boneless beef
　chuck, cut into 2-inch
　pieces
½ teaspoon salt
¼ teaspoon black pepper
2 tablespoons vegetable oil
1 medium onion, sliced
1 medium green bell pepper,
　sliced
3 garlic cloves, minced
1 (14½-ounce) can diced
　peeled tomatoes, juices
　reserved

2 cups Brown Beef Stock
　(page 264) or reduced-
　sodium canned broth
2 tablespoons tomato paste
2 teaspoons chili powder, or
　to taste
1 teaspoon ground cumin
2 tablespoons minced cilantro

1. Season beef with salt and black pepper. In a large nonreactive flameproof casserole, heat oil over medium-high heat. Add beef in batches and cook, turning occasionally, until browned on all sides, 6 to 8 minutes per batch. Transfer beef to a platter.

2. Reduce heat to medium. Add onion, bell pepper, and garlic and cook, stirring occasionally, until softened, about 5 minutes. Add tomatoes with their juices, beef stock, tomato paste, chili powder, and cumin. Return beef to casserole. Bring to a boil. Reduce heat to low, cover, and simmer, stirring occasionally, until beef is tender, about 1½ hours.

3. Skim cooking liquid. Sprinkle stew with cilantro just before serving.

262   BRISKET OF BEEF WITH CARROT, SWEET POTATO, AND DRIED PRUNES

Prep: 10 minutes   Stand: 15 minutes
Cook: 2 hours 13 minutes to 2 hours 15 minutes   Serves: 6

2 tablespoons vegetable oil
1 (3-pound) brisket of beef
½ teaspoon salt
¼ teaspoon pepper
2 medium onions, minced
4 garlic cloves, minced
3 tablespoons flour
4 cups Simple Beef Stock (page 264) or reduced-sodium canned broth
1 bay leaf

1 teaspoon dried thyme leaves
½ teaspoon dried marjoram
1 cinnamon stick
4 whole cloves
2 teaspoons grated orange zest
8 ounces pitted prunes
½ cup orange juice
1 pound carrots, peeled and sliced
1 pound sweet potatoes, peeled and sliced

1. Preheat oven to 350°F. In a large flameproof casserole, heat oil over medium-high heat. Season brisket with salt and pepper. Add to casserole and cook until browned on both sides, 8 to 10 minutes. Transfer brisket to a platter and pour off all but 2 tablespoons fat.

2. Reduce heat to medium. Add onion and garlic to casserole and cook, stirring occasionally, until softened, about 3 minutes. Add flour and cook, stirring constantly, 2 minutes without allowing to color. Add beef stock, bay leaf, thyme, marjoram, cinnamon stick, cloves, and orange zest. Return brisket to casserole. Bring to a boil, cover, and braise in oven 1 hour.

3. Meanwhile, place prunes in a medium bowl. Add orange juice and let stand 15 minutes.

4. Add prunes with juice and carrots to casserole, cover, and braise 30 minutes longer. Add sweet potatoes, cover, and braise, until potatoes are tender, about 30 minutes longer. Remove and discard bay leaf and cinnamon stick before serving.

263   BOILED BEEF WITH VEGETABLES

Prep: 10 minutes   Cook: 3 hours 20 minutes to 3 hours 25 minutes
Serves: 6

This is the uptown version of corned beef and cabbage; the French call it *pot au feu*. While it is often prepared with assorted meats and chicken, we have created a simplified version and concentrated on the beef and basic vegetables. Traditionally, the meat and vegetables are removed from the stock and accompanied by coarse-grained mustard, horseradish, and pickles as condiments, with a salad and crusty bread on the side. The stock is often served as a separate soup course by itself.

3 pounds rump roast, in
     1 piece
2 large onions, each stuck
     with 3 whole cloves
1 large carrot, peeled and
     sliced, plus 4 medium
     carrots, peeled
5 large celery ribs, 1 sliced, 4
     whole
8 garlic cloves, halved
12 sprigs of fresh parsley
8 black peppercorns

1 bay leaf
1 teaspoon dried thyme leaves
6 cups Simple Beef Stock
     (page 264) or reduced-
     sodium canned broth
4 medium leeks (white part
     only), well rinsed, halved
     lengthwise and crosswise
4 medium turnips, peeled and
     quartered
1 teaspoon salt

1. In a soup pot, combine beef, onions, sliced carrot, sliced celery, garlic, parsley, peppercorns, bay leaf, thyme, and beef stock. Add enough water to just cover and bring to a boil. Reduce heat to low and simmer, partially covered, skimming surface frequently, 3 hours.

2. Remove beef and set aside. Strain cooking stock and discard solids. Return broth to pot and skim off fat. Cut remaining carrots and celery in half lengthwise, then cut in half crosswise. Tie carrots, celery, and leeks in separate bundles with white kitchen string.

3. Bring stock in pot to a boil. Lower bundles of carrots, celery, and leeks into broth. Return beef to pot. Reduce heat to medium-low and cook, partially covered, 10 minutes. Remove beef to a cutting board and cover loosely with foil. Add turnips and season stock with salt. Continue to simmer, partially covered, until vegetables and meat are tender, 10 to 15 minutes longer.

4. Carve meat against grain into thin slices. Arrange on a platter. Remove strings from vegetable bundles and arrange vegetables around meat. Moisten platter with a little stock and serve. Reserve remaining stock for another use.

264 MUSTARD-BRAISED SHORT RIBS WITH HORSERADISH

Prep: 10 minutes
Cook: 2 hours 31 minutes to 2 hours 34 minutes   Serves: 6

Serve this dish with a vegetable puree, such as potato and celery root, or a puree of butternut squash.

2   tablespoons vegetable oil
4   pounds beef short ribs, chopped into 3-inch pieces
1   teaspoon salt
½   teaspoon pepper
2   medium onions, minced
1   large carrot, peeled and minced
4   garlic cloves, minced
2   cups Simple Beef Stock (page 264) or reduced-sodium canned broth

1   teaspoon dried thyme leaves
½   teaspoon dried sage
1   bay leaf
2   tablespoons Dijon mustard
2   tablespoons prepared horseradish
3   tablespoons minced fresh parsley

1. In a large flameproof casserole, heat oil over medium-high heat. Add beef ribs, salt, and pepper in 3 batches and cook until browned on all sides, 7 to 8 minutes per batch. Transfer ribs to a platter. Reduce heat to medium.

2. Add onions, carrot, and garlic to casserole and cook, stirring frequently, until softened, about, 5 minutes. Add beef stock, thyme, sage, and bay leaf. Return ribs to casserole. Bring to a boil. Reduce heat to medium-low, cover, and simmer until ribs are tender, about 2 hours.

3. Transfer ribs to a serving dish. Skim fat from liquid and discard. Discard bay leaf. Add mustard and horseradish to stock and simmer, stirring occasionally, 5 minutes. Pour sauce over ribs and sprinkle with parsley.

265   PROVENÇAL BEEF STEW WITH OLIVES

Prep: 10 minutes   Cook: 2 hours 1 minute to 2 hours 10 minutes
Serves: 4 to 6

This aromatic stew makes a wonderful Sunday dinner. Serve it with steamed potatoes and peas.

2 pounds boneless chuck, cut into 2-inch pieces
½ cup flour
1 teaspoon salt
½ teaspoon pepper
3 tablespoons olive oil
2 medium onions, minced
6 garlic cloves, minced
1½ cups dry red wine
4 cups Simple Beef Stock (page 264) or reduced-sodium canned broth

2 tablespoons tomato paste
1 tablespoon minced fresh rosemary or 1 teaspoon dried
1 bay leaf
2 teaspoons grated orange zest
4 whole cloves
4 carrots, peeled and cut into ½-inch-thick slices
1 cup pitted black olives
3 tablespoons minced fresh parsley

1. Dredge beef to coat lightly with flour; shake off excess flour. Season with salt and pepper.

2. In a large nonreactive flameproof casserole, heat oil over medium-high heat. Add beef in 2 batches and cook, turning occasionally, until browned on all sides, 5 to 7 minutes per batch. Transfer beef to a platter. Reduce heat to medium. Add onions and garlic to pan and cook, stirring occasionally, until softened, about 5 minutes.

3. Stir in wine and boil 1 minute. Add beef stock, tomato paste, rosemary, bay leaf, orange zest, and cloves. Return beef to casserole. Bring to a boil. Reduce heat to low, cover, and simmer, stirring occasionally, until meat is tender, about 1½ hours.

4. Add carrots and simmer 10 minutes. Add olives and simmer until carrots are tender, 5 to 10 minutes longer. Remove and discard bay leaf, garnish with parsley, and serve.

266 BOLLITO MISTO
Prep: 10 minutes   Cook: 3 hours 15 minutes   Serves: 8

A variety of meats "boiled" in a flavorful broth is one of the great dishes of northern Italy.

6 cups Brown Beef Stock (page 264) or reduced-sodium canned broth	1 teaspoon salt
	½ teaspoon pepper
	2 pounds brisket of beef
2 medium onions, each studded with 3 cloves	2 medium tomatoes, peeled, seeded, and chopped
2 medium celery ribs, sliced	2 pounds boneless veal rump, tied
1 medium carrot, peeled and sliced	1 whole (3-pound) chicken, trussed
1½ teaspoons dried thyme leaves	Italian Green Sauce (recipe follows)
1 teaspoon dried rosemary	
1 bay leaf	

1. In a large nonreactive soup pot, combine beef stock, onions studded with cloves, celery, carrot, thyme, rosemary, bay leaf, ½ teaspoon salt, and ¼ teaspoon pepper. Bring to a boil. Add brisket and tomatoes. Reduce heat to low, cover, and simmer, skimming surface occasionally, 1½ hours.

2. Add veal and simmer, skimming surface occasionally, 45 minutes.

3. Add chicken and remaining ½ teaspoon salt and ¼ teaspoon pepper and simmer, still covered, skimming surface occasionally, until juices run clear and all meats are tender, about 1 hour.

4. Transfer meats and chicken to a cutting board. Cut meat into slices and chicken into serving pieces. Arrange on a large platter. Strain cooking broth and ladle enough over meats and chicken to moisten generously. Reserve remaining broth for another use. Pass Italian Green Sauce on the side.

267 ITALIAN GREEN SAUCE
Prep: 15 minutes   Cook: none   Makes: about 1⅓ cups

¼ cup minced fresh parsley	2 teaspoons Dijon mustard
3 tablespoons minced drained capers	2 teaspoons red wine vinegar
	½ teaspoon salt
4 anchovy fillets, minced	1 cup extra-virgin olive oil
2 garlic cloves, minced	

1. In a medium bowl, combine parsley, capers, anchovies, garlic, mustard, vinegar, and salt. Stir to dissolve salt and mix well.

2. Whisk in olive oil in a thin stream. Whisk sauce until well blended.

268   OXTAIL AND TOMATO RAGOUT

Prep: 10 minutes   Cook: 3 hours 20 minutes to 3 hours 57 minutes
Serves: 4 to 6

Although the cooking time is quite long for this stew, it is virtually unattended. Serve this flavorful ragout with mashed potatoes or hot cooked rice.

3 tablespoons vegetable oil
4 to 4½ pounds oxtails,
    chopped into 2-inch
    sections
1 teaspoon salt
½ teaspoon pepper
2 medium onions, chopped
2 medium carrots, peeled and
    chopped
2 medium celery ribs,
    chopped
3 garlic cloves, chopped
1 cup dry red wine

6 cups Simple Beef Stock
    (page 264) or reduced-
    sodium canned broth
1 (35-ounce) can Italian-style
    plum tomatoes, juices
    reserved
1 teaspoon dried thyme leaves
1 teaspoon dried basil
½ teaspoon dried oregano
1 bay leaf
2 tablespoons flour
¼ cup port or water

1. In a large nonreactive flameproof casserole, heat 2 tablespoons oil over medium-high heat. Add oxtails, salt, and pepper in 2 batches and cook, adding remaining oil as needed, until browned on all sides, 6 to 8 minutes per batch. Transfer oxtails to a platter.

2. Reduce heat to medium. Add onions, carrots, celery, and garlic to pan and cook, stirring frequently, until softened, 3 to 4 minutes. Stir in wine and boil 1 minute. Add beef stock, tomatoes with their juices, thyme, basil, oregano, and bay leaf. Return oxtails to casserole. Bring to a boil, reduce heat to medium-low, cover, and simmer, skimming and stirring occasionally, until meat is tender, 3 to 3½ hours.

3. Transfer oxtails to a cutting board, remove meat from bones, and discard bones. Strain cooking liquid and skim off fat. Return liquid to pot and bring to a boil.

4. In a small bowl, combine flour and port. Gradually add to simmering stock and cook until slightly thickened, 2 to 3 minutes. Return meat to casserole and cook until heated through, 2 to 3 minutes.

269   TANGERINE BEEF STEW ASIAN STYLE

Prep: 10 minutes   Cook: 1 hour 59 minutes to 2 hours 4 minutes
Serves: 4 to 6

Serve this stew with cooked Chinese egg noodles.

2 tablespoons vegetable oil
3 scallions, sliced
1 tablespoon minced fresh
    ginger
3 garlic cloves, minced
1½ pounds boneless beef
    chuck, cut into 1-inch
    pieces
2½ cups Brown Beef Stock
    (page 264) or reduced-
    sodium canned broth
2 strips of dried tangerine or
    fresh orange zest

¼ cup soy sauce
¼ cup dry sherry
1 (4-inch) cinnamon stick
1 tablespoon sugar
½ teaspoon salt
¼ teaspoon aniseed, crushed
1 pound turnips, peeled and
    cut into 1-inch pieces
1 tablespoon cornstarch
2 tablespoons minced cilantro
    or fresh parsley

1. In a large saucepan or flameproof casserole, heat oil over medium heat. Add scallions, ginger, and garlic and cook, stirring frequently, until softened, 2 to 3 minutes. Add beef in 2 batches and cook, turning occasionally, until browned on all sides, 5 to 7 minutes per batch. Add beef stock, tangerine zest, soy sauce, sherry, cinnamon stick, sugar, salt, and aniseed. Bring to a boil. Reduce heat to low, cover, and simmer, stirring occasionally, until beef is tender, 1½ hours.

2. Add turnips, cover, and simmer until tender, about 15 minutes longer.

3. In a small bowl, blend cornstarch with 2 tablespoons cold water. Stir into simmering liquid and bring to a boil, stirring until smooth, about 2 minutes. Remove and discard tangerine zest and cinnamon stick. Sprinkle with cilantro just before serving.

270   CAJUN BEEF STEW
Prep: 10 minutes   Cook: 1 hour 49 minutes to 2 hours 26 minutes
Serves: 4 to 6

2   pounds boneless chuck, cut
    into 1½-inch pieces
1½   teaspoons black pepper
1   teaspoon cayenne, or more
    to taste
½   teaspoon salt
3   tablespoons vegetable oil
2   medium onions, minced
2   medium celery ribs, sliced
1   medium green bell pepper,
    diced
3   garlic cloves, minced

1   tablespoon flour
1   (8-ounce) can tomato sauce
1½   cups Simple Beef Stock
    (page 264) or reduced-
    sodium canned broth
1   (14½-ounce) can plum
    tomatoes, juices reserved
1   teaspoon dried thyme leaves
1   bay leaf
2   tablespoons minced fresh
    parsley

1. Season beef with black pepper, cayenne, and salt. In a large nonreactive flameproof casserole, heat oil over medium-high heat. Add beef in 2 batches and cook, turning occasionally, until browned on all sides, 6 to 8 minutes per batch. Transfer beef to a platter.

2. Reduce heat to medium. Add onions, celery, green pepper, and garlic to pan. Cook, stirring occasionally, until softened, 5 to 7 minutes. Add flour and cook, stirring constantly, without allowing to color, 1 to 2 minutes. Stir in tomato sauce, beef stock, tomatoes with their juices, thyme, and bay leaf.

3. Return beef to casserole. Bring to a boil. Reduce heat to medium-low, cover, and cook until beef is tender, 1½ to 2 hours. Skim fat from cooking liquid and discard with bay leaf. Sprinkle with parsley before serving.

271   VEAL STEW WITH ONIONS, MUSHROOMS, AND SPINACH IN MUSTARD CREAM
Prep: 10 minutes   Cook: 11 minutes   Serves: 6

1   recipe Veal Stew with
    Onions and Mushrooms
    (page 196)
2   tablespoons butter
2   tablespoons minced
    shallots

1   pound trimmed and well
    rinsed spinach leaves
    or 1 (10-ounce) package
    frozen spinach leaves,
    thawed and squeezed dry
2   tablespoons Dijon mustard

1. In a large saucepan, heat veal stew over medium heat.

2. In a large skillet, melt butter over medium heat. Add shallots and cook, stirring constantly, 1 minute. Add spinach and cook, stirring frequently, until wilted and moisture is evaporated, about 5 minutes. Chop spinach. Add spinach and mustard to stew and simmer, stirring occasionally, until heated through, about 5 minutes.

272   VEAL STEW WITH ONIONS AND MUSHROOMS

Prep: 10 minutes   Cook: 1 hour 45 minutes   Serves: 6

Serve this creamy stew with steamed rice or pasta.

3 pounds boneless veal shoulder, cut into 2-inch pieces	1 teaspoon dried thyme leaves
	1 bay leaf
1 large onion	6 cups Chicken Stock (page 262) or reduced-sodium canned broth
4 whole cloves	
1 large carrot, peeled and quartered	½ pound fresh mushrooms
	4 teaspoons lemon juice
1 medium celery rib, quartered	18 small white onions
	¼ cup flour
6 garlic cloves	1 cup heavy or light cream
1 teaspoon salt	⅛ teaspoon grated nutmeg
12 sprigs of fresh parsley	2 tablespoons minced fresh parsley
8 black peppercorns	

1. Place veal in a large soup pot and add enough cold water to cover. Bring to a boil. Reduce heat to medium and simmer 5 minutes. Drain veal into a colander, rinse under cold running water, and return to soup pot. Stud onion with cloves and add to pot along with carrot, celery, garlic, and salt. Tie parsley, peppercorns, thyme, and bay leaf in a cheesecloth bag and add to pot. Pour in chicken stock and enough water to cover veal and vegetables by 1 inch. Bring to a boil. Reduce heat to low and simmer, partially covered and skimming often, until veal is tender, about 1½ hours.

2. Meanwhile, place whole mushrooms in a medium saucepan. Add 2 tea-spoons lemon juice and enough cold water to cover. Bring to a boil, reduce heat to medium-low, and cook until tender, 5 minutes. With a slotted spoon, transfer mushrooms to a bowl. Pour mushroom cooking liquid into stew.

3. Place pearl onions in another medium saucepan and add enough cold water to cover. Bring to a boil, reduce heat to medium, cover, and cook until tender, about 20 minutes. With a slotted spoon, transfer onions to bowl containing mushrooms. Pour onion cooking liquid into stew.

4. With a slotted spoon, transfer veal to bowl containing vegetables. Strain cooking liquid through a fine sieve, pressing hard on solids; return broth to soup pot. Boil over high heat until reduced to 4 cups, about 5 minutes. Return veal and vegetables to soup pot.

5. In a small bowl, stir together flour and cream until smooth and well blended. Bring stew to a boil. Stir in flour and cream and bring to a boil. Reduce heat to medium-low and simmer until slightly thickened, 5 min-utes, stirring frequently. Stir in remaining 2 teaspoons lemon juice and nut-meg. Season with additional salt to taste. Sprinkle with parsley just before serving.

273   QUICK VEAL STEW WITH MADEIRA
Prep: 10 minutes   Cook: 13 to 18 minutes   Serves: 4

Although quickly assembled and cooked, this stew is good enough for company. Serve with rice and crisp green beans.

1 **pound veal scallops, cut into strips**
¼ **cup flour**
½ **teaspoon salt**
¼ **teaspoon pepper**
2 **tablespoons olive oil**
1 **tablespoon butter**
½ **cup minced shallots**
½ **cup Madeira or dry red wine**
1 **teaspoon dried sage**
1 **teaspoon dried thyme leaves**
2 **cups Veal Stock (page 267) or reduced-sodium canned beef broth**

1 **tablespoon arrowroot or cornstarch**
¼ **pound baked ham, cut into strips**
1 **(6-ounce) jar roasted red peppers, drained and cut into strips**
2 **tablespoons minced fresh parsley**

1. Dredge veal to coat lightly with flour; shake off excess flour. Season veal with salt and pepper.

2. In a large nonstick skillet, heat olive oil over medium-high heat. Add veal and cook, turning occasionally, until browned on all sides, 3 to 4 minutes. Transfer veal to a plate. Keep warm.

3. Reduce heat to medium. Add butter to skillet and heat until melted. Add shallots and and cook, stirring constantly, until golden, about 2 minutes.

4. Add ⅓ cup Madeira, sage, and thyme, bring to a boil, and cook until mixture is reduced by half, 1 to 2 minutes. Add veal stock and boil until mixture is reduced to 2 cups, 2 to 3 minutes longer.

5. In a small bowl, combine arrowroot and remaining Madeira. Whisk mixture into stock and simmer, stirring constantly, until slightly thickened, about 2 minutes. Return veal to skillet. Add ham and red peppers and simmer, stirring frequently, until heated through, 3 to 5 minutes. Sprinkle with parsley just before serving.

274   VEAL STEW WITH LEEKS AND WILD MUSHROOMS

Prep: 20 minutes   Cook: 1 hour 44 minutes to 1 hour 50 minutes
Serves: 6

Splurge on this stew in the fall, when wild mushrooms are plentiful and slightly more affordable.

2   tablespoons butter
2   tablespoons extra-virgin
      olive oil
1½ pounds veal shoulder, cut
      into 1½-inch cubes
¾   teaspoon salt
½   teaspoon pepper
2   garlic cloves, minced
3   medium leeks (white and
      tender green), well rinsed
      and thinly sliced
1   tablespoon flour
½   cup dry white wine
1½ cups Chicken Stock (page
      262) or reduced-sodium
      canned broth

6   fresh sage leaves or
      ½ teaspoon dried
2   large sprigs of fresh thyme
      or ½ teaspoon dried
      thyme leaves
½   pound cremini or white
      button mushrooms,
      thinly sliced
¼   pound oyster, chanterelle,
      or shiitake mushrooms,
      trimmed and sliced
1   pound small red potatoes,
      scrubbed and cut in half
      or quartered

1. In a large nonreactive flameproof casserole, melt 1 tablespoon butter in 1 tablespoon olive oil over medium-high heat. Season veal with salt and pepper. Add to pan in 2 batches and cook, turning, until browned all over, 5 to 7 minutes per batch. As veal browns, remove to a plate.

2. Add garlic and leeks to casserole and cook, stirring, until soft, 3 to 5 minutes. Add flour and cook, stirring constantly, 1 minute without allowing to color. Stir in wine and cook 2 minutes. Return veal to pan. Stir in chicken stock, sage, and thyme. Reduce heat to low, cover, and simmer 1 hour.

3. Meanwhile, in a large skillet, melt remaining 1 tablespoon butter in remaining 1 tablespoon olive oil over high heat. Add cremini and oyster mushrooms and cook, stirring frequently, until mushrooms are lightly browned, about 3 minutes.

4. Add mushrooms and potatoes to stew, cover, and simmer until meat and potatoes are tender, about 25 minutes.

275 VEAL STEW WITH BALSAMIC VINEGAR

Prep: 15 minutes   Cook: 1 hour 22 minutes to 1 hour 31 minutes
Serves: 4

¼ pound thick slices of bacon
1½ pounds boneless veal
shoulder, cut into 1½-inch
pieces
½ teaspoon salt
¼ teaspoon pepper
2 tablespoons butter
2 medium onions, minced
1 large carrot, peeled and
minced
3 garlic cloves, minced
2 tablespoons flour
¼ cup balsamic vinegar

1 cup dry red wine
1½ cups Simple Beef Stock
(page 264) or reduced-
sodium canned broth
1 (14½-ounce) can Italian
peeled tomatoes, drained
and chopped
1 teaspoon dried rosemary
1 teaspoon dried thyme leaves
1 bay leaf
2 tablespoons minced fresh
parsley

1. In a large nonreactive flameproof casserole, cook bacon over medium heat until crisp, 3 to 4 minutes. With a slotted spoon, transfer bacon to paper towels to drain.

2. Add veal, salt, and pepper in 2 batches and cook, turning occasionally, until lightly browned on all sides, 5 to 7 minutes per batch. Transfer veal to a platter and pour off and discard fat from pan.

3. Add butter to casserole and heat until melted. Add onions, carrot, and garlic. Cook, stirring frequently, until onions are golden, 5 to 7 minutes. Add flour and cook, stirring without allowing to color, 1 to 2 minutes. Stir in vinegar and wine. Bring to a boil and cook 1 minute.

4. Add stock, tomatoes, rosemary, thyme, and bay leaf. Return veal to pan and bring to a boil. Reduce heat to medium-low, cover, and cook until veal is tender, about 1 hour.

5. Skim fat from surface and simmer until cooking liquid is slightly thickened, 2 to 3 minutes. Remove and discard bay leaf. Crumble reserved bacon and sprinkle over stew with parsley.

276   HUNGARIAN VEAL STEW

Prep: 10 minutes   Cook: 2 hours 7 minutes to 2 hours 11 minutes
Serves: 6

Serve this goulash with parsleyed buttered noodles and a tossed green salad.

3 tablespoons vegetable oil
3 pounds boneless veal shoulder, cut into 1-inch pieces
2 medium onions, chopped
1 large green bell pepper, chopped
½ pound fresh mushrooms, sliced
3 garlic cloves, minced
2 tablespoons sweet Hungarian paprika
½ cup dry white wine

3 cups Simple Beef Stock (page 264) or reduced-sodium canned broth
1 (14½-ounce) can Italian peeled tomatoes, drained and chopped
½ teaspoon dried thyme leaves
1 bay leaf
1 teaspoon salt
¼ teaspoon pepper
1 tablespoon flour
1 cup sour cream
Minced fresh dill

1. In a large nonreactive flameproof casserole, heat oil over medium-high heat. Add veal in 3 batches without crowding and cook, turning occasionally, until browned all over, 7 to 8 minutes per batch. With a slotted spoon, transfer veal to a platter.

2. Add onions and bell pepper to pan, reduce heat to medium, and cook, stirring occasionally, until softened, about 5 minutes. Add mushrooms and garlic and cook, stirring frequently, until mushrooms are tender, 5 minutes longer. Add paprika and cook, stirring constantly, 2 minutes. Add wine, beef stock, tomatoes, thyme, bay leaf, salt, and pepper. Bring to a boil. Reduce heat to low, cover, and simmer, stirring occasionally, until veal is tender, about 1½ hours.

3. In a small bowl, blend flour with 2 tablespoons cold water. Stir into stew and bring to a boil, stirring until thickened, 2 to 3 minutes. Reduce heat to low and stir in sour cream. Cook just until heated through, about 2 minutes. Garnish with dill just before serving.

277   VEAL AND SUCCOTASH STEW WITH TARRAGON

Prep: 20 minutes   Cook: 1 hour 26 minutes to 1 hour 44 minutes
Serves: 4 to 6

1½ pounds boneless veal
    shoulder, cut into 1½-inch
    pieces
⅓ cup flour
½ teaspoon salt
¼ teaspoon black pepper
2 tablespoons vegetable oil
1 medium onion, minced
1 medium celery rib, minced
3 garlic cloves, minced
½ cup dry white wine
2 cups Veal Stock (page 267)
    or reduced-sodium
    canned beef broth
1 tablespoon minced fresh
    tarragon or 1 teaspoon
    dried

½ teaspoon dried thyme leaves
1 bay leaf
1 cup light cream or milk
2 cups fresh or 1 (10-ounce)
    package frozen baby lima
    beans
2 cups fresh or 1 (10-ounce)
    package frozen corn
    kernels
1 (6-ounce) jar roasted red
    peppers, drained and
    chopped
¼ cup minced fresh parsley

1. Dredge veal to coat lightly with flour; shake off excess flour. Season veal with salt and black pepper.

2. In a large nonreactive flameproof casserole, heat oil over medium heat. Add veal in 2 batches and cook, turning occasionally, until golden brown on all sides, 5 to 6 minutes per batch. Transfer veal to a platter.

3. Add onion, celery, and garlic to pan. Cook, stirring occasionally, until softened, about 5 minutes.

4. Stir in wine, bring to a boil, and cook 1 minute. Add veal stock, tarragon, thyme, and bay leaf. Return veal to pan. Bring to a boil, reduce heat to medium-low, cover, and simmer until meat is tender, 1 to 1¼ hours.

5. Stir in cream and lima beans and bring to a boil. Reduce heat to medium-low, cover, and simmer, stirring occasionally, 6 minutes. Add corn and red peppers and simmer, covered, until all vegetables are tender, 4 to 5 minutes. Remove and discard bay leaf. Stir in parsley just before serving.

278   GROUND VEAL, SAGE, AND PARMESAN MEATBALLS IN MARINARA SAUCE

Prep: 15 minutes   Cook: 18 minutes   Serves: 4

Serve these meatballs over spaghetti or tubular pasta, such as penne or fusilli.

2/3 cup fresh bread crumbs
1/4 cup milk
3 tablespoons olive oil
1 medium onion, minced
1 pound ground veal
1 large egg, lightly beaten
1/3 cup grated Parmesan cheese

2 tablespoons minced fresh parsley
1 large garlic clove, minced
1/2 teaspoon salt
1/4 teaspoon pepper
2 cups marinara sauce

1. In a small bowl, soak bread crumbs in milk.

2. In a large skillet, heat 1 tablespoon olive oil over medium heat. Add onion and cook, stirring frequently, until golden, about 3 minutes.

3. In a large bowl, combine onion mixture, bread crumb mixture, veal, egg, Parmesan cheese, parsley, garlic, salt, and pepper. Mix with hands until well blended and form into 1½-inch meatballs (makes about 18 meatballs).

4. In a large nonreactive skillet, heat remaining 2 tablespoons olive oil over medium heat. Add meatballs and cook, turning occasionally, until browned on all sides, about 10 minutes. Add marinara sauce. Bring to a boil, simmer 5 minutes, and serve.

279   VEAL SHANKS WITH FENNEL

Prep: 10 minutes   Cook: 2 hours 42 minutes to 2 hours 44 minutes
Serves: 4

4 (2-inch-thick) pieces of veal shanks (about 8 ounces each)
1/2 teaspoon salt
1/4 teaspoon pepper
1/2 cup flour
3 tablespoons olive oil
1 large onion, chopped
1 large carrot, peeled and chopped
3 garlic cloves, chopped

1 cup dry white wine
3 cups Veal Stock (page 267) or reduced-sodium canned chicken broth
1 teaspoon dried rosemary
1 teaspoon fennel seed, crushed
1 bay leaf
2 fennel bulbs, cut into wedges, fronds reserved

1. Season veal with salt and pepper. Dredge veal to coat lightly with flour; shake off excess flour.

2. In a large flameproof casserole, heat olive oil over medium-high heat. Add veal and cook until browned on all sides, 6 to 8 minutes. Transfer veal to a platter.

3. Add onion, carrot, and garlic to casserole. Cook, stirring occasionally, until softened, about 5 minutes.

4. Stir in wine, bring to a boil, and cook 1 minute. Add veal stock, rosemary, fennel seed, and bay leaf. Return veal to casserole and bring to a boil. Reduce heat to medium-low, cover, and cook until meat is just tender, about 2 hours. Add fennel wedges and simmer until meat is very tender, about 30 minutes longer. Meanwhile, mince 1 tablespoon fennel fronds. Skim fat from surface and discard with bay leaf. Sprinkle with minced fennel fronds just before serving.

---

280 VEAL, TOMATO, AND GREEN OLIVE STEW

Prep: 10 minutes   Cook: 1 hour 46 minutes to 1 hour 48 minutes
Serves: 4 to 6

1½ pounds boneless veal shoulder, cut into 1½-inch pieces
½ cup flour
½ teaspoon salt
¼ teaspoon pepper
3 tablespoons vegetable oil
2 medium onions, sliced
1 large red bell pepper, stemmed and sliced
3 garlic cloves, minced
½ cup dry white wine
1 (28-ounce) can peeled plum tomatoes, drained and chopped

1 cup Veal Stock (page 267) or reduced-sodium canned beef broth
½ teaspoon dried oregano
½ teaspoon dried basil
1 bay leaf
½ cup pitted green olives, halved
2 tablespoons minced fresh basil (optional)

1. Dredge veal to coat lightly with flour; shake off excess flour. Season veal with salt and pepper.

2. In a large nonreactive flameproof casserole, heat oil over medium-high heat. Add veal in 2 batches and cook, turning occasionally, until lightly browned, 5 to 6 minutes per batch. Transfer veal to a platter.

3. Add onions, bell pepper, and garlic to pan. Cook, stirring frequently, until softened, about 5 minutes. Stir in wine and boil 1 minute. Add tomatoes, veal stock, oregano, basil, and bay leaf. Return veal to casserole and bring to a boil. Reduce heat to medium-low, cover, and cook 1 hour.

4. Add olives and simmer until veal is tender, about 30 minutes longer. Skim fat from surface and discard with bay leaf. Sprinkle with minced fresh basil just before serving.

281   BRAISED VEAL SHANKS

Prep: 10 minutes   Cook: 1 hour 52 minutes to 1 hour 59 minutes
Serves: 8

Known in Italy as *osso bucco*, this hearty stew provides a perfect winter meal. Classically it is served with *risotto Milanese*—Italian rice flavored with a pinch of saffron and Parmesan cheese. It can also be served with a simple rice pilaf or hot cooked pasta.

4 pounds veal shank, cut into
    8 (2-inch-thick) pieces and
    tied with string (ask your
    butcher to do this)
⅔ cup flour
1 teaspoon salt
½ teaspoon pepper
¼ cup olive oil
2 medium onions, chopped
1 large celery rib, sliced
1 small carrot, peeled and
    diced
6 garlic cloves, minced
½ cup dry white wine

3 cups Simple Beef Stock
    (page 264) or reduced-
    sodium canned broth
1 (14½-ounce) can peeled
    tomatoes, drained and
    chopped
2 teaspoons tomato paste
1 teaspoon dried thyme leaves
1 teaspoon dried rosemary
1 bay leaf
2 tablespoons cornstarch
    Gremolata (recipe follows)

1. Dredge veal to coat lightly with flour; shake off excess flour. Season veal with ½ teaspoon salt and ¼ teaspoon pepper. In a large nonreactive flame-proof casserole, heat oil over medium-high heat. Add veal in 2 batches without crowding and cook, turning occasionally, until browned all over, 8 to 10 minutes per batch. Transfer veal to a plate.

2. Add onions, celery, carrot, and garlic to pan and cook over medium heat, stirring occasionally, until vegetables are softened, 5 to 7 minutes. Add wine, beef stock, tomatoes, tomato paste, thyme, rosemary, bay leaf, and remaining ½ teaspoon salt and ¼ teaspoon pepper. Return veal to casserole. Bring to a boil. Reduce heat to medium-low, cover, and cook until veal is tender, about 1½ hours.

3. Transfer veal to a serving dish and remove strings. Remove and discard bay leaf. Skim off fat from liquid and bring liquid to a boil.

4. In a small bowl, blend cornstarch with ¼ cup cold water. Stir into boiling liquid and cook, stirring constantly, until slightly thickened, 1 to 2 minutes. Spoon sauce over veal and sprinkle Gremolata on top.

GREMOLATA
Makes: ⅓ cup

2 tablespoons grated lemon
    zest

¼ cup minced fresh parsley
1 garlic clove, finely minced

In a small bowl, combine lemon zest, parsley, and garlic. Mix well.

Chapter 11

Pork Stews

Breeders are now producing leaner and trimmer hogs, making today's pork lower in calories and higher in protein. Pork is not only one of our most nutritious and versatile meats, it is also economical. Just about every part of the pig is edible and delicious. To recognize quality in pork, look for finely grained pink meat with some marbling.

The best cuts of pork for stewing are shoulder and picnic cuts because of their firm texture and high flavor. As with beef and veal, these cuts require long, slow, moist cooking and are far less expensive than their prime neighbors, such as loin. However, if you are especially concerned about fat, you could substitute boneless loin, in which case the cooking time will be 20 to 30 minutes less.

Included in this chapter are several recipes using smoked ham and sausage. Smoked ham is fully cooked and essentially needs only reheating or enough simmering to impart its smoky flavor. Be mindful of the salt content in ham and take care to season with discretion. Smoked sausages, such as kielbasa and chorizo, also need to be handled carefully. Their taste will depend upon the curing process, resulting in either a mildly smoked meat or not. As with all the recipes in the book, choose the meat that best suits your tastes and your needs.

282   PORK STEW WITH CLAMS
Prep: 15 minutes   Cook: 55 to 65 minutes   Serves: 6

1 cup dry white wine
1 teaspoon salt
½ teaspoon black pepper
4 garlic cloves, minced
⅛ teaspoon ground cloves
¼ teaspoon crushed hot red
   pepper
3 pounds boneless pork loin,
   cut into 1-inch cubes
5 tablespoons olive oil
1½ cups Simple Beef Stock
   (page 264) or reduced-
   sodium canned broth

1 large onion, minced
1 medium green bell pepper,
   chopped
1 (28-ounce) can whole
   tomatoes, drained and
   chopped
1 tablespoon tomato paste
1 bay leaf
1 teaspoon dried thyme leaves
12 cherrystone clams, scrubbed
3 tablespoons minced cilantro
   or fresh parsley

1. In a large bowl, combine wine, ½ teaspoon salt, ¼ teaspoon black pepper, garlic, cloves, and hot red pepper. Add pork and toss to coat with marinade. Cover and marinate in refrigerator overnight.

2. Drain pork, reserving marinade; pat pork dry with paper towels. In a large skillet, heat 3 tablespoons oil over medium-high heat. Add pork in 3 batches without crowding and cook, turning occasionally, until browned outside and white throughout, 6 to 8 minutes per batch. Transfer pork to a plate.

3. Add reserved marinade to pan and bring to a boil, scraping up brown bits from the pan. Boil over high heat until marinade is reduced by half, about 3 minutes. Add beef stock and boil until liquid is reduced to 1 cup, 3 to 5 minutes. Return pork to skillet and set aside.

4. In a large nonreactive flameproof casserole, heat remaining 2 tablespoons oil over medium-high heat. Add onion and bell pepper. Cook, stirring occasionally, until softened, 3 to 5 minutes. Add tomatoes, tomato paste, bay leaf, thyme, and remaining ½ teaspoon salt and ¼ teaspoon black pepper. Reduce heat to medium-low and cook, stirring occasionally, 15 minutes.

5. Add clams. Cover casserole and cook over medium-high heat until clams have opened, about 8 minutes. Remove and discard bay leaf. Discard any clams that have not opened. Add pork mixture to casserole. Bring to a simmer and cook until heated through, 5 minutes. Sprinkle with cilantro just before serving.

283 PORK AND SWEET POTATO PIE

Prep: 15 minutes   Cook: 2 hours 14 minutes to 3 hours 5 minutes
Serves: 6

This is a delicious dish for informal home entertaining. It can be completely prepared ahead of time and reheated just before serving.

2½ **pounds boneless pork shoulder, cut into 2-inch pieces**
½ **cup flour**
1½ **teaspoons salt**
¾ **teaspoon pepper**
¼ **cup vegetable oil**
1 **large onion, sliced**
3 **garlic cloves, minced**
½ **cup dry white wine**
2 **cups Brown Beef Stock (page 264), Brown Chicken Stock (page 263), or reduced-sodium canned beef broth**

½ **teaspoon dried thyme leaves**
½ **teaspoon dried rosemary**
½ **teaspoon dried sage**
1 **bay leaf**
⅛ **teaspoon ground cloves**
1 **tablespoon Dijon mustard**
3 **pounds sweet potatoes**
1 **teaspoon grated lemon zest**
¼ **teaspoon grated nutmeg**
2 **tablespoons butter, melted**

1. Dredge pork to coat lightly with flour; shake off excess flour. Season with ½ teaspoon salt and ¼ teaspoon pepper. In a large flameproof casserole, heat oil over medium-high heat. Add pork in 3 batches and cook, stirring frequently, until browned on all sides, 6 to 8 minutes. Transfer to a platter.

2. Add onion to casserole. Reduce heat to medium and cook, stirring frequently, until softened, 5 minutes. Add garlic and cook, stirring constantly, 1 minute. Stir in wine, beef stock, thyme, rosemary, sage, bay leaf, cloves, ½ teaspoon salt, and ¼ teaspoon pepper.

3. Return pork to casserole. Bring to a boil. Reduce heat to medium-low, cover, and cook, stirring and skimming surface occasionally, until pork is tender, 1 to 1½ hours. Remove and discard bay leaf. Stir in mustard.

4. Meanwhile, prick sweet potatoes with fork and bake at 400°F. 30 to 35 minutes, or until softened. Remove from oven and let cool slightly. Leave oven on.

5. Cut potatoes in half lengthwise, scoop out centers, and place in a large bowl. Add lemon zest, nutmeg, and remaining ½ teaspoon salt and ¼ teaspoon pepper. Mash potatoes and mix well.

6. Spoon sweet potatoes over pork in casserole, spreading evenly. Drizzle melted butter over potatoes. Bring to a boil and transfer to oven. Bake 20 to 30 minutes, until sweet potatoes are piping hot.

284 PORK AND GREEN CHILE STEW

Prep: 10 minutes   Cook: 2 hours 3 minutes to 2 hours 7 minutes
Serves: 6

Serve this New Mexican stew with warmed flour tortillas.

2 pounds boneless pork shoulder, cut into 1½-inch pieces
½ teaspoon salt
¼ teaspoon pepper
3 tablespoons vegetable oil
2 medium onions, chopped
3 garlic cloves, minced
2 teaspoons ground cumin
2 teaspoons dried oregano

1½ cups Chicken Stock (page 262) or reduced-sodium canned broth
6 canned peeled tomatillos, chopped
2 (7-ounce) cans mild or hot green chiles, seeded and chopped, juices reserved
2 to 3 teaspoons lime juice
2 tablespoons minced cilantro

1. Season pork with salt and pepper. In a large flameproof casserole, heat oil over medium-high heat. Add pork in 2 batches and cook, stirring frequently, until browned on all sides, 6 to 8 minutes. Transfer pork to a platter.

2. Reduce heat to medium. Add onions and garlic to pan. Cook, stirring occasionally, until softened but not browned, 5 minutes. Add cumin and oregano and cook, stirring constantly, 1 minute. Stir in chicken stock.

3. Return pork to casserole. Bring to a boil. Reduce heat to medium-low, cover, and cook until meat is tender, about 1½ hours. Add tomatillos and chiles with their juices, cover, and simmer 15 minutes longer. Stir in lime juice and cilantro just before serving.

285 PORK, SWEET POTATO, AND SPINACH STEW

Prep: 10 minutes   Cook: 1 hour 59 minutes to 2 hours 4 minutes
Serves: 4

1½ pounds boneless pork shoulder, cut into 1½-inch pieces
¼ cup flour
½ teaspoon salt
¼ teaspoon pepper
3 tablespoons vegetable oil
1 medium onion, sliced
3 garlic cloves, minced
2 cups Chicken Stock (page 262) or reduced-sodium canned broth

1 teaspoon dried savory
1 bay leaf
¼ teaspoon crushed hot red pepper (optional)
1 pound sweet potatoes, peeled and cut into 1-inch dice
1 pound spinach, rinsed, tough stems removed, and coarsely chopped

1. Dredge pork to coat lightly with flour; shake off excess flour. Season pork with salt and pepper.

2. In a large flameproof casserole, heat oil over medium-high heat. Add pork in 2 batches and cook, stirring frequently, until browned on all sides, 6 to 8 minutes. Transfer pork to a platter.

3. Reduce heat to medium. Add onion and garlic and cook, stirring occasionally, until golden, 7 to 8 minutes. Add chicken stock, savory, bay leaf, and crushed hot pepper. Return pork to casserole. Bring to a boil. Reduce heat to medium-low, cover, and cook until pork is tender, 1¼ hours.

4. Add sweet potatoes, cover, and simmer until heated through, 20 minutes. Add spinach, cover, and simmer until spinach is wilted, about 5 minutes longer. Remove and discard bay leaf before serving.

---

286   CIDER PORK STEW WITH APPLES

Prep: 10 minutes   Cook: 1 hour 24 minutes to 1 hour 58 minutes
Serves: 6

Pork and fruit have an affinity for one another. Here we have paired pork with apples and have concentrated the flavors by using apple cider.

3 tablespoons vegetable oil	1 cup apple cider
2½ pounds boneless pork shoulder, cut into 2-inch pieces	1 large tart apple, such as Granny Smith, peeled, cored, and sliced
1 large onion, sliced	1 tablespoon tomato paste
1 large celery rib, sliced	½ teaspoon dried thyme leaves
4 garlic cloves, minced	½ teaspoon dried rosemary
3 tablespoons flour	½ teaspoon dried sage
2 cups Simple Beef Stock (page 264), Brown Chicken Stock (page 263), or reduced-sodium canned beef broth	1 teaspoon salt
	½ teaspoon pepper
	2 tablespoons minced fresh parsley

1. In a large flameproof casserole, heat oil over medium-high heat. Add pork in 2 batches without crowding and cook, stirring frequently, until browned all over, 6 to 8 minutes. Transfer pork to a platter.

2. Add onion and celery to pan. Reduce heat to medium and cook, stirring frequently, until softened but not browned, 5 minutes. Add garlic and flour and cook, stirring frequently, 2 minutes. Stir in beef stock, apple cider, apple, tomato paste, thyme, rosemary, sage, salt, and pepper. Return pork to casserole and bring to a boil. Reduce heat to medium-low, cover, and cook, stirring and skimming occasionally, until pork is tender, 1 to 1½ hours.

3. With a slotted spoon, transfer pork to a serving dish. In a food processor or blender, puree sauce from casserole, in batches as necessary, until smooth. Return puree to pan and bring to a boil. Reduce heat to low and simmer 3 minutes. Return pork to pan and cook until heated through, about 2 minutes. Sprinkle with parsley just before serving.

287 NEW ENGLAND BOILED DINNER

Prep: 10 minutes   Cook: 1 hour 29 minutes to 1 hour 31 minutes
Serves: 4

1 (2-pound) boneless smoked
   pork butt
1 large bay leaf
1 teaspoon black peppercorns
1 pound medium red
   potatoes, quartered

¾ pound carrots, peeled,
   halved lengthwise, and
   cut into 3-inch pieces
1 small head of cabbage
   (about 1¼ pounds), cored
   and cut into 4 wedges

1. Place pork in a large flameproof casserole. Add enough water to cover. Add bay leaf and peppercorns. Bring to a boil. Reduce heat to medium-low and simmer 5 minutes. Transfer pork to a cutting board. Remove and discard netting.

2. Return pork to casserole, cover, and cook until tender, 1 hour. Add potatoes and cook 8 minutes. Add carrots and cook 6 minutes longer. Add cabbage and cook until all vegetables are tender, 10 to 12 minutes. Remove and discard bay leaf before serving.

288 PORK STEW WITH JUNIPER, POTATOES, AND HERBS

Prep: 20 minutes   Cook: 1 hour 41 minutes to 1 hour 42 minutes
Serves: 6

For a great cold-weather dinner, serve this stew with hot buttered noodles and a mixed green salad.

1 tablespoon extra-virgin
   olive oil
1 tablespoon butter
1½ pounds pork loin, cut into
   1½-inch cubes
¾ teaspoon salt
½ teaspoon pepper
1 medium onion, finely
   chopped
2 garlic cloves, minced
2 tablespoons flour
½ cup dry red wine
1½ cups Chicken Stock (page
   262) or reduced-sodium
   canned broth

½ teaspoon dried sage
½ teaspoon dried thyme leaves
½ teaspoon dried rosemary
5 juniper berries, lightly
   crushed
1 pound red potatoes, cut into
   1-inch dice
2 medium carrots, peeled and
   sliced ½ inch thick
2 tablespoons chopped
   parsley

1. In a large flameproof casserole, heat olive oil and butter over high heat. Season pork with salt and pepper. Add to pot in 2 batches and cook, stirring frequently, until browned on all sides, about 5 minutes per batch. Remove pork to a plate.

2. Add onion to pan and cook, stirring frequently, until softened, 3 minutes. Add garlic and flour and cook, stirring without allowing to color, 1 to 2 minutes. Stir in wine, reduce heat to medium-low, and cook 2 minutes. Stir in chicken stock, pork, herbs, and juniper berries, cover, and simmer 1 hour.

3. Add potatoes and carrots, cover, and simmer 25 minutes longer, or until pork and potatoes are tender. Stir in parsley just before serving.

---

289 PORK AND SAUERKRAUT STEW
Prep: 15 minutes   Cook: 57 minutes   Serves: 4

This is a quick version of the classic French dish *choucroute garnie*. Serve it with dark bread, pickles, and mustard. If smoked pork chops are not available, use fresh pork chops, browned first, and slice up 2 additional knockwurst.

3 tablespoons vegetable oil
2 medium onions, minced
1 large carrot, peeled and sliced
1 (1-pound) bag fresh sauerkraut, drained and rinsed
2 cups Chicken Stock (page 262) or reduced-sodium canned broth
⅔ cup dry white wine
8 juniper berries
1 teaspoon caraway seed

1 bay leaf
½ teaspoon salt
¼ teaspoon pepper
1½ pounds medium boiling potatoes, peeled and cut into quarters
4 smoked pork chops
2 knockwurst, sliced ½ inch thick
½ pound garlic sausage, such as kielbasa, sliced ½ inch thick

1. In a large nonreactive flameproof casserole, heat oil over medium-high heat. Add onions and carrot and cook, stirring occasionally, until onions are softened, about 5 minutes. Stir in sauerkraut and cook 2 minutes longer. Stir in chicken stock, wine, juniper berries, caraway seed, bay leaf, salt, pepper, and potatoes. Bring to a boil. Reduce heat to low, cover, and simmer 30 minutes.

2. Add pork chops, knockwurst, and sausage, arranging sauerkraut and potatoes over and around meats. Cover and simmer until potatoes are softened and meats are heated through, about 20 minutes. Remove and discard bay leaf before serving.

290 RED CABBAGE AND SMOKED SAUSAGE STEW

Prep: 10 minutes   Cook: 46 to 49 minutes   Serves: 4 to 6

2 tablespoons butter
1 pound smoked sausage,
    such as kielbasa, sliced
2 medium onions, thinly
    sliced
1 large head of red cabbage
    (about 2 pounds), cored
    and shredded
1 large tart apple, such as
    Granny Smith, peeled,
    cored, and sliced

¼ cup red wine vinegar
1 cup Simple Beef Stock (page
    264) or reduced-sodium
    canned broth
1 bay leaf
1 teaspoon caraway seed
½ teaspoon salt
¼ teaspoon pepper

1. In a large nonreactive flameproof casserole, melt butter over medium heat. Add sausage and cook, turning occasionally, until lightly browned on both sides, 4 to 6 minutes. Transfer sausage to a plate.

2. Add onions to casserole and cook, stirring occasionally, until golden, 7 to 8 minutes. Add red cabbage and cook, stirring occasionally, 5 minutes. Add apple, red wine vinegar, beef stock, bay leaf, caraway seed, salt, and pepper. Return sausage to pan. Bring to a boil. Reduce heat to low, cover, and simmer, stirring occasionally, until cabbage is tender, about 30 minutes. Remove and discard bay leaf before serving.

291 PORK, RICE, AND TOMATO STEW

Prep: 10 minutes   Cook: 2 hours 19 minutes to 2½ hours   Serves: 6

¼ cup olive oil
3 pounds boneless pork
    shoulder, cut into 1½-inch
    pieces
1 large onion, sliced
3 garlic cloves, minced
½ cup dry white wine
2 cups Simple Beef Stock
    (page 264), Brown
    Chicken Stock (page 263),
    or reduced-sodium
    canned beef broth
1 (14½-ounce) can tomatoes,
    drained and cut up

1 bay leaf
1 teaspoon ground cumin
1 teaspoon dried thyme leaves
1 tablespoon tomato paste
1 teaspoon salt
½ teaspoon pepper
1½ cups long-grain white rice
½ cup grated Parmesan cheese
8 large pimiento-stuffed
    olives, chopped
3 tablespoons minced fresh
    parsley
1 tablespoon drained
    chopped capers

1. Preheat oven to 350°F. In a large nonreactive flameproof casserole, heat oil over medium-high heat. Add pork in 3 batches and cook, stirring frequently, until browned on all sides, 6 to 8 minutes. Transfer to a platter.

2. Add onion to casserole. Reduce heat to medium and cook, stirring frequently, until softened, 5 minutes. Add garlic and cook, stirring frequently, until softened, 1 minute. Stir in wine, beef stock, tomatoes, bay leaf, cumin, thyme, tomato paste, salt, and pepper. Return meat to casserole. Bring to a boil.

3. Place casserole in oven and bake 1½ hours. Add rice, cover, and bake 25 to 30 minutes longer, or until liquid is absorbed. Remove and discard bay leaf. Stir in Parmesan cheese, olives, parsley, and capers and serve.

---

292 PORK STEWED IN RED WINE WITH PRUNES AND SAGE

Prep: 10 minutes   Cook: 1 hour 58 minutes to 2 hours 4 minutes
Serves: 6

¼ cup vegetable oil
3 pounds boneless pork
  shoulder, cut into 2-inch
  pieces
1 medium onion, chopped
3 garlic cloves, minced
3 tablespoons flour
2 cups dry red wine
1 cup Simple Beef Stock (page
  264), Brown Chicken
  Stock (page 263), or
  reduced-sodium canned
  beef broth

1 teaspoon dried sage
½ teaspoon dried thyme leaves
½ teaspoon dried rosemary
1 bay leaf
1 teaspoon salt
½ teaspoon pepper
1 cup pitted prunes

1. In a nonreactive large flameproof casserole, heat oil over medium-high heat. Add pork in 3 batches and cook, stirring frequently, until browned on all sides, 6 to 8 minutes per batch. Transfer pork to a platter.

2. Add onion to pan, reduce heat to medium, and cook, stirring occasionally, until golden, about 5 minutes. Add garlic and flour and cook, stirring without allowing to color, 2 minutes. Stir in wine, beef stock, sage, thyme, rosemary, bay leaf, salt, and pepper. Return pork to pan and bring to a boil. Reduce heat to medium-low, cover, and simmer 1 hour.

3. Add prunes and simmer until pork is tender, about 30 minutes. Remove and discard bay leaf.

4. With a slotted spoon, transfer pork and prunes to a serving dish. Bring cooking liquid to a boil and cook until slightly thickened, about 3 minutes. Spoon over meat and prunes.

293   LENTIL STEW WITH SMOKED HAM
Prep: 15 minutes   Cook: 45 to 50 minutes   Serves: 4

Smoked sausage, such as kielbasa or knockwurst, may be substituted for the ham, if desired.

2   tablespoons butter
1   pound smoked ham, cut
    into 1-inch pieces
1   large onion, chopped
1   large carrot, peeled and
    chopped
1   medium celery rib, chopped
2   garlic cloves, minced
1   bay leaf
½   pound dried lentils, rinsed
    and picked over

1   (14½-ounce) can diced
    peeled tomatoes, juices
    reserved
4   cups Simple Beef Stock
    (page 264) or reduced-
    sodium canned broth
½   teaspoon salt
¼   teaspoon pepper
¼   cup chopped parsley

1. In a large saucepan, melt butter over medium heat. Add ham and cook, stirring frequently, until browned on all sides, 5 minutes. Transfer ham to a plate.

2. Add onion, carrot, celery, and garlic and cook, stirring constantly, until vegetables are softened, 5 minutes. Add bay leaf, lentils, tomatoes with their juices, beef stock, salt, and pepper. Bring to a boil, skimming any foam from surface of liquid. Add ham. Reduce heat to medium-low, cover, and simmer until lentils are tender, 35 to 40 minutes. Remove and discard bay leaf. Stir in parsley just before serving.

294   SAUSAGE, KALE, AND POTATO STEW
Prep: 10 minutes   Cook: 35 minutes   Serves: 6

If kale is not available, collard greens, turnip greens, or a combination of the two can be substituted.

1   tablespoon olive oil
1   pound linguiça, chorizo, or
    kielbasa sausage, thinly
    sliced
1   large onion, chopped
1   medium carrot, peeled and
    minced
3   garlic cloves, minced
4   cups Chicken Stock (page
    262) or reduced-sodium
    canned broth

1   (14½-ounce) can peeled
    plum tomatoes, chopped,
    juices reserved
1   pound red potatoes, peeled
    and cut into ½-inch dice
1   pound kale, well rinsed,
    tough stems removed,
    and sliced
1   (10½-ounce) can chickpeas,
    rinsed and drained
    Salt and pepper

1. In a large nonreactive flameproof casserole, heat olive oil over medium heat. Add sausage and cook, turning occasionally, until browned on all sides, 5 minutes. Transfer sausage to a plate.

2. Add onion, carrot, and garlic to pan and cook, stirring frequently, until onion is softened, 5 minutes. Add chicken stock, tomatoes with their juices, and potatoes.

3. Return sausage to casserole. Bring to a boil, skimming away foam from surface of liquid. Add ham. Reduce heat to medium-low, cover, and simmer 15 minutes. Add kale and chickpeas, cover, and simmer just until potatoes are softened and kale is tender, about 10 minutes longer. Season with salt and pepper to taste.

295   PORK, PUMPKIN, AND TURNIP STEW

Prep: 10 minutes   Cook: 2 hours 2 minutes to 2 hours 8 minutes
Serves: 6 to 8

If fresh pumpkin is unavailable, substitute butternut squash instead. For a heartier meal, serve this stew with hot cooked rice.

3 tablespoons vegetable oil
2 pounds boneless pork shoulder, cut into 1½-inch pieces
2 medium onions, minced
3 garlic cloves, minced
1 (14½-ounce) can diced tomatoes, juices reserved
1½ to 2 cups Brown Beef Stock (page 264) or reduced-sodium canned broth

1 teaspoon salt
½ teaspoon pepper
1 pound turnips, peeled and cut into 1-inch pieces
4 cups chopped turnip greens
1 medium pumpkin (about 2 pounds), seeded, peeled, and cut into 1-inch pieces

1. In a large nonreactive flameproof casserole, heat oil over medium-high heat. Add pork in 2 batches and cook, turning, until browned on all sides, 6 to 8 minutes. Transfer pork to a platter.

2. Reduce heat to medium. Add onions and garlic. Cook, stirring occasionally, until onions are golden, 5 to 7 minutes. Add tomatoes with their juices, beef stock, salt, and pepper. Return pork to casserole. Bring to a boil. Reduce heat to medium-low, cover, and cook 1 hour.

3. Add turnips, cover, and simmer 15 minutes. Add greens and pumpkin, cover, and simmer until pork and pumpkin are tender, about 30 minutes longer.

296   PORK STEW IN COCONUT MILK

Prep: 15 minutes   Cook: 1 hour 22 minutes to 1 hour 55 minutes
Serves: 6

Tamarind paste, which can be found in many East Indian and oriental supermarkets, adds a tantalizing sweet-and-sour flavor to this deliciously different stew.

3 tablespoons vegetable oil	1 teaspoon grated lemon zest
2½ pounds boneless pork shoulder, cut into 1½-inch pieces	1 teaspoon ground cumin
	½ teaspoon ground turmeric
	1 (15-ounce) can unsweetened coconut milk
1 medium onion, quartered	
1 garlic clove	½ cup Chicken Stock (page 262) or reduced-sodium canned broth
1 tablespoon minced fresh ginger	
1½ teaspoons ground coriander	3 bay leaves
1½ teaspoons dark brown sugar	½ teaspoon salt
1 teaspoon tamarind paste (optional)	¼ teaspoon pepper

1. In a large flameproof casserole, heat oil over medium-high heat. Add pork in 3 batches and cook, stirring frequently, until browned on all sides, 7 to 8 minutes. Transfer pork to a platter.

2. In a food processor, combine onion, garlic, ginger, coriander, brown sugar, tamarind paste, lemon zest, cumin, turmeric, and 1 cup coconut milk and process until well blended. Add to casserole and cook over medium heat, stirring constantly, 1 minute. Return pork to pan and add chicken stock, bay leaves, salt, pepper, and remaining coconut milk. Bring to a boil. Reduce heat to medium-low, cover, and cook until pork is tender, 1 to 1½ hours. Remove and discard bay leaves before serving.

Chapter 12

Lamb Stews

Succulent and rich-tasting, lamb is ideally suited for stew. The Irish and French have made their versions famous, as in Irish Lamb and Potato Stew—simple but delicious fare—and *navarin printanier,* presented here as Lamb Stew with Spring Vegetables—which celebrates the mild, young lamb of the season by pairing it with the tenderest and most flavorful vegetables of the season.

What follows is a selection of recipes from many cuisines, hopefully broadening the horizons of lamb possibilities. There's Greek Lamb and Orzo Stew, Moroccan Lamb Stew with Green Olives and Artichokes, and Lamb Stew Ratatouille. These dishes combine lamb with fragrant herbs and pungent spices.

The best cuts to use for stewing lamb are shoulder, neck, and shank. Although many of the recipes call for boneless lamb shoulder, you may leave the bones in if you prefer—just be sure to increase the overall weight of the lamb used in the recipe. The bones will only add flavor.

Shanks are probably the most savory of all these cuts. They are particularly economical because they are so meaty. Combined with potatoes and vegetables, they make the perfect Sunday dinner.

297   LAMB COUSCOUS

Prep: 30 minutes   Cook: 1 hour 32 minutes to 2 hours 4 minutes
Serves: 4

This is a wonderful dish for entertaining. For a festive presentation, spoon the couscous into a lightly oiled bowl or mold and invert it onto the center of a shallow platter. Spoon the lamb stew around the couscous and sprinkle with parsley.

2 tablespoons vegetable oil	1 teaspoon salt
1½ pounds boneless lamb	½ teaspoon pepper
shoulder, cut into 1½-inch	2 medium carrots, peeled and
pieces	sliced
2 medium onions, chopped	1 medium to large red potato,
3 garlic cloves, minced	cut into 1-inch dice
1 (14½-ounce) can Italian	1 medium zucchini, cut into
peeled tomatoes,	1-inch pieces
chopped, juices reserved	1 medium yellow squash, cut
1½ teaspoons ground cumin	into 1-inch pieces
1 teaspoon ground ginger	1 (10½-ounce) can chickpeas,
½ teaspoon dried rosemary	drained
½ teaspoon dried thyme leaves	2 cups couscous, cooked
1 cinnamon stick	according to package
4 cups Lamb Stock (page 265)	directions
or reduced-sodium	Harissa (recipe follows)
canned beef broth	

1. In a large nonreactive flameproof casserole, heat 1 tablespoon oil over medium-high heat. Add lamb in 2 batches stirring occasionally and adding remaining 1 tablespoon oil as needed, and cook until browned on all sides, 7 to 8 minutes. Transfer lamb to a platter.

2. Add onions to pot, reduce heat to medium, and cook, stirring frequently, until softened, 5 minutes. Add garlic, tomatoes with their juices, cumin, ginger, rosemary, thyme, cinnamon stick, lamb stock, salt, and pepper.

3. Return lamb to casserole. Bring to a boil. Reduce heat to low, cover, and simmer, stirring and skimming surface occasionally, until lamb is tender, 1 to 1½ hours. Add carrots and potato, cover, and simmer 8 minutes. Add zucchini, yellow squash, and chickpeas. Simmer until vegetables are tender, about 5 minutes longer. Remove and discard cinnamon stick. Serve with couscous and top each serving with tablespoonfuls of Harissa.

298 HARISSA

Prep: 15 minutes   Cook: 5 minutes   Makes: 1 cup

This is a fiery condiment particularly good with couscous. Use it sparingly.

1 tablespoon cumin seed	15 whole cloves
1 tablespoon coriander seed	1 teaspoon black peppercorns
1 teaspoon cardamom seed	1 teaspoon cayenne
2 tablespoons pequin chiles	1½ teaspoons salt
or 1 tablespoon crushed	3 large garlic cloves
hot red pepper	½ cup olive oil

1. In a small dry skillet, combine cumin, coriander, cardamom, chiles, cloves, and peppercorns; cook over medium heat until lightly toasted, 5 minutes, stirring constantly. Let cool slightly.

2. In a small food processor or coffee grinder, crush toasted spices. Add cayenne, salt, and garlic and process until blended.

3. Transfer mixture to a covered container or jar with lid. Add oil; cover tightly and shake to blend. Store in refrigerator up to 2 weeks.

299 MOROCCAN LAMB STEW WITH GREEN OLIVES AND ARTICHOKES

Prep: 10 minutes   Cook: 1 hour 50 minutes   Serves: 6

Lamb bones contribute lots of flavor to stews; here's one made with shoulder chops.

2 tablespoons butter	3 pounds lamb shoulder
2 medium onions—1	chops, cut ¾ inch thick
chopped, 1 sliced	10 baby (or 3 large) artichokes
½ teaspoon ground turmeric	½ cup pitted oil-cured green
1 teaspoon ground ginger	olives
¼ teaspoon cayenne	3 tablespoons lemon juice
1 teaspoon ground cumin	½ teaspoon salt
½ teaspoon pepper	

1. In a large flameproof casserole, melt butter over medium heat. Stir in chopped onion, spices, and seasonings. Add lamb chops and stir to coat with seasoning mixture. Stir in 2 cups water and bring to a boil. Reduce heat to low, cover, and simmer 1 hour.

2. Meanwhile, if using large artichokes, remove and discard outer leaves. Quarter large artichokes and remove the chokes.

3. Stir in sliced onion, cover, and simmer 30 minutes longer. Stir in artichokes and simmer, uncovered, until lamb and artichokes are tender, about 20 minutes. Stir in olives, lemon juice, and salt just before serving.

300   LAMB AND BARLEY STEW

Prep: 15 minutes   Cook: 1 hour 47 minutes to 1 hour 51 minutes
Serves: 4

Serve this stew with a fresh green salad and hot, crusty bread.

1½ **pounds boneless lamb**
  shoulder, cut into 1½-inch
  pieces
½ **cup flour**
½ **teaspoon salt**
¼ **teaspoon black pepper**
3 **tablespoons vegetable oil**
2 **medium onions, chopped**
1 **large carrot, peeled and**
  chopped

4 **garlic cloves, minced**
3 **cups Lamb Stock (page 265)**
  or reduced-sodium
  canned beef broth
1 **(14½-ounce) can tomatoes,**
  chopped, juices reserved
1 **teaspoon dried thyme leaves**
⅔ **cup medium pearl barley**
2 **tablespoons minced fresh**
  dill

1. Dredge lamb to coat lightly with flour; shake off excess flour. Season lamb with salt and pepper.

2. In a large nonreactive flameproof casserole, heat oil over medium-high heat. Add lamb in 2 batches and cook, turning occasionally, until browned on all sides, 6 to 8 minutes. Transfer lamb to a platter.

3. Reduce heat to medium. Add onions, carrot, and garlic. Cook, stirring occasionally, until onions are softened, 5 minutes. Add lamb stock, tomatoes with their juices, and thyme. Return lamb to casserole. Bring to a boil. Reduce heat to medium-low, cover, and simmer 45 minutes. Add barley and simmer until lamb is tender and barley is cooked, about 45 minutes longer. Stir in dill just before serving.

301   GROUND LAMB, CORN, AND BELL PEPPER STEW

Prep: 10 minutes   Cook: 27 to 28 minutes   Serves: 6

Complement this quick stew with hot freshly baked corn bread.

2 **tablespoons vegetable oil**
1½ **pounds lean ground lamb**
1 **large red bell pepper, diced**
2 **medium onions, chopped**
3 **garlic cloves, minced**
4 **cups frozen corn kernels**
1 **(14½-ounce) can crushed**
  tomatoes, juices reserved

1 **teaspoon ground cumin**
1 **teaspoon dried oregano**
½ **teaspoon salt**
¼ **teaspoon black pepper**
⅛ **teaspoon cayenne**
2 **tablespoons minced cilantro**
  or fresh parsley

1. In a large nonreactive flameproof casserole, heat oil over medium heat. Add ground lamb and cook, stirring occasionally, until browned, 7 to 8 minutes.

2. Add bell pepper, onions, and garlic and cook, stirring occasionally, until softened, 5 minutes.

3. Add corn, tomatoes with their juices, cumin, oregano, salt, black pepper, and cayenne. Bring to a boil. Reduce heat to medium-low, cover, and simmer, skimming surface occasionally, 15 minutes. Stir in cilantro just before serving.

---

302 ORANGE-FLAVORED LAMB STEW WITH WALNUTS

Prep: 10 minutes   Cook: 2 hours 29 minutes to 2 hours 34 minutes
Serves: 4

3 pounds boneless lamb shoulder, cut into 2-inch pieces
½ cup flour
1 teaspoon salt
½ teaspoon pepper
¼ cup olive oil
2 medium onions, chopped
1 large celery rib, sliced
6 garlic cloves, chopped
1 cup dry white wine
1 (14½-ounce) can peeled whole tomatoes, juices reserved

3 cups Lamb Stock (page 265) or reduced-sodium canned beef broth
3 (3 x 1-inch) strips of orange zest plus 2 teaspoons grated
12 sprigs of fresh parsley
1 teaspoon dried thyme leaves
1 teaspoon dried rosemary
1 large bay leaf
⅔ cup toasted walnut halves or pignoli nuts
2 tablespoons minced fresh parsley

1. Dredge lamb to coat lightly with flour; shake off excess flour. Sprinkle lamb with ½ teaspoon salt and ¼ teaspoon pepper.

2. In a large nonreactive flameproof casserole, heat 2 tablespoons oil over medium-high heat. Add lamb in 3 batches and cook, stirring occasionally and adding remaining 2 tablespoons oil as needed, until browned on all sides, 7 to 8 minutes per batch. Transfer lamb to a plate.

3. Add onions, celery, and garlic to casserole and cook over medium heat, stirring frequently, until tender, about 5 minutes. Add wine, tomatoes with their juices, lamb stock, orange zest, parsley, thyme, rosemary, bay leaf, and remaining ½ teaspoon salt and ¼ teaspoon pepper. Return lamb to casserole. Bring to a boil. Reduce heat to low, cover, and simmer until lamb is tender, about 2 hours.

4. With a slotted spoon, remove lamb from casserole and set aside. Skim fat from liquid in saucepan. Remove and discard bay leaf and orange zest.

5. In a food processor, puree cooking liquid and vegetables until smooth. Return to pan. Add lamb and grated orange zest. Bring to a boil and cook, stirring constantly, until slightly thickened, 3 to 5 minutes. Sprinkle with walnuts and parsley just before serving.

303 LAMB STEW WITH DRIED APRICOTS AND GINGER

Prep: 10 minutes   Stand: 15 minutes
Cook: 1 hour 49 minutes to 1 hour 54 minutes   Serves: 4

⅔ cup dried apricots, diced
1 cup hot water
2 tablespoons vegetable oil
1½ pounds boneless lamb shoulder, cut into 1½-inch pieces
½ teaspoon salt
¼ teaspoon black pepper
1 medium onion, sliced
3 garlic cloves, minced
1 tablespoon minced fresh ginger

1½ cups Lamb Stock (page 265) or reduced-sodium canned beef broth
2 tablespoons tomato paste
1 teaspoon dried rosemary
1 bay leaf
1 (10½-ounce) can chickpeas, rinsed and drained
⅓ cup sliced toasted almonds

1. In a small heatproof bowl, cover apricots with hot water and let stand until apricots are plumped, about 15 minutes. Drain apricots, reserving liquid.

2. In a large nonreactive flameproof casserole, heat oil over medium-high heat. Season lamb with salt and black pepper. Add to casserole in 2 batches and cook, stirring occasionally, until browned on all sides, 6 to 8 minutes per batch. Transfer lamb to a platter.

3. Add onion, garlic, and ginger to casserole. Cook, stirring occasionally, until golden, 7 to 8 minutes. Stir in reserved apricot liquid, lamb stock, tomato paste, rosemary, and bay leaf.

4. Return lamb to casserole. Bring to a boil. Reduce heat to medium-low, cover, and simmer until lamb is tender, about 1¼ hours. Add chickpeas and simmer until heated through, about 15 minutes. Remove and discard bay leaf. Sprinkle with almonds just before serving.

304 LAMB STEW WITH WHITE BEANS

Prep: 15 minutes   Stand: 12 hours
Cook: 1 hour 31 minutes to 2 hours 4 minutes   Serves: 6 to 8

For a quicker version of this hearty stew, substitute 2 (10½-ounce) cans rinsed and drained Great Northern white beans for the dried beans. Simply add the canned beans during the last 10 minutes of cooking. If you are using dried beans, remember to put the beans up to soak the night before.

1 pound small dried white beans, rinsed and picked over
2 bay leaves
2 teaspoons dried thyme leaves
2 medium onions—1 whole stuck with 3 whole cloves, 1 chopped
1 carrot, peeled and quartered
3 tablespoons vegetable oil
2½ pounds boneless lamb shoulder, cut into 2-inch pieces

1 medium celery rib, chopped
3 garlic cloves, minced
1 (14½-ounce) can Italian peeled tomatoes, juices reserved
2 cups Lamb Stock (page 265) or reduced-sodium canned beef broth
1 tablespoon tomato paste
1 teaspoon salt
½ teaspoon pepper
2 tablespoons minced fresh parsley

1. Place the beans in a large bowl and add enough water to cover by at least 2 inches. Let stand at least 12 hours or overnight. Drain and rinse before using.

2. In a large saucepan, combine beans, 1 bay leaf, 1 teaspoon thyme, whole onion with cloves, carrot, and enough water to cover. Bring to a boil. Reduce heat to low and simmer, skimming surface and stirring occasionally, until beans are tender, 1 to 1½ hours. Drain beans. Remove and discard bay leaf, cloves, onion, and carrots.

3. Meanwhile, in a large nonreactive flameproof casserole, heat 1 tablespoon oil over medium-high heat. Add lamb in 3 batches and cook, stirring occasionally and adding remaining 2 tablespoons oil as needed, until lamb is browned on all sides, 7 to 8 minutes per batch. Transfer lamb to a platter.

4. Add chopped onion and celery to pot and cook, stirring occasionally, until softened, 5 minutes. Add garlic, tomatoes with their juices, lamb stock, tomato paste, remaining bay leaf and thyme, salt, and pepper. Bring to a boil. Return lamb to casserole. Reduce heat to low, cover, and simmer, skimming surface and stirring occasionally, until lamb is tender, 1 to 1½ hours.

5. Add beans to casserole and simmer until heated through, about 5 minutes. Remove and discard bay leaf. Sprinkle with parsley just before serving.

305   IRISH LAMB AND POTATO STEW
Prep: 30 minutes   Cook: 2 hours   Serves: 4

3   pounds boneless lamb
shoulder, cut into 2-inch
pieces
6   medium red potatoes,
peeled and sliced ¼ inch
thick
2   medium onions, sliced
4   medium carrots, peeled and
sliced

1   teaspoon dried rosemary
1   teaspoon dried thyme leaves
2   teaspoons salt
1   teaspoon pepper
4   cups Lamb Stock (page 265)
or reduced-sodium
canned beef broth

1. Preheat oven to 350°F. In a greased 3-quart flameproof casserole dish, layer lamb, half of the potatoes, the onions, and carrots, seasoning each layer with rosemary, thyme, salt, and pepper. End with a layer of potatoes. Add lamb stock and, if necessary, additional water to come up to, but not cover, top potato layer. Cover with sheet of greased foil.

2. Bake 1½ hours. Uncover and bake 30 minutes longer, or until lamb is tender and potatoes are browned.

306   BRAISED LAMB SHANKS WITH POTATOES AND VEGETABLES
*Prep: 20 minutes   Cook: 1 hour 19 minutes to 1 hour 21 minutes
Serves: 4*

Lamb shanks, considered a secondary cut of meat, are not only less expensive than their primary brothers but, to our minds, are far more flavorful. Although they require long, slow cooking time, this stew is primarily unattended.

3   tablespoons olive oil
2   pounds lamb shanks
½   cup flour
2   large onions, chopped
4   garlic cloves, minced
3   medium red potatoes,
peeled and cut into 1-inch
dice
4   small white turnips, peeled
and cut into 1-inch pieces
2   large carrots, peeled and
sliced ½ inch thick

2   cups Lamb Stock (page 265)
or reduced-sodium
canned beef broth
½   cup dry white wine
1   teaspoon dried rosemary
1   bay leaf
½   teaspoon salt
¼   teaspoon pepper
2   tablespoons minced fresh
parsley

1. Preheat oven to 350°F. In a large nonreactive flameproof casserole, heat oil over medium-high heat. Dredge lamb to coat lightly with flour; shake off excess flour. Add lamb to casserole in 2 batches and cook until browned on all sides, 7 to 8 minutes per batch. Transfer lamb to a platter.

2. Add onions to casserole. Reduce heat to medium and cook, stirring occasionally, until golden, 5 minutes. Add garlic, potatoes, turnips, carrots, lamb stock, wine, rosemary, bay leaf, salt, and pepper. Return lamb to casserole. Bring to a boil.

3. Cover casserole and place in oven. Bake, stirring occasionally, until meat is tender, about 1 hour. Skim fat from sauce and remove and discard bay leaf. Sprinkle with parsley just before serving.

---

307 GREEK LAMB AND ORZO STEW

Prep: 15 minutes   Cook: 2 hours 18 minutes to 2 hours 52 minutes
Serves: 6

This stew is enriched with the classic Greek lemon and egg sauce known as avgolemono. For a complete meal, precede the stew with a Greek salad and accompany it with a loaf of crusty bread.

3 tablespoons olive oil	1½ teaspoons dried rosemary
3 pounds boneless lamb shoulder, cut into 2-inch pieces	1 teaspoon dried thyme leaves
	1 bay leaf
	1 teaspoon salt
2 medium onions, chopped	¼ teaspoon pepper
1 medium carrot, peeled and chopped	½ cup orzo
	2 eggs
1 large celery rib, chopped	¼ cup lemon juice
2 tablespoons flour	½ cup heavy cream
5 cups Lamb Stock (page 265) or reduced-sodium canned beef broth	3 tablespoons minced fresh dill

1. In a large nonreactive flameproof casserole, heat 1 tablespoon olive oil over medium-high heat. Add lamb in 3 batches and cook, stirring frequently and adding remaining 2 tablespoons olive oil as needed, until browned on all sides, 7 to 8 minutes per batch. Transfer lamb to a platter.

2. Add onions, carrot, and celery to casserole. Reduce heat to medium and cook, stirring occasionally, until onions are softened, 5 minutes. Reduce heat to medium-low. Add flour and cook, stirring constantly without allowing to color, 2 to 3 minutes. Add lamb stock, rosemary, thyme, bay leaf, salt, and pepper.

3. Return lamb to casserole. Bring to a boil. Reduce heat to low and simmer, skimming surface and stirring occasionally, 1½ to 2 hours.

4. Add orzo, cover, and simmer until orzo is tender, about 15 minutes.

5. In a small bowl, whisk together eggs and lemon juice. Remove 1 cup hot stock from pot and gradually add to egg mixture, whisking constantly. Return to casserole and whisk until blended. Whisk in cream. Cook over medium-low heat, stirring constantly until slightly thickened, about 5 minutes. Remove and discard bay leaf. Stir in dill just before serving.

308   LAMB STEW WITH BROWNED ONIONS AND DIJON MUSTARD

Prep: 15 minutes   Cook: 2 hours 5 minutes to 2 hours 8 minutes
Serves: 4

Serve this stew with steamed potatoes and fresh peas.

3 tablespoons olive oil
2½ pounds boneless lamb
    shoulder, cut into 2-inch
    pieces
2 large onions, thinly sliced
1 teaspoon dried rosemary
3 garlic cloves, minced
2 tablespoons flour
½ cup dry white wine
2 cups Lamb Stock (page 265)
    or reduced-sodium
    canned beef broth

1 (14½-ounce) can Italian-style
    peeled tomatoes,
    chopped, juices reserved
1 teaspoon salt
½ teaspoon pepper
3 tablespoons minced fresh
    parsley
2 tablespoons Dijon mustard

1. In a large nonreactive flameproof casserole, heat 1 tablespoon olive oil over medium-high heat. Add lamb in 3 batches and cook, stirring occasionally and adding remaining 2 tablespoons olive oil as needed, until browned on all sides, 7 to 8 minutes. Transfer lamb to a platter.

2. Add onions and rosemary to pan. Reduce heat to medium-low and cook, stirring occasionally, until onion is golden, about 10 minutes. Add garlic and flour and cook, stirring constantly, until garlic is fragrant, 2 minutes. Stir in wine, lamb stock, tomatoes with their juices, salt, and pepper.

3. Return lamb to casserole. Bring to a boil over medium-high heat. Reduce heat to low and simmer, stirring occasionally, until meat is tender, about 1½ hours. Add parsley and mustard, simmer, stirring constantly, 2 minutes, and serve.

309 LAMB STEW WITH SPRING VEGETABLES

Prep: 30 minutes   Cook: 1 hour 37 minutes to 1 hour 41 minutes
Serves: 4

Known in France as *navarin printanier*, this delicious stew is served with the first vegetables of spring. Vary the vegetables according to taste and preference, choosing vegetables with contrasting textures and colors for best appearance.

2 tablespoons vegetable oil
2 pounds boneless lamb
    shoulder, cut into 1½-inch
    pieces
1 medium onion, chopped
1 small carrot, peeled and
    chopped
2 to 3 tablespoons flour
1 teaspoon salt
½ teaspoon pepper
4 cups Lamb Stock (page 265)
    or reduced-sodium
    canned beef broth
½ cup dry white wine
1 (14½-ounce) can Italian
    peeled tomatoes, drained
    and chopped

3 garlic cloves, minced
1 teaspoon dried rosemary
½ teaspoon dried thyme leaves
1 bay leaf
½ pound small white onions,
    peeled
½ pound baby carrots, peeled
1 cup frozen peas
½ pound small white turnips,
    peeled
2 tablespoons chopped
    parsley

1. In a large nonreactive flameproof casserole, heat oil over medium-high heat. Add lamb in 2 batches and cook, stirring occasionally, until browned on all sides, 7 to 8 minutes per batch. Transfer lamb to a platter. Add chopped onion and carrot to pan. Reduce heat to medium and cook, stirring frequently, until softened, about 5 minutes. Add flour, salt, and pepper and cook, stirring, without allowing to color, 1 to 2 minutes. Add lamb stock, wine, tomatoes, garlic, rosemary, thyme, and bay leaf. Return lamb to casserole. Bring to a boil, stirring, until liquid thickens slightly, 2 to 3 minutes. Reduce heat to low, cover, and simmer, stirring occasionally, until lamb is tender, about 1 hour.

2. Skim as much fat as possible from cooking liquid. Bring to a boil. Add whole onions. Reduce heat to medium, cover, and cook, stirring occasionally, until golden, 5 minutes. Add baby carrots and cook 5 minutes. Add peas and turnips and cook until vegetables are tender, about 5 minutes longer.

3. If sauce is thin, combine 1 tablespoon flour with 2 tablespoons water in small bowl. Add to sauce and simmer, stirring occasionally, until slightly thickened, 1 to 2 minutes. Remove and discard bay leaf. Pour sauce over lamb and vegetables, sprinkle with parsley, and serve.

310   LAMB STEW RATATOUILLE

Prep: 30 minutes   Cook: 1 hour 14 minutes to 1 hour 16 minutes
Serves: 4 to 6

This is an excellent way to use leftover lamb.

6 tablespoons olive oil
1 small to medium eggplant (about ¾ pound), cut into 1-inch cubes
1 large green bell pepper, cut into 1-inch pieces
1 large onion, chopped
1 medium zucchini, cut into ½-inch-thick slices
1 (14½-ounce) can Italian peeled tomatoes, chopped, juices reserved
1 cup Lamb Stock (page 265) or reduced-sodium canned beef broth

1 pound cooked lamb, cut into 1-inch cubes
3 garlic cloves, minced
1 tablespoon tomato paste
1 teaspoon dried thyme leaves
1 teaspoon dried basil
1 bay leaf
½ teaspoon salt
¼ teaspoon black pepper
2 tablespoons minced fresh parsley

1. In a large nonstick skillet, heat 2 tablespoons oil over medium-high heat. Add eggplant and cook, stirring occasionally, until golden, about 5 minutes. Transfer to a 2-quart nonreactive flameproof casserole.

2. Heat 2 tablespoons oil in same skillet. Add green pepper and onion and cook, stirring occasionally, until vegetables are softened, 6 to 8 minutes. Transfer to casserole.

3. Heat remaining 2 tablespoons oil in same skillet. Add zucchini and cook, stirring occasionally, until softened, about 3 minutes. Transfer to casserole.

4. Preheat oven to 350°F. Add tomatoes with their juices, lamb stock, cooked lamb, garlic, tomato paste, thyme, basil, bay leaf, salt, and black pepper to casserole and stir to combine. Cover and bake 1 hour. Remove and discard bay leaf. Sprinkle with parsley.

311   LAMB STEW WITH ARTICHOKES, SOUR CREAM, AND DILL

Prep: 10 minutes   Cook: 2 hours 11 minutes to 2 hours 17 minutes
Serves: 6

Serve this stew with hot buttered egg noodles or rice.

3 tablespoons vegetable oil
3 pounds boneless lamb
    shoulder, cut into 2-inch
    pieces
1 medium onion, chopped
½ pound mushrooms, sliced
3 garlic cloves, minced
2 tablespoons flour
3 cups Lamb Stock (page 265)
    or reduced-sodium
    canned beef broth

¼ cup minced fresh dill
1 teaspoon salt
½ teaspoon pepper
1 (10-ounce) package frozen
    artichoke hearts, thawed
½ cup sour cream

1. In a large flameproof casserole, heat oil over medium-high heat. Add lamb in 3 batches and cook, stirring frequently, until browned on all sides, 7 to 8 minutes per batch. Transfer lamb to a platter.

2. Add onion to pan. Reduce heat to medium and cook, stirring occasionally, until softened, 5 minutes. Add mushrooms and garlic and cook, stirring occasionally, until mushrooms are tender, 5 minutes longer. Reduce heat to medium-low. Add flour and cook, stirring constantly, without allowing to color, 2 to 3 minutes. Add lamb stock, 2 tablespoons dill, salt, and pepper.

3. Return lamb to sauce pot. Bring to a boil. Reduce heat to low and simmer, stirring occasionally, until lamb is tender, about 1½ hours.

4. Add artichoke hearts and simmer until tender, 8 to 10 minutes. Stir in sour cream and remaining 2 tablespoons dill just before serving.

Chapter 13

Fish Stews

There are few dishes as exciting and gratifying as a great seafood stew. It's a full meal, full of lightly cooked fish bathed in a wonderful broth. In this chapter, stews run the gamut to fit any menu or budget, from elegant to homey, from pricey to very inexpensive.

For elegant entertaining, try the French Fish Stew with Aioli, a traditional French soup lightly thickened with garlic mayonnaise. For relaxed entertaining and enough to feed a large crowd, try the Louisiana Oyster and Sausage Stew. If your family enjoys a variety of seafood, long-simmered Italian-Style Stewed Squid with Tomatoes and Swiss Chard might be just the thing for a delicious and nutritious change of pace. Here the squid is slowly cooked until it becomes very tender and almost melts into the dish.

When purchasing your fish, try to get the freshest available. Go to a reliable fish store and take a look around before buying. If they don't have the particular fish you are after, talk to the fishmonger. He or she should be able to recommend a similar fish for your recipe. Make sure fillets and steaks look shiny and clear as opposed to dull and opaque. Ask for a sniff to make sure there is no fishy smell. If you are purchasing shellfish, see that it's alive and has been kept very cold, preferably on ice. If the fish is frozen, defrost it slowly in the refrigerator. Chances are, if it has been handled properly, frozen fish will taste almost as wonderful as fresh.

312 LOBSTER AND ROASTED PEPPER STEW WITH GARLIC TOASTS

Prep: 45 minutes
Cook: 1 hour 18 minutes to 1 hour 20 minutes   Serves: 6

Roasted peppers and lobster make a great combination of colors and flavors.

¼ cup olive oil
3 garlic cloves, quartered
1 (35-ounce) can peeled plum tomatoes, chopped, juices reserved
1 (28-ounce) can crushed tomatoes in thick puree
1 cup Quick Fish Stock (page 265) or canned clam juice
¼ teaspoon crushed hot red pepper

2 red or yellow bell peppers
2 live whole lobsters (1¼ pounds each)
1 pound small red potatoes, cut in half
¼ cup chopped parsley
Garlic Toasts (recipe follows)

1. In a large nonreactive flameproof casserole, heat oil over medium heat. Add garlic and cook, stirring constantly, until golden and fragrant, 1 to 2 minutes. Stir in chopped and crushed tomatoes with their liquid, fish stock, and hot red pepper. Bring to a boil, reduce heat to low, and simmer 30 minutes.

2. Meanwhile, preheat broiler. Place bell peppers on a large baking sheet and broil, turning occasionally, 2 to 3 inches from heat, until charred, about 15 minutes. Place peppers in paper bag and let cool slightly before removing peel and seeds. Chop peppers.

3. Add peppers to pan along with lobsters and potatoes. Cover and simmer, stirring occasionally, until potatoes are softened, 45 minutes. Transfer lobsters to a large bowl and remove and chop all meat, reserving juices and discarding shells.

4. Return lobster meat and juices to pot and simmer to heat through, 2 to 3 minutes. Stir in parsley and serve sprinkled with Garlic Toasts.

313 GARLIC TOASTS

Prep: 5 minutes   Cook: 6 minutes   Serves: 6

3 tablespoons extra-virgin olive oil

12 thin slices of French bread
3 garlic cloves, cut in half

In a large skillet, heat olive oil over high heat. Add half of the bread slices and cook until golden brown on both sides, about 3 minutes. Immediately rub both sides of toasted bread with half of the garlic and place on paper towels to drain. Repeat with remaining bread slices and garlic. Serve hot.

314   SPICY TOMATO AND MONKFISH STEW WITH ORANGE GREMOLATA

Prep: 20 minutes   Cook: 1 hour 46 minutes   Serves: 6

Gremolata is usually made with lemon. The orange zest here is a nice variation.

2 tablespoons butter
2 tablespoons extra-virgin olive oil
1 large onion, chopped
1 red bell pepper, chopped
3 garlic cloves, minced
½ teaspoon crushed hot red pepper
2 bay leaves
¼ teaspoon sugar
1 teaspoon salt
1 cup dry white wine

2 (28-ounce) cans diced peeled tomatoes in juice
2 cups Quick Fish Stock (page 265) or reserved canned clam juice
2 pounds monkfish or other firm white fish fillets (striped bass, red snapper, rock cod), cut into 1-inch pieces
Orange Gremolata (recipe follows)

1. In a large nonreactive flameproof casserole, melt butter in oil over medium-high heat. Add onion and bell pepper and cook, stirring frequently about 5 minutes. Add garlic, hot red pepper, bay leaves, sugar, and salt and cook, stirring constantly, until garlic is fragrant, 1 minute. Stir in wine and simmer 5 minutes.

2. Add tomatoes with their juices and fish stock and bring to a boil. Reduce heat to medium-low and simmer 1½ hours.

3. Stir in fish and simmer until fish flakes easily when tested with a fork, about 5 minutes. Remove and discard bay leaves. Ladle stew into bowls and serve sprinkled with Orange Gremolata.

ORANGE GREMOLATA

Makes: ⅓ cup

1 teaspoon grated orange zest
⅓ cup chopped parsley

1 large garlic clove, coarsely chopped

In a food processor or blender, combine orange zest, parsley, and garlic and process until well blended.

315   SHRIMP ÉTOUFFÉE
Prep: 20 minutes   Cook: 30 minutes   Serves: 4

Étouffée means smothered. Étouffées are usually made with either shrimp or crawfish.

¼ cup vegetable oil
¼ cup flour
1 large onion, chopped
1 medium green bell pepper, chopped
2 medium celery ribs, chopped
2 garlic cloves, minced
½ teaspoon salt

½ teaspoon black pepper
¼ teaspoon cayenne
2 cups Quick Fish Stock (page 265) or canned clam juice
1 pound medium shrimp, shelled and deveined
4 scallions (green part only), thinly sliced
Savory Rice (page 144)

1. In a large, heavy saucepan, heat oil over high heat. Gradually stir in flour with a whisk or wooden spoon. Cook, stirring constantly, until mixture is medium brown in color, about 5 minutes.

2. Remove saucepan from heat and add onion, green pepper, celery, and garlic. Stir 2 minutes and return saucepan to heat. Stir in salt, black pepper, cayenne, and fish stock and bring to a boil. Reduce heat to medium-low and simmer 20 minutes.

3. Stir in shrimp and scallions and simmer until shrimp turn pink, about 3 minutes. Serve with Savory Rice.

316   SIMPLE MUSSEL STEW
Prep: 10 minutes   Cook: 6 minutes   Serves: 4

2 dozen mussels, cleaned and debearded
1½ cups milk
½ cup heavy cream
1 bay leaf
2 shallots, quartered

½ teaspoon salt
¼ teaspoon pepper
2 to 3 drops Tabasco sauce
2 tablespoons chopped parsley
2 tablespoons butter

1. Place mussels in a large soup pot over high heat. Cover and steam until mussels open, removing them as they open, about 6 minutes. Discard any mussels that do not open. Remove mussels from shells and strain liquid from pot, reserving both mussels and liquid.

2. In a large flameproof casserole, combine milk, cream, bay leaf, shallots, and mussel liquid. Bring to a boil.

3. Turn off the heat and stir in mussels, salt, pepper, Tabasco sauce, parsley, and butter. Remove and discard bay leaf and serve.

317   OYSTER STEW
Prep: 10 minutes   Cook: none   Stand: 10 minutes   Serves: 4

This is a thin stew that makes a rich, elegant first course.

1½ cups milk
½ cup heavy cream
1 bay leaf
2 shallots, quartered
½ teaspoon dried thyme leaves
2 dozen medium oysters,
    shucked, liquor reserved

½ teaspoon salt
¼ teaspoon pepper
2 to 3 drops Tabasco sauce
2 tablespoons butter

1. In a large soup pot, combine milk, cream, bay leaf, shallots, thyme, and oyster liquor. Bring to a boil.

2. Turn off the heat and add oysters, salt, pepper, Tabasco sauce, and butter. Cover and let stand 10 minutes, or until oysters curl. Remove and discard bay leaf. Stir before serving.

318   LOUISIANA OYSTER AND SAUSAGE STEW
Prep: 15 minutes   Cook: 28 minutes   Stand: 5 minutes   Serves: 6

Oysters and smoked sausages are usually found together in jambalaya, but they combine to make a great stew as well.

1 tablespoon vegetable oil
½ pound smoked sausage
    (andouille or kielbasa)
2 tablespoons butter
1 large onion, chopped
1 greed bell pepper, chopped
4 scallions, chopped
3 garlic cloves, minced
1 teaspoon salt
½ teaspoon black pepper

¼ teaspoon cayenne
½ teaspoon chili powder
½ teaspoon dried thyme leaves
1 cup long-grain white rice
4 cups Chicken Stock (page
    262) or reduced-sodium
    canned broth
12 small oysters, shucked,
    liquor reserved

1. In a large flameproof casserole, heat oil over medium-high heat. Add sausage and cook, turning occasionally, until browned on all sides, about 10 minutes. Remove sausage to a cutting board and cut into ½-inch-thick slices.

2. Add butter to casserole and melt over medium heat. Add onion, green pepper, scallions, and garlic and cook, stirring frequently, until vegetables are softened, 5 minutes. Add salt, black pepper, cayenne, chili powder, thyme, sausage, and rice and cook, stirring constantly, 1 minute. Add chicken stock and bring to a boil. Reduce heat to low, cover, and simmer until rice is almost tender, about 12 minutes.

3. Stir in oysters with their liquor, cover, and remove from heat. Let stand until oysters curl, about 5 minutes, before serving.

319 ITALIAN-STYLE STEWED SQUID WITH TOMATOES AND SWISS CHARD

Prep: 25 minutes   Cook: 1 hour 23 minutes   Serves: 4

3 tablespoons extra-virgin
olive oil
3 large garlic cloves, minced
2 shallots, minced
3 tablespoons chopped
parsley
1 cup dry white wine
2 cups Quick Fish Stock (page
265) or canned clam juice
¾ teaspoon salt
1 pound squid, cleaned and
cut into ½-inch rings

2 plum tomatoes, peeled,
seeded, and chopped
1 cup chopped Swiss chard
leaves
½ teaspoon pepper
1 (10-ounce) package frozen
artichoke hearts
Parmesan Toasts (recipe
follows)

1. In a large nonreactive flameproof casserole, heat olive oil over medium heat. Add garlic, shallots, and 2 tablespoons parsley and cook, stirring constantly, until shallots are softened, 3 minutes. Stir in wine, stock, salt, and squid and bring to a boil.

2. Reduce heat to low and simmer until squid are tender, about 40 minutes. Stir in tomatoes, Swiss chard, and pepper and simmer, stirring occasionally, 20 minutes. Stir in artichokes and simmer until tender, 20 minutes longer. Stir in remaining 1 tablespoon parsley and serve with Parmesan Toasts.

320 PARMESAN TOASTS

Prep: 5 minutes   Cook: 3 to 4 minutes   Serves: 4

8 (½-inch-thick) slices of
sourdough baguette
2 garlic cloves, peeled and cut
in half

3 tablespoons grated
Parmesan cheese
Pinch of cayenne

1. Preheat broiler. Place bread slices on baking sheet and broil 2 minutes. Turn bread slices over and rub each slice with garlic. In a small bowl, combine Parmesan cheese and cayenne; sprinkle over bread.

2. Broil until lightly toasted, 1 to 2 minutes longer.

321   FRENCH FISH STEW WITH AIOLI
Prep: 5 minutes   Cook: 9 minutes   Serves: 6

Many times, this type of fish stew, called *bourride*, is served as two courses; first the soup, then the fish. Here, we've combined the two.

12 thin slices of French bread
 6 cups Quick Fish Stock (page
      265) or 4 cups canned
      clam juice diluted with
      2 cups water
 ½ teaspoon dried thyme leaves
 2 bay leaves

 1 pound white fish fillets (cod,
      flounder, halibut,
      haddock, or striped bass),
      cut into 2-inch pieces
    Aioli (recipe follows)
 2 tablespoons chopped
      parsley

1. Preheat broiler. Place bread slices on baking sheet and broil 1 to 2 inches from heat until lightly toasted on both sides, about 2 minutes on each side.

2. In a large soup pot, combine fish stock, thyme, and bay leaves and bring to a boil. Reduce heat to low, add fish, and simmer until fish flakes easily when tested with a fork, about 3 minutes.

3. Place bread on large platter and with slotted spoon, transfer fish to bread slices. Cover and keep warm.

4. Whisk 1 cup stock into half of the Aioli and transfer to soup pot. (Reserve remaining Aioli for serving.) Cook stock over low heat, stirring constantly, until slightly thickened, about 2 minutes. Remove from heat. Remove and discard bay leaves.

5. Place 2 fish-covered toast slices in each soup bowl. Ladle thickened stock over fish and sprinkle with parsley. Serve with remaining Aioli.

322   AIOLI
Prep: 15 minutes   Cook: none   Serves: 6

This is made just like a fresh mayonnaise. Be sure to refrigerate it no longer than 2 days.

 3 garlic cloves, peeled
 3 egg yolks
 ¼ teaspoon salt

 1 cup olive oil
 2 tablespoons lemon juice

Crush garlic through a garlic press or chop very finely. Transfer garlic to a food processor or blender and add egg yolks and salt. With machine on, slowly drizzle in oil until well blended and thick. Transfer sauce to a small bowl and whisk in lemon juice.

323   KOREAN-STYLE FISH AND BEAN CURD STEW

Prep: 20 minutes   Stand: 15 minutes   Cook: 10 minutes   Serves: 4

Traditionally, this dish contains beef. Here, the meat has been omitted and is replaced with fish and shellfish. Miso, a flavoring of Japanese origin, adds a pungent winelike flavor to this stew. Look for miso in your local health food store.

6 dried shiitake mushrooms
2 teaspoons Asian sesame oil
½ red bell pepper, cut into ½-inch pieces
1 medium zucchini, thinly sliced
3 garlic cloves, minced
3 tablespoons miso (preferably red)
2 cups Quick Fish Stock (page 265) or canned clam juice

¼ teaspoon cayenne
2 teaspoons sugar
½ pound firm bean curd, cut into ½-inch pieces
12 mussels, cleaned and debearded
½ pound firm white fish (cod, halibut, snapper), cut into 1-inch pieces
3 scallions, thinly sliced

1. In a medium heatproof bowl, place mushrooms and cover with 1 cup boiling water. Let stand 15 minutes. Remove and discard stems. Thinly slice mushrooms and reserve soaking liquid.

2. In a large saucepan, heat sesame oil over medium heat. Add bell pepper, zucchini, mushrooms, and garlic and cook, stirring frequently, until vegetables are softened, about 5 minutes.

3. Stir several tablespoons mushroom soaking liquid into miso and pour into pot along with fish stock and remaining soaking liquid. Add cayenne, sugar, bean curd, mussels, fish, and scallions and simmer until mussels open and fish flakes easily when tested with a fork, about 5 minutes. Discard any mussels that have not opened before serving.

324   RED WINE FISH STEW

Prep: 30 minutes   Cook: 41 minutes   Serves: 4

A classic French fish stew, this combines freshwater fish and red wine.

5 tablespoons butter
1 small onion, chopped
1 medium carrot, peeled and
    chopped
1 medium celery rib, chopped
½ cup chopped ham
1 garlic clove, minced
1 bay leaf
½ teaspoon dried thyme leaves
⅛ teaspoon ground allspice
4 stems of fresh parsley
2 cups dry red wine
    (preferably Burgundy or
    Côtes de Rhône)
2 cups Quick Fish Stock (page
    265) or canned clam juice

1 tablespoon flour
½ pound fresh mushrooms,
    trimmed and sliced
1 cup frozen baby onions,
    thawed
1 pound freshwater fish (bass,
    perch, carp, eel, trout, or
    catfish), cut into ¾-inch
    pieces
½ teaspoon salt
½ teaspoon pepper
2 tablespoons chopped
    parsley

1. In a large nonreactive flameproof casserole, melt 3 tablespoons butter over medium heat. Add onion, carrot, celery, ham, and garlic and cook, stirring frequently, until browned, about 8 minutes. Stir in bay leaf, thyme, allspice, parsley stems, wine, and fish stock. Bring to a boil, reduce heat to medium-low, and simmer 15 minutes. Strain through a fine sieve, pressing on the solids, and return liquid to pot. Discard solids.

2. In a small bowl, combine flour and 1 tablespoon butter and work with fingers or wooden spoon until well blended. Pinch off small pieces of butter mixture and whisk into stock, bringing stock to a boil each time mixture is added. Keep adding butter mixture, and heating until all of butter mixture is used and stew is slightly thickened, about 5 minutes.

3. In a large skillet, melt remaining 1 tablespoon butter over medium heat. Add mushrooms and onions and cook until browned and tender, about 10 minutes. Stir into stock, along with fish. Simmer until fish flakes easily when tested with a fork, about 3 minutes. Stir in salt and pepper and serve sprinkled with parsley.

325   ZUPPA DI PESCE WITH BASIL AND GARLIC BRUSCHETTA

Prep: 30 minutes   Cook: 38 minutes   Serves: 6

There are countless versions of zuppa di pesce. We have chosen one that uses fresh fennel—a wonderful complement to the seafood. If fresh fennel is not available, substitute 2 chopped celery ribs and 1 teaspoon crushed fennel seed instead.

¼ cup olive oil
1 cup minced fennel bulb
1 medium leek (white part only), well rinsed and sliced
1 medium onion, chopped
4 garlic cloves, minced
1 teaspoon dried thyme leaves
1 teaspoon dried basil
½ teaspoon dried oregano
1 cup dry white wine
1 (28-ounce) can crushed tomatoes, juices reserved
8 cups Quick Fish Stock (page 265) or reduced-sodium canned chicken broth
1 teaspoon salt

½ teaspoon pepper
½ pound squid, cleaned and cut into ½-inch rings
1 pound mussels, scrubbed and debearded
1 (¾-pound) lobster tail, cut into 1-inch-thick slices
1 pound large shrimp, shelled and deveined
2 pounds white fish fillets, such as red snapper or bass, cut into 2-inch pieces
3 tablespoons minced fresh parsley
   Basil and Garlic Bruschetta (recipe follows)

1. In a large nonreactive soup pot, heat olive oil over medium heat. Add fennel, leek, onion, garlic, thyme, basil, and oregano and cook, stirring occasionally, until leek and onion are golden, 5 minutes. Stir in wine, tomatoes, fish stock, salt, and pepper. Bring to a boil. Add squid. Reduce heat to low, cover, and simmer until squid is tender, about 20 minutes.

2. Return soup to a boil over medium-high heat. Add mussels, lobster, and shrimp, cover, and cook 5 minutes. Add fish fillets, cover, and cook until mussels have opened and fish just flakes easily when tested with a fork, about 8 minutes longer. Discard any mussels that have not opened. Sprinkle with parsley and serve with Basil and Garlic Bruschetta.

326   BASIL AND GARLIC BRUSCHETTA
Prep: 10 minutes   Cook: 2 to 4 minutes   Serves: 6

These toasts are delicious on their own or can be topped with fresh tomatoes tossed with a little olive oil and garlic.

12 slices of Italian bread
2 large garlic cloves, crushed
¼ cup extra-virgin olive oil

¼ cup chopped fresh basil
1 teaspoon salt
½ teaspoon pepper

1. Preheat broiler. Arrange bread on a baking sheet. Broil 4 inches from heat until golden, 1 to 2 minutes.

2. In a small bowl, combine garlic, olive oil, basil, salt, and pepper. Brush onto untoasted side of bread and broil until golden brown, 1 to 2 minutes.

327   GREEK SHELLFISH STEW
Prep: 20 minutes   Cook: 19 minutes   Serves: 6

You can use any shellfish or firm white fish fillets in this dish.

¼ cup extra-virgin olive oil
1 large onion, chopped
1 celery rib, chopped
1 medium carrot, peeled and
     chopped
2 garlic cloves, minced
1 teaspoon dried thyme leaves
½ teaspoon dried oregano
1 (28-ounce) can crushed
     tomatoes in thick puree
½ cup Quick Fish Stock (page
     265) or canned clam juice

3 tablespoons red wine
     vinegar
½ teaspoon salt
¼ teaspoon crushed hot red
     pepper
2 dozen mussels, cleaned and
     debearded
1 pound medium shrimp,
     shelled and deveined
2 tablespoons chopped
     parsley

1. In a large nonreactive flameproof casserole, heat oil over medium-high heat. Add onion, celery, and carrot and cook, stirring occasionally, until vegetables are softened, about 8 minutes. Stir in garlic, thyme, and oregano and cook, stirring constantly, 1 minute. Add tomatoes, fish stock, vinegar, salt, and hot red pepper. Bring to a boil, reduce heat to low, and simmer 5 minutes.

2. Stir in mussels, shrimp, and parsley and simmer until shrimp turn pink and mussels open, about 5 minutes longer. Discard any mussels that have not opened before serving.

328   CIOPPINO

Prep: 45 minutes   Cook: 1 hour 47 minutes to 1 hour 49 minutes
Serves: 6

San Francisco claims to be the birthplace of this famous American seafood stew.

2 tablespoons butter
2 tablespoons extra-virgin
  olive oil
1 large onion, chopped
1 green bell pepper, chopped
3 garlic cloves, minced
¼ teaspoon crushed hot red
  pepper
½ teaspoon dried thyme leaves
½ teaspoon dried oregano
2 bay leaves
1 teaspoon salt
¼ teaspoon sugar
1 cup dry white wine
2 (28-ounce) cans diced peeled
  tomatoes, juices reserved

2 cups Quick Fish Stock (page
  265) or canned clam juice
1 pound firm white fish fillets
  (striped bass, red
  snapper, rock cod), cut
  into 1-inch pieces
12 littleneck or Manila clams in
  the shell, well rinsed
1 cooked Dungeness crab or
  lobster, cracked
1 pound large shrimp, shelled
  and deveined
12 mussels, cleaned and
  debearded
½ cup chopped parsley

1. In a large nonreactive flameproof casserole, melt butter in oil over medium-high heat. Add onion and green pepper and cook, stirring frequently, until softened, 3 to 5 minutes. Add garlic, hot red pepper, thyme, oregano, bay leaves, salt, and sugar. Cook, stirring constantly, 1 minute. Stir in wine and simmer 5 minutes.

2. Add tomatoes and fish stock and bring to a boil. Reduce heat to medium-low and simmer to reduce slightly, 1½ hours.

3. Stir in fish and clams and simmer 3 minutes. Gently stir in crab, shrimp, mussels, and parsley and cook until mussels open, about 5 minutes longer. Before serving, discard any mussels and clams that don't open.

329 TUSCAN SEAFOOD STEW

Prep: 25 minutes   Cook: 26 minutes   Serves: 4

Traditionally, Tuscans make this stew, which they call *"cacciucco,"* with the same number of fish as there are *c*'s in the name.

3 tablespoons extra-virgin olive oil
1 large red onion, chopped
4 garlic cloves, chopped
¼ teaspoon crushed hot red pepper
½ cup red wine
½ teaspoon sugar
1 (28-ounce) can crushed tomatoes in thick puree
2 cups Quick Fish Stock (page 265) or 1 cup clam juice diluted with 1 cup water
12 littleneck or Manila clams in the shell, well rinsed

½ pound firm-fleshed white fish (monkfish, snapper, halibut)
½ pound squid, cleaned and cut into ½-inch rings
¼ pound large shrimp, shelled and deveined
12 mussels, scrubbed and debearded
½ teaspoon salt
½ teaspoon pepper
¼ cup chopped fresh basil
Anchovy Toasts (recipe follows)

1. In a large nonreactive flameproof casserole, heat olive oil over medium heat. Add onion and cook, stirring occasionally, until softened, about 5 minutes. Add garlic and hot red pepper and cook, stirring constantly, 1 minute. Stir in wine and simmer 2 minutes longer.

2. Add sugar, tomatoes, and fish stock and bring to a boil. Reduce heat to medium and cook 10 minutes. Stir in clams and white fish and cook 3 minutes. Stir in squid, shrimp, mussels, salt, and pepper and cook until shrimp turn pink and mussels open, about 5 minutes longer. Discard any clams and mussels that have not opened. Serve sprinkled with basil and topped with Anchovy Toasts.

330 ANCHOVY TOASTS

Prep: 5 minutes   Cook: 2 minutes   Serves: 4

8 thin slices of French bread
2 garlic cloves, cut in half
2 tablespoons chopped parsley

1 anchovy fillet, minced
2 tablespoons extra-virgin olive oil

1. Rub bread with garlic. Chop parsley and anchovy together until well combined and spread onto one side of bread slices.

2. Heat oil in large skillet over medium heat and add bread slices, parsley side up. Cook until bread is browned and golden on bottom, about 2 minutes. Remove to paper towels to drain. Serve hot.

331   INDONESIAN FISH CURRY
Prep: 20 minutes   Cook: 8 minutes   Serves: 4

This curry is very rich but only slightly spicy. If you like lots of heat, increase the cayenne.

2 tablespoons vegetable oil
4 shallots, thinly sliced
½ red bell pepper, cut into
    ½-inch dice
2 garlic cloves, minced
1 tablespoon grated fresh
    ginger
1½ teaspoons ground coriander
1 teaspoon ground cumin
¼ teaspoon cayenne
½ teaspoon ground turmeric
½ teaspoon salt
2 (13½-ounce) cans
    unsweetened coconut
    milk

1 cup Quick Fish Stock (page
    265) or reduced-sodium
    canned chicken broth
1 pound firm white fish (cod,
    halibut, swordfish), cut
    into ¾-inch pieces
1 cup fresh or thawed frozen
    peas
2 tablespoons lime juice
3 tablespoons chopped
    cilantro
8 basil leaves, shredded

1. In a large flameproof casserole, heat oil over medium-high heat. Add shallots and red pepper and cook until softened, stirring frequently, 5 minutes.

2. Add garlic, ginger, spices, and salt and cook, stirring constantly, 1 minute. Stir in coconut milk, fish stock, fish, and peas and bring to a boil. Reduce heat to medium-low and cook until fish flakes easily when tested with a fork, 2 minutes. Stir in lime juice just before serving and serve topped with cilantro and basil.

Chapter 14

Mainly Meatless Stews

Meatless meals are not just for vegetarians any-more. As we all try to cut down on fat, more vegetables, beans, and grains naturally become a larger part of our diet. And stews are a great way to mix and match these healthful ingredients.

Some of the recipes in this chapter—Brown Rice, Sweet Potato, and Lentil Stew or Wheat Berry, White Bean, and Mushroom Stew—are strictly vegetarian. Others—Black-Eyed Peas and Greens or Creole Red Beans and Rice—contain small amounts of meat used as a flavoring. There are elegant recipes like Italian Rice and Peas and Moroccan Vegetable Ragout, and earthy recipes like Roasted Corn, Pepper, and White Bean Stew and Two-Mushroom and Potato Stew.

Many of these stews are made with vegetable stock or water. However, where we felt the flavor called for it, we included chicken stock. Since you can now buy defatted, reduced-sodium chicken broth, we feel it is a perfectly appro-priate ingredient in mostly meatless meals. However, if you are a strict vegetarian, you can, of course, substitute vegetable broth.

While vegetables are quick-cooking, as are vegeta-ble stews, those that contain beans and grains take a bit more time. A number of the following stews use canned beans as a convenience. Where dried beans are called for, the first step requires soaking them overnight. If you forget, remember the quick-soaking beans method: Place the beans in a large pot with enough cold water to cover by at least 2 inches. Bring to a boil over medium heat. Boil for 2 minutes. Remove from the heat, cover, and let stand for 1 to 2 hours; then proceed with your recipe.

332 BROWN RICE, SWEET POTATO, AND LENTIL STEW

Prep: 20 minutes   Cook: 1 hour 36 minutes   Serves: 6

1 tablespoon vegetable oil
1 large onion, chopped
2 garlic cloves, minced
¼ teaspoon ground cloves
¼ teaspoon ground coriander
¼ teaspoon cinnamon
⅛ teaspoon crushed hot red pepper
1 cup brown rice
½ cup lentils, rinsed and picked over

2 plum tomatoes, peeled, seeded, and chopped
½ teaspoon salt
1 large sweet potato, peeled and cut into ½-inch dice
1 tablespoon chopped fresh mint
2 tablespoons chopped cilantro

1. In a large flameproof casserole, heat oil over medium-high heat. Add onion and cook, stirring frequently, until golden, about 5 minutes. Stir in garlic, spices, and red pepper and stir 1 minute. Add rice, lentils, tomatoes, salt, and 5 cups water. Bring to a boil. Reduce heat to medium-low, cover, and simmer 1 hour.

2. Stir in sweet potato and simmer until softened, about 30 minutes longer. Stir in mint and cilantro just before serving.

333 BULGUR STEW WITH CARAMELIZED APPLES AND ONIONS

Prep: 15 minutes   Cook: 1 hour 6 minutes to 1 hour 8 minutes Serves: 6

3 tablespoons butter
2 large onions, thinly sliced
1 Golden Delicious apple, cored, peeled, and chopped
2 garlic cloves, minced
¼ teaspoon cinnamon
⅛ teaspoon ground cardamom

⅛ teaspoon saffron powder
1½ teaspoons sugar
¾ teaspoon salt
½ teaspoon pepper
1 cup bulgur
6 cups Vegetable Stock (page 266) or canned broth

1. In a large skillet, heat 2 tablespoons butter over medium heat. Add onions and cook, stirring occasionally, until onions are softened and caramelized, about 40 minutes. Stir in apple and cook until softened, 20 minutes longer.

2. Meanwhile, in a large flameproof casserole, heat remaining 1 tablespoon butter over medium heat. Add garlic and spices and stir 1 minute. Stir in sugar, salt, pepper, bulgur, and vegetable stock and bring to a boil. Reduce heat to low, cover, and simmer until bulgur is tender, about 15 minutes. Stir in onions and apples and heat thoroughly, stirring occasionally, 6 to 8 minutes.

334   LENTIL AND BUTTERNUT SQUASH STEW

Prep: 15 minutes   Cook: 42 to 43 minutes   Serves: 4 to 6

This simple soup can be made with any variety of other winter squash, such as acorn, pumpkin, calabaza, or delicata.

2 tablespoons olive oil
1 large onion, chopped
2 garlic cloves, minced
1 teaspoon ground cumin
3 (2 x 1-inch) pieces of orange zest
1 (14½-ounce) can diced peeled tomatoes, juices reserved

1 cup dried lentils, rinsed and picked over
½ pound butternut or acorn squash, peeled and cut into ½-inch chunks (about 1½ cups)
¾ teaspoon salt
½ teaspoon pepper

1. In a large nonreactive flameproof casserole, heat oil over medium-high heat. Add onion and cook, stirring occasionally, until softened, 2 to 3 minutes. Stir in garlic, cumin, and orange zest. Add tomatoes with their juices, lentils, and 3 cups water. Cover and bring to a boil. Reduce heat to medium-low and simmer 25 minutes.

2. Add squash, salt, and pepper. Simmer until squash is softened, about 15 minutes, and serve.

335   ITALIAN RICE AND PEAS

Prep: 10 minutes   Cook: 32 to 38 minutes   Serves: 4

Risi e bisi simply means rice and peas. Traditionally, it's a very soupy risotto.

4 to 5 cups Chicken Stock (page 262) or 1 (14¾-ounce) can reduced-sodium broth diluted with 2 cups water
2 tablespoons butter
2 tablespoons olive oil
1 small onion, finely chopped

4 anchovy fillets, minced
1 cup Arborio rice
½ cup dry white wine
1½ cups fresh or thawed frozen tiny peas
½ cup grated Parmesan cheese
½ teaspoon pepper

1. In a large saucepan, bring chicken stock just to a boil. Meanwhile, in a large nonreactive soup pot, melt butter in oil over medium heat. Add onion and cook, stirring occasionally, until softened, 2 to 3 minutes. Add anchovies and stir 1 minute longer. Add rice and cook, stirring constantly, until golden, 2 minutes.

2. Stir in wine and cook 5 minutes. Stir in 1 cup chicken stock and simmer, uncovered, stirring frequently, until liquid is absorbed, about 5 minutes. Keep adding stock, ½ cup at a time, and stir frequently until almost all of liquid is absorbed and rice is tender but chewy, 15 to 20 minutes. Add peas, Parmesan cheese, and pepper and stir 2 minutes longer.

336   CHICKPEA, CAULIFLOWER, AND SWISS CHARD TAGINE

Prep: 15 minutes   Cook: 40 minutes   Stand: 5 minutes   Serves: 4

For optimum flavor, make sure you use fresh paprika for this dish.

3 tablespoons vegetable oil
1 large onion, chopped
2 garlic cloves, minced
4 cups (1-inch pieces) cut-up cauliflower florets
5 cups finely chopped Swiss chard (stalks and leaves)
1 (15-ounce) can chickpeas, rinsed and drained

1 tablespoon grated fresh ginger
½ cup chopped cilantro
2½ teaspoons ground cumin
2½ teaspoons sweet Hungarian paprika
1 teaspoon salt
½ teaspoon pepper
½ cup long-grain white rice

1. In a large saucepan, combine oil, onion, garlic, cauliflower, Swiss chard, chickpeas, ginger, ¼ cup cilantro, cumin, paprika, salt, pepper, and ¼ cup water. Bring to a boil. Reduce heat to low, cover tightly, and simmer 20 minutes.

2. Add rice and ¼ cup water. Cover tightly and simmer until rice is tender, about 20 minutes. Sprinkle with remaining cilantro and let stand 5 minutes before serving.

337   INDIAN SPICED CAULIFLOWER STEW

Prep: 20 minutes   Cook: 32 to 33 minutes   Serves: 4

2 tablespoons vegetable oil
1 small onion, finely chopped
6 thin slices fresh ginger
2 teaspoons ground cumin
2 teaspoons ground coriander
1 teaspoon sugar
½ teaspoon salt
   Pinch of cayenne
1 small head of cauliflower, cut into small florets (about 4 cups)

1 large sweet potato (about 1 pound), peeled and cut into ¾-inch dice
3 plum tomatoes, seeded and chopped
½ cup frozen peas

1. In a large flameproof casserole, heat oil over medium-high heat. Add onion and cook, stirring occasionally, until lightly browned, about 5 minutes.

2. Add all remaining ingredients except peas. Stir in 1 cup water and bring to a boil. Reduce heat to low, cover, and simmer, stirring occasionally, until vegetables are very tender, about 25 minutes. Stir in peas and simmer until tender, 2 to 3 minutes longer.

338 BLACK-EYED PEAS AND GREENS

Prep: 20 minutes   Stand: 12 hours   Cook: 1½ hours   Serves: 6

Black-eyed peas are also known as cowpeas. Remember to put the peas up to soak the night before.

2 cups dried black-eyed peas, rinsed and picked over
½ teaspoon salt
4 thick slices of bacon, cut into ½-inch pieces
1 large onion, chopped
2 medium celery ribs, sliced
1 large green bell pepper, cut into ½-inch chunks
2 garlic cloves, chopped

3 bay leaves
½ teaspoon dried thyme leaves
½ teaspoon dried basil
½ teaspoon dried marjoram
⅛ teaspoon cayenne
4 cups Chicken Stock (page 262) or reduced-sodium canned broth
2 cups chopped mustard greens

1. Place dried beans in a large bowl and add enough water to cover by at least 2 inches. Let stand at least 12 hours or overnight. Drain and rinse beans before using.

2. Place beans in a large flameproof casserole. Add enough water to cover by 2 inches. Bring to a boil, reduce heat to medium-low, and simmer 20 minutes. Add salt and continue cooking until beans are tender, about 10 minutes longer. Drain beans, reserving 1 cup liquid. Transfer beans to a medium bowl.

3. In same pot, cook bacon over medium-high heat, stirring occasionally, until crisp, about 5 minutes. Remove to paper towels to drain. Increase heat to high. Add onion, celery, and green pepper to pot. Cook, stirring constantly, until vegetables are softened, about 10 minutes. Stir in garlic, bay leaves, seasonings, chicken stock, reserved bean liquid, and beans and bring to a boil. Reduce heat to medium-low and simmer 30 minutes.

4. Stir in mustard greens and cook until wilted, 15 minutes longer. Remove and discard bay leaves before serving.

339 SAVOY CABBAGE AND RICE STEW WITH CHICKEN SAUSAGE

Prep: 25 minutes   Cook: 53 to 55 minutes   Serves: 4

1 tablespoon extra-virgin
    olive oil
½ pound chicken sausage or
    Italian pork sausage links
1 medium onion, chopped
1 medium carrot, peeled and
    chopped
2 large garlic cloves, finely
    chopped
1 medium head of Savoy
    cabbage, finely shredded
    (about 8 cups)

½ cup dry white wine
1 cup Arborio rice
6 cups Chicken Stock (page
    262) or reduced-sodium
    canned broth
¾ teaspoon salt
½ teaspoon pepper

1. In a large saucepan, heat oil over medium heat. Add sausage and cook, turning occasionally, until browned on all sides, about 10 minutes. Remove to a cutting board and cut into slices ½ inch thick. Add onion and carrot to saucepan and cook, stirring occasionally, until onion is softened, 3 to 4 minutes. Stir in garlic and cook 1 minute longer. Add cabbage and cook, stirring frequently, until cabbage is wilted, 4 to 5 minutes.

2. Stir in wine and simmer 5 minutes. Stir in rice and chicken stock and bring to a boil. Reduce heat to medium-low and cook until rice is tender, about 30 minutes. Stir in sausage, salt, and pepper and serve.

340 CURRIED KASHA AND MUSHROOM STEW

Prep: 20 minutes   Cook: 29 to 33 minutes   Serves: 4

Kasha and toasted buckwheat groats are one and the same—look for them in your local health food store.

½ cup toasted buckwheat
    groats
1 egg, lightly beaten
1 teaspoon salt
6 cups Chicken Stock (page
    262), Vegetable Stock
    (page 266), or reduced-
    sodium canned chicken
    broth
1 tablespoon vegetable oil

1 large onion, chopped
1 medium carrot, peeled and
    chopped
1 medium celery rib, chopped
½ pound fresh mushrooms,
    chopped
2 teaspoons curry powder
½ teaspoon ground cumin
    Pinch of cayenne

1. In a large saucepan, combine groats and egg. Stir over medium heat until dry, 3 to 5 minutes. Add ½ teaspoon salt and 1 cup chicken stock and bring to a boil. Reduce heat to low, cover, and simmer 5 minutes, or until liquid is absorbed.

2. Meanwhile, in a large saucepan, heat oil over high heat. Add onion, carrot, celery, and mushrooms and cook, stirring constantly, until vegetables are softened, about 10 minutes. Stir in curry powder, cumin, cayenne, and remaining ½ teaspoon salt and chicken stock and bring to a boil. Reduce heat to medium-low and simmer 5 minutes. Stir in groats mixture, heat thoroughly, stirring occasionally, 6 to 8 minutes, and serve.

341   CRANBERRY BEAN, PEPPER, AND SAUSAGE STEW

Prep: 25 minutes   Stand: 12 hours   Cook: 1 hour 25 minutes
Serves: 6

Remember to put the beans up to soak the night before.

1½ cups dried cranberry beans, rinsed and picked over
1 teaspoon salt
1 tablespoon olive oil
½ pound sweet Italian sausage links
1 large onion, chopped
3 large yellow or red bell peppers (or a combination), cut into 1-inch chunks

3 garlic cloves, chopped
1 (28-ounce) can Italian peeled tomatoes, chopped, juices reserved
2 cups Chicken Stock (page 262) or reduced-sodium canned broth
2 sprigs of fresh thyme or ½ teaspoon dried thyme leaves
½ teaspoon black pepper

1. Place dried beans in a large bowl and add enough water to cover by at least 2 inches. Let stand at least 12 hours or overnight. Drain and rinse beans before using.

2. In a large nonreactive flameproof casserole, place beans. Add enough water to cover by 2 inches. Bring to a boil, reduce heat to low, and simmer 20 minutes. Add ½ teaspoon salt and continue cooking until beans are tender, about 10 minutes. Drain and set beans aside.

3. In same pot, heat oil over medium-high heat. Add sausage and cook, turning occasionally, until browned on all sides, about 10 minutes. Remove sausage to a cutting board and cut into ½-inch-thick slices.

4. Add onion, bell peppers, and garlic to pot and cook, stirring frequently, until vegetables are softened, about 5 minutes. Add tomatoes with their juices, chicken stock, thyme, sausage, beans, and pepper. Simmer until stew has thickened, about 40 minutes, and serve.

342 PUMPKIN AND WHITE BEAN STEW
Prep: 20 minutes   Cook: 41 minutes   Serves: 4

If you wish, you can make this soup with butternut, delicata, or acorn squash instead of the pumpkin.

2 tablespoons olive oil
2 medium leeks (white and tender green), well rinsed and thinly sliced
2 medium celery ribs, finely chopped
3 garlic cloves, minced
1 tablespoon chopped fresh sage or 1 teaspoon dried
1 teaspoon chopped fresh thyme leaves or ¼ teaspoon dried thyme leaves

1 bay leaf
½ cup dry white wine
2 cups cut-up peeled pumpkin or winter squash
1 (15½-ounce) can Great Northern beans, rinsed and drained
4 cups Chicken Stock (page 262) or reduced-sodium canned broth
½ teaspoon salt
½ teaspoon pepper

1. In a large nonreactive saucepan, heat heat olive oil over medium-high heat. Add leeks and celery and cook, stirring occasionally, until vegetables are softened, about 8 minutes. Stir in garlic, sage, thyme, and bay leaf. Stir in wine and simmer until liquid is reduced by half, about 3 minutes.

2. Add pumpkin, beans, chicken stock, salt, and pepper and bring to a boil. Reduce heat to medium-low and cook until pumpkin is very soft, about 30 minutes. Remove and discard bay leaf before serving.

343 ROASTED CORN, PEPPER, AND WHITE BEAN STEW
Prep: 25 minutes   Cook: 46 to 48 minutes   Serves: 4

4 ears of corn
2 medium red bell peppers
1 tablespoon extra-virgin olive oil
1 large onion, chopped
3 garlic cloves, chopped
1 sprig of fresh rosemary or ½ teaspoon dried
2 sprigs of fresh thyme or ½ teaspoon dried thyme leaves

5 cups Vegetable Stock (page 266) or canned broth
1 teaspoon sugar
½ teaspoon salt
Pinch of cayenne
1 (10½-ounce) can Great Northern or white beans, drained
2 tablespoons chopped cilantro

1. Preheat broiler. Place corn and peppers on baking sheet and broil 2 to 3 inches from heat source, turning occasionally, until blackened on all sides, about 15 minutes. Remove corn and let cool. Place peppers in paper bag and let cool.

2. Scrape kernels from corn, reserving cobs. Peel, seed, and dice peppers.

3. In a soup pot, heat olive oil over medium-high heat. Add onion and cook, stirring occasionally, until golden, 5 minutes. Add garlic, rosemary, thyme, vegetable stock, sugar, salt, cayenne, and corn cobs. Bring to a boil. Reduce heat to medium-low, cover, and simmer 10 minutes. Remove cobs and stir in corn kernels, beans, and peppers. Cook until corn is tender, 10 minutes longer, Remove half of soup from pot, place in blender or food processor, and puree until smooth. Stir puree into soup in saucepan and heat thoroughly, 2 to 3 minutes. Serve garnished with cilantro.

---

344 GARBANZO BEAN STEW WITH GREENS AND SAUSAGES

Prep: 15 minutes   Cook: 35 minutes   Serves: 6

This easy soup makes a great lunch when served with crusty bread.

- 1 tablespoon olive oil
- ½ pound Italian pork or chicken sausage links
- 1 large onion, finely chopped
- 3 garlic cloves, minced
- ¼ teaspoon crushed hot red pepper
- 1 teaspoon crushed fennel seed
- 1 teaspoon chopped fresh rosemary
- ¼ cup chopped parsley
- 1 (14½-ounce) can chopped peeled tomatoes, juices reserved
- 4 cups Chicken Stock (page 262) or reduced-sodium canned broth
- 1 (15-ounce) can garbanzo beans, rinsed and drained
- 2 cups chopped fresh spinach or Swiss chard leaves
- ½ teaspoon black pepper
- ¼ teaspoon salt

1. In a large nonreactive flameproof casserole, heat oil over medium-high heat. Add sausage and cook, turning occasionally, until browned on all sides, about 10 minutes. Remove to a cutting board and cut into 1-inch slices.

2. Add onion to casserole and cook, stirring occasionally, until golden, about 8 minutes. Stir in garlic, red pepper, fennel, rosemary, and 2 tablespoons parsley. Add tomatoes with their juices, sausage, chicken stock, and beans. Reduce heat to medium-low and simmer 15 minutes.

3. Stir in spinach, pepper, salt, and remaining 2 tablespoons parsley, cook until spinach is wilted, 2 minutes longer, and serve.

345 MOROCCAN VEGETABLE RAGOUT
Prep: 25 minutes   Cook: 43 to 45 minutes   Serves: 6

Here's another stew that is long on ingredients but prepares itself once everything is in the pot. Serve over couscous.

¼ cup olive oil
1 Spanish onion, chopped
½ teaspoon ground ginger
½ teaspoon ground cumin
¼ teaspoon cinnamon
¼ teaspoon salt
Pinch of saffron or ground saffron
1 pound carrots (about 5 medium), peeled and cut into 1-inch pieces

1 pound small turnips, peeled and cut into 1-inch pieces
1 pound medium zucchini, cut into 1½-inch pieces
4 plum tomatoes, seeded and chopped
1 cup Vegetable Stock (page 266) or water
2 tablespoons chopped cilantro

In a large nonreactive flameproof casserole, heat oil over medium-high heat. Add onion and cook, stirring occasionally, until softened, 3 to 5 minutes. Add all remaining ingredients except cilantro and stir well. Bring to a boil. Reduce heat to low, cover, and simmer until vegetables are very soft, about 40 minutes. Stir in cilantro just before serving.

346 HUNGARIAN PARSNIP, CARROT, AND CABBAGE STEW
Prep: 20 minutes   Cook: 49 to 50 minutes   Serves: 8

2 tablespoons vegetable oil
1 large onion, chopped
2 garlic cloves, minced
2 tablespoons sweet Hungarian paprika
¼ teaspoon ground cumin
1 teaspoon salt
1 teaspoon sugar
2 tablespoons flour
½ medium head of green cabbage, shredded (about 6 cups)
1 large russet potato, peeled and cut into ½-inch dice

2 medium parsnips, peeled and cut into 1-inch pieces
3 medium carrots, peeled and cut into 1-inch pieces
5 cups Chicken Stock (page 262) or reduced-sodium canned broth
3 tablespoons chopped parsley
½ teaspoon pepper
½ cup sour cream

1. In a large flameproof casserole, heat oil over medium-high heat. Add onion and cook, stirring occasionally, until golden, 3 to 4 minutes. Add garlic, paprika, cumin, salt, sugar, and flour and cook, stirring constantly, 1 minute. Stir in cabbage, potato, parsnips, carrots, and chicken stock and bring to a boil.

2. Reduce heat to low and simmer, partially covered, 30 minutes. Uncover and simmer until vegetables are very soft and mixture has thickened about 15 minutes longer. Stir in parsley and pepper and top with dollops of sour cream just before serving.

---

347 TWO-MUSHROOM AND POTATO STEW
Prep: 20 minutes   Stand: 15 minutes
Cook: 50 to 51 minutes   Serves: 4

Here's a hearty vegetarian stew. Serve it with polenta or rice and a green salad with Gorgonzola for a great meal.

1 ounce dried mushrooms
2 tablespoons butter
1 large onion, finely chopped
1 medium celery rib, finely chopped
2 garlic cloves, minced
1 pound button or cremini mushrooms, cut in half or quartered, if large
½ cup dry white wine
1 cup Vegetable Stock (page 266), Chicken Stock (page 262), or canned vegetable broth

1 tablespoon tomato paste
1 sprig of fresh thyme or ½ teaspoon dried thyme leaves
1 imported bay leaf
½ teaspoon salt
½ teaspoon pepper
2 red or baking potatoes (about 1½ pounds), peeled and cut into 1-inch dice

1. Place dried mushrooms in a small heatproof bowl and cover with 1 cup boiling water. Let stand 15 minutes. Finely chop mushroom caps; discard stems and reserve soaking liquid.

2. In a large saucepan, melt butter over medium-high heat. Add onion, celery, and garlic and cook, stirring occasionally, until softened, 3 to 4 minutes. Add fresh and dried mushrooms and cook, stirring occasionally, until mushrooms start to brown, about 5 minutes. Stir in wine and simmer 2 minutes.

3. Add vegetable stock, mushroom soaking liquid, tomato paste, thyme, bay leaf, salt, pepper, and potatoes and bring to a boil. Reduce heat to low and simmer until vegetables are very soft and mixture has thickened, about 40 minutes. Remove and discard bay leaf before serving.

348 ITALIAN WINTER VEGETABLE STEW
Prep: 20 minutes   Cook: 45 minutes   Serves: 4

Though this stew has a long list of ingredients, once they are chopped, your work is over; simply throw them in the pot and they cook up into a delicious stew.

¼ cup extra-virgin olive oil
4 garlic cloves, thinly sliced
1 large Spanish onion, chopped
2 medium celery ribs, chopped
2 medium zucchini (about 1 pound), cut into 1-inch pieces
2 yellow or red bell peppers, cut into 1-inch pieces
1 large eggplant (about 1 pound), cut into 1-inch pieces

4 cups torn kale leaves
1 (14½-ounce) can Italian peeled tomatoes, drained and chopped
1 teaspoon salt
¼ teaspoon crushed hot red pepper
1 teaspoon dried rosemary leaves
3 tablespoons chopped parsley
¼ cup grated Parmesan cheese

1. In a large nonreactive flameproof casserole, combine all ingredients except parsley and Parmesan cheese. Stir in ¼ cup water and bring to a boil. Reduce heat to medium-low, cover, and cook, stirring occasionally, 30 minutes. Uncover and cook until mixture has reduced slightly, 15 minutes more.

2. To serve, stir in parsley, ladle into bowls, and sprinkle with Parmesan cheese.

349 MILLET, LENTIL, AND BARLEY STEW WITH MIXED HERB GREMOLATA
Prep: 25 minutes   Cook: 36 to 38 minutes   Serves: 8

Gremolata is a traditional Italian seasoning made with parsley, lemon, and garlic. Here we've used several herbs in addition to the parsley.

½ cup millet
2 tablespoons extra-virgin olive oil
3 leeks (white and tender green), well rinsed and thinly sliced
2 medium celery ribs, chopped
4 large carrots, peeled and chopped

½ cup lentils, rinsed and picked over
½ cup pearl barley
9 cups Vegetable Stock (page 266) or canned broth
½ teaspoon salt
½ teaspoon pepper
1 teaspoon lemon juice
Mixed Herb Gremolata (recipe follows)

1. In a large saucepan or flameproof casserole, toast millet over medium-high heat until it begins to pop, about 5 minutes. Remove to a bowl.

2. Heat oil in same soup pot over medium-high heat. Add leeks, celery, and carrots and cook, stirring occasionally, until vegetables are softened, 6 to 8 minutes. Stir in millet, lentils, barley, vegetable stock, salt, and pepper. Bring to a boil. Reduce heat to low, cover, and simmer until lentils are tender, about 25 minutes.

3. Stir in lemon juice and ladle stew into soup bowls. Sprinkle with Mixed Herb Gremolata before serving.

MIXED HERB GREMOLATA
Makes: ½ cup

2 teaspoons grated lemon zest
½ cup parsley leaves
3 tablespoons mixed fresh
    herb leaves (thyme,
    oregano, sage)

1 large garlic clove, coarsely
    chopped

Place all ingredients in a food processor or blender and puree until smooth.

350   CORN AND SQUASH STEW
Prep: 20 minutes   Cook: 29 to 30 minutes   Serves: 4

To make this satisfying stew a complete meal, stir in some cooked or canned black beans and serve with freshly steamed rice.

2 tablespoons vegetable oil
1 large onion, chopped
3 garlic cloves, minced
½ chipotle chile packed in
    adobo sauce, finely
    chopped
1 tablespoon chili powder
1 teaspoon ground cumin
¼ teaspoon salt
1 (14½-ounce) can chopped
    tomatoes, drained
1 pound acorn squash, peeled
    and cut into 1-inch
    chunks (about 3 cups)

2 cups Vegetable Stock (page
    266) or canned broth
2 medium zucchini, cut into
    1-inch chunks
2 cups fresh or frozen corn
    kernels
3 scallions, finely chopped
½ cup shredded Monterey
    Jack cheese

1. In a large nonreactive flameproof casserole, heat oil over medium-high heat. Add onion and cook, stirring occasionally, until golden, 3 to 4 minutes. Add garlic, chipotle chile, chili powder, and cumin and cook, stirring constantly, 1 minute. Stir in salt, tomatoes, acorn squash, and vegetable stock and bring to a boil. Reduce heat to low and simmer 10 minutes.

2. Stir in zucchini and corn and simmer, until vegetables are cooked, 15 minutes longer. Stir in scallions and sprinkle with Monterey Jack cheese just before serving.

351   CREOLE RED BEANS AND RICE

Prep: 20 minutes   Stand: 12 hours   Cook: 3 hours   Serves: 12 to 14

The traditional Monday evening meal in New Orleans, this hearty one-dish meal is a great crowd-pleaser. Or prepare it for your family and freeze any leftovers for a quick in-a-minute dinner. Since tasso, a spicy-hot, highly seasoned cut of cured pork, can be difficult to find outside of Louisiana, you may substitute smoked ham here instead. Remember to put the beans up to soak the night before.

2 pounds dried red kidney beans, rinsed and picked over
1 pound spicy smoked pork sausage (andouille or kielbasa), sliced ½ inch thick
1 ham bone
¾ pound tasso or smoked ham, cut into ½-inch pieces
2 large onions, chopped
2 large green bell peppers, chopped
2 medium celery ribs, chopped
3 garlic cloves, chopped
2 bay leaves
1 teaspoon dried thyme leaves
1 bunch of scallions, sliced
¼ cup chopped parsley
6 cups cooked long-grain white rice

1. Place dried beans in a large bowl and add enough water to cover by at least 2 inches. Let stand at least 12 hours or overnight. Drain and rinse beans before using.

2. In a large stockpot, combine all ingredients except scallions, parsley, and rice. Add enough water to cover and bring to a boil over high heat. Reduce heat to low and simmer, stirring occasionally, until beans are tender and mixture has thickened, about 3 hours. Remove and discard bay leaves.

3. Stir in scallions and parsley and serve with rice.

352 WHEAT BERRY, WHITE BEAN, AND MUSHROOM STEW

Prep: 20 minutes   Stand: 15 minutes
Cook: 1 hour 41 minutes   Serves: 6

½ ounce dried imported mushrooms
2 tablespoons extra-virgin olive oil
2 leeks (white and tender green), well rinsed and thinly sliced
2 medium celery ribs, thinly sliced
4 large carrots, peeled and thinly sliced
¼ pound fresh mushrooms, sliced
3 garlic cloves, minced

2 bay leaves
3 sprigs of fresh summer savory or ½ teaspoon dried
7 cups Vegetable Stock (page 266) or reduced-sodium canned broth
1½ cups wheat berries, rinsed
¼ teaspoon salt
½ teaspoon pepper
1 (10½-ounce) can navy or Great Northern beans, drained and rinsed
½ cup chopped parsley

1. In a medium heatproof bowl, cover dried mushrooms with 1 cup boiling water. Let stand 15 minutes or until softened. Strain liquid through cheese-cloth-lined strainer or coffee filter. Reserve liquid and chop mushrooms.

2. In a large flameproof casserole, heat oil over medium-high heat. Add leeks, celery, carrots, and fresh mushrooms and cook, stirring occasionally, until vegetables are softened, about 10 minutes. Add garlic, bay leaves, and savory and stir 1 minute. Stir in vegetable stock, wheat berries, salt, pepper, and chopped mushrooms. Bring to a boil, reduce heat to low, and simmer 1 hour.

3. Stir in beans and parsley and simmer until vegetables are softened, 30 minutes or longer. Remove and discard bay leaves before serving.

353   GARBURE
Prep: 20 minutes   Stand: 12 hours
Cook: 1 hour 35 minutes to 1 hour 40 minutes   Serves: 10 to 12

This classic French stew typically features preserved goose or duck; if you can't find any, substitute smoked sausage. Remember to put the beans up to soak the night before.

1½ cups dried white navy or
    Great Northern beans,
    rinsed and picked over
1 pork hock or ham bone
4 garlic cloves, minced
1 large onion, chopped
3 carrots, peeled and thinly
    sliced
3 leeks (white and tender
    green), well rinsed and
    thinly sliced

2 bay leaves
1 teaspoon dried thyme leaves
6 sprigs of fresh parsley, plus
    ½ cup chopped parsley
½ medium head of green
    cabbage, thinly sliced
2 large red potatoes, cut into
    ½-inch dice
1 piece goose confit, cubed, or
    1 cup chopped smoked
    sausage

1. Place dried beans in a large bowl and add enough water to cover by at least 2 inches. Let stand at least 12 hours or overnight. Drain and rinse before using.

2. In a large saucepan or flameproof casserole, combine beans, pork hock, garlic, onion, carrots, leeks, bay leaves, thyme, parsley stems, and 8 cups of water. Bring to a boil. Cover, reduce heat to low, and simmer 1 hour.

3. Add cabbage and potatoes and continue cooking until vegetables are tender, 15 to 20 minutes. Stir in goose and cook 20 minutes longer. Remove and discard bay leaves and parsley stems. Sprinkle with chopped parsley just before serving.

Chapter 15

Basic Stocks

The stock is the foundation upon which a good soup or stew is built. A good flavorful stock makes the difference between an ordinary soup and a memorable one.

Included here are the most essential stocks: chicken, beef, veal, and lamb in addition to a variety of others. They are easily made from leftover chicken or meat bones, with the addition of vegetables, herbs, and water. Although several hours are required to make a flavorful stock, these stocks can simmer on your stovetop with minimal supervision. All of the stocks will keep in the refrigerator for days or can be frozen for several months.

If you don't have the time to prepare these basic stocks from start to finish, we have included "quick" alternatives using canned broth. When using canned broth, be sure to look for the reduced-sodium variety. Many canned broths are quite salty and need to be used with caution.

---

354   QUICK CHICKEN STOCK
Prep: 5 minutes   Cook: 30 minutes   Makes: 4 cups

If you have the giblets to the chicken, add them to the soup pot, eliminating the liver.

1 medium onion, minced	12 stems of fresh parsley
2 celery ribs, chopped	½ teaspoon dried thyme leaves
1 small carrot, chopped	8 black peppercorns
5 cups reduced-sodium	3 whole cloves
canned chicken broth	1 bay leaf
½ cup dry white wine	

1. In a large nonreactive saucepan, combine onion, celery, carrot, chicken broth, wine, parsley, thyme, peppercorns, cloves, and bay leaf. Bring to a boil. Reduce heat to medium-low, cover, and simmer 30 minutes.

2. Strain stock through a fine sieve into a medium bowl, pressing hard on solids. Let stock cool, then cover and refrigerate.

355   CHICKEN STOCK
Prep: 10 minutes   Cook: 3 hours 5 minutes to 4 hours 5 minutes
Makes: 8 cups

4 pounds meaty chicken bones, such as chicken backs, wings, necks, or a combination, chopped into 3-inch pieces

2 medium leeks (white part only), well rinsed and chopped

2 large onions

2 carrots, quartered

2 celery ribs, cut into 1-inch slices

3 garlic cloves

12 stems of fresh parsley

2 teaspoons dried thyme leaves

12 black peppercorns

6 cloves

2 bay leaves

1. In a soup pot, place bones and add enough water to cover. Bring to a boil, reduce heat to medium-low, and simmer 5 minutes. Drain and rinse.

2. Return bones to soup pot. Add leeks, onions, carrots, celery, garlic, parsley, thyme, peppercorns, cloves, and bay leaves. Add 12 cups cold water. Bring to a boil, reduce heat to low, and simmer, skimming surface frequently, until stock is reduced to 8 cups, 3 to 4 hours.

3. Strain stock through a fine sieve into a large bowl, pressing hard on solids. Let stock cool, then cover and refrigerate. Remove fat from top of stock before using.

356   QUICK BROWN CHICKEN STOCK
Prep: 5 minutes   Cook: 40 to 42 minutes   Makes: 4 cups

2 tablespoons vegetable oil

2 medium onions, chopped

2 celery ribs, chopped

1 medium carrot, peeled and minced

4 garlic cloves, chopped

½ cup dry white wine

5 cups reduced-sodium canned chicken broth

1 tablespoon tomato paste

12 stems of fresh parsley

1 teaspoon dried thyme leaves

12 black peppercorns

3 whole cloves

1 bay leaf

1. In a large nonreactive saucepan, heat oil over medium heat. Add onions, celery, carrot, and garlic and cook, stirring frequently, until golden brown, 10 to 12 minutes. Stir in wine, chicken broth, tomato paste, parsley, thyme, peppercorns, cloves, and bay leaf. Bring to a boil. Reduce heat to medium-low, cover, and simmer 30 minutes.

2. Strain stock through a fine sieve into a medium bowl, pressing hard on solids. Let stock cool, then cover and refrigerate.

357 BROWN CHICKEN STOCK

Prep: 10 minutes   Cook: 3 hours 50 minutes to 4 hours 55 minutes
Makes: 8 cups

4 pounds meaty chicken bones, such as backs, wings, necks, or a combination, chopped into 3-inch pieces
2 large onions, quartered
2 medium carrots, quartered
1 whole head of garlic, halved crosswise
2 celery ribs, cut into 1-inch pieces

2 cups chopped fresh tomatoes or 1 (28-ounce) can tomatoes, drained and chopped
15 stems of fresh parsley
2 teaspoons dried thyme leaves
12 peppercorns
6 whole cloves
2 bay leaves

1. Preheat oven to 450°F. Place bones in a large roasting pan. Roast 25 minutes. Add onions, carrots, and garlic to pan. Roast 25 to 30 minutes longer, stirring occasionally, or until vegetables are browned.

2. Transfer bones and vegetables to a large nonreactive soup pot. Add 1 cup water to baking pan. Bring to a boil, occasionally scraping browned bits off bottom of pan, and add to soup pot. Add celery, tomatoes, parsley, thyme, peppercorns, cloves, bay leaves, and 12 cups cold water to soup pot. Bring to a boil, reduce heat to low, and simmer, skimming surface frequently, until stock has reduced to 8 cups, 3 to 4 hours.

3. Strain stock through a fine sieve into a large bowl, pressing hard on solids. Let cool, then cover and refrigerate.

358 QUICK BROWN MEAT STOCK

Prep: 5 minutes   Cook: 40 to 42 minutes   Makes: 4 cups

2 tablespoons vegetable oil
2 medium onions, chopped
2 medium celery ribs, chopped
1 medium carrot, peeled and chopped
4 garlic cloves, chopped
½ cup dry white wine

5 cups reduced-sodium canned beef broth
1 tablespoon tomato paste
12 stems of fresh parsley
1 teaspoon dried thyme leaves
12 black peppercorns
3 whole cloves
1 bay leaf

1. In a large nonreactive saucepan, heat oil over medium heat. Add onions, celery, carrot, and garlic and cook, stirring frequently, until golden brown, 10 to 12 minutes. Stir in wine, beef broth, tomato paste, parsley, thyme, peppercorns, cloves, and bay leaf. Bring to a boil. Reduce heat to medium-low, cover, and simmer 30 minutes.

2. Strain stock through a fine sieve into a medium bowl, pressing hard on solids. Let stock cool, then cover and refrigerate.

359 BROWN BEEF STOCK
Prep: 10 minutes   Cook: 4 hours 50 minutes to 5 hours 55 minutes
Makes: 8 cups

4 to 5 pounds meaty beef
    bones, cut from the
    shank, neck, leg, or
    knuckle, sawed into 2-
    inch pieces
2 large onions, quartered
2 medium carrots, quartered
1 whole head of garlic, halved
    crosswise
2 celery ribs, cut into 1-inch
    pieces

2 cups chopped fresh
    tomatoes or 1 (28-ounce)
    can tomatoes, drained
    and chopped
15 stems of fresh parsley
2 teaspoons dried thyme
    leaves
12 black peppercorns
6 whole cloves
2 bay leaves

1. Preheat oven to 450°F. Place bones in roasting pan. Roast 25 minutes. Add onions, carrots, and garlic to pan. Roast 25 to 30 minutes longer, stirring frequently, or until vegetables are browned.

2. Transfer bones and vegetables to a large nonreactive soup pot. Add 1 cup water to baking pan. Bring to a boil, occasionally scraping browned bits off bottom of pan, and add to soup pot. Add celery, tomatoes, parsley, thyme, peppercorns, cloves, bay leaves, and 12 cups cold water to soup pot. Bring to a boil, reduce heat to low, and simmer, skimming surface frequently, until stock has reduced to 8 cups, 4 to 5 hours.

3. Strain stock through a fine sieve into a bowl, pressing hard on solids. Let stock cool, then cover and refrigerate.

360 SIMPLE BEEF STOCK
Prep: 10 minutes   Cook: 4 hours 5 minutes to 5 hours 5 minutes
Makes: 8 cups

4 to 5 pounds meaty beef
    bones, cut from the
    shank, neck, leg, or
    knuckle, sawed into 2-
    inch pieces
2 large onions
2 carrots, quartered
2 medium celery ribs, cut into
    1-inch slices

6 garlic cloves
12 stems of fresh parsley
2 teaspoons dried thyme
    leaves
12 black peppercorns
3 bay leaves

1. In a soup pot, combine bones with enough water to cover. Bring to a boil, reduce heat to low, and simmer 5 minutes. Drain and rinse.

2. Return bones to soup pot. Add onions, carrots, celery, garlic, parsley, thyme, peppercorns, and bay leaves. Add 12 cups cold water. Bring to a boil, reduce heat to low, and simmer, skimming surface frequently, until stock is reduced to 8 cups, 4 to 5 hours.

3. Strain stock through a fine sieve into a large bowl, pressing hard on solids. Let stock cool, then cover and refrigerate. Remove fat from top of stock before using.

361   QUICK FISH STOCK
Prep: 5 minutes   Cook: 20 minutes   Makes: 4 cups

1½ cups bottled clam juice
⅔ cup dry white wine
1 large onion or leek (white part only), well rinsed and minced

12 stems of fresh parsley
½ teaspoon dried thyme leaves
6 black peppercorns
1 bay leaf

1. In a large nonreactive saucepan, combine clam juice, wine, onion, parsley, thyme, peppercorns, and bay leaf with 2½ cups cold water. Bring to a boil, reduce heat to low, and simmer, stirring frequently, 20 minutes.

2. Strain stock through a fine sieve into a large bowl, pressing hard on solids. Let stock cool, then cover and refrigerate.

362   LAMB STOCK
Prep: 10 minutes   Cook: 4 hours 5 minutes to 5 hours 5 minutes   Makes: 8 cups

4 to 5 pounds meaty lamb bones, cut from the shank, neck, breast, or leg, sawed into 2-inch pieces
2 large onions
2 carrots, peeled and quartered
2 celery ribs, cut into 1-inch pieces

3 garlic cloves
12 stems of fresh parsley
2 teaspoons dried thyme leaves
2 teaspoons dried rosemary
1 teaspoon black peppercorns
3 bay leaves

1. In a soup pot, combine bones with enough cold water to cover. Bring to a boil, reduce heat to medium-low, and cook 5 minutes. Drain and rinse.

2. Return bones to soup pot. Add onions, carrots, celery, garlic, parsley, thyme, rosemary, peppercorns, and bay leaves. Add 12 cups cold water. Bring to a boil, reduce heat to low, and simmer, skimming surface frequently, until stock is reduced to 8 cups, 4 to 5 hours.

3. Strain stock through a fine sieve into a large bowl, pressing hard on solids. Let stock cool, then cover and refrigerate. Remove fat from top of stock before using.

363 BROWN VEGETABLE STOCK

Prep: 10 minutes   Cook: 2 hours 25 minutes to 2 hours 30 minutes
Makes: 8 cups

3 medium onions, quartered
2 large leeks (white part only),
   well rinsed and sliced
2 medium carrots, quartered
1 whole head of garlic, halved
   crosswise
3 tablespoons vegetable oil
2 celery ribs, cut into 1-inch
   pieces
2 cups chopped fresh
   tomatoes or 1 (28-ounce)
   can tomatoes, drained
   and chopped

½ pound mushrooms, sliced
1 teaspoon dried thyme leaves
12 black peppercorns
6 whole cloves
2 bay leaves
12 stems of fresh parsley

1. Preheat oven to 450°F. In a large roasting pan, toss onions, leeks, carrots, and garlic with oil until coated. Roast 25 to 30 minutes, stirring several times, until browned.

2. Transfer vegetables to a large nonreactive soup pot. Add 1 cup water to roasting pan, bring to a boil, scraping bottom of pan occasionally to remove browned bits, and add to soup pot. Add celery, tomatoes, mushrooms, thyme, peppercorns, cloves, bay leaves, parsley, and 12 cups cold water to soup pot. Bring to a boil, reduce heat to low, and simmer, stirring frequently, until stock is reduced to 8 cups, about 2 hours.

3. Strain stock through a fine sieve into a large bowl, pressing hard on solids. Let stock cool, then cover and refrigerate.

364 VEGETABLE STOCK

Prep: 10 minutes   Cook: 2 hours 10 minutes   Makes: 8 cups

3 tablespoons vegetable oil
2 large onions, chopped
2 large leeks (white part only),
   well rinsed and chopped
2 medium carrots, peeled and
   chopped
2 medium celery ribs, sliced

1 large red potato, cubed
½ pound mushrooms, sliced
8 garlic cloves
1 teaspoon dried thyme leaves
8 black peppercorns
1 bay leaf
12 stems of fresh parsley

1. In a soup pot, heat oil over medium heat. Add onions, leeks, carrots, celery, potato, mushrooms, and garlic. Cook, stirring frequently, until vegetables are very soft, about 10 minutes. Add 12 cups cold water, thyme, peppercorns, bay leaf, and parsley. Bring to a boil, reduce heat to medium-low , and cook until stock is reduced to 8 cups, about 2 hours.

2. Strain stock through a fine sieve into a large bowl, pressing hard on solids. Let stock cool, then cover and refrigerate.

365   VEAL STOCK
Prep: 10 minutes   Cook: 4 hours 5 minutes to 5 hours 5 minutes
Makes: 8 cups

Stock keeps, covered and refrigerated, 1 week if brought to a boil every 2 days. Cool to warm, uncovered, before refrigerating again. Or it may be frozen up to 2 months.

5 **pounds veal bones, cracked**	3 **garlic cloves**
2 **large onions**	12 **stems of fresh parsley**
2 **carrots, peeled and**	2 **teaspoons dried thyme**
quartered	**leaves**
2 **celery ribs, cut into 1-inch**	1 **teaspoon black peppercorns**
pieces	3 **bay leaves**

1. In a soup pot, combine bones with enough cold water to cover. Bring to a boil, reduce heat to medium-low, and cook 5 minutes. Drain and rinse.

2. Return bones to soup pot. Add onions, carrots, celery, garlic, parsley, thyme, peppercorns, and bay leaves. Add 12 cups cold water. Bring to a boil, reduce heat to low, and simmer, skimming surface frequently, until stock is reduced to 8 cups, 4 to 5 hours.

3. Strain stock through a fine sieve into a large bowl, pressing hard on solids. Let stock cool, then cover and refrigerate. Remove fat from top of stock before using.

Index

About the Authors

Georgia Downard, a former food editor of *Gourmet* magazine and current Culinary Director of the Television Food Network, is author of *The Big Broccoli Book* and *The Big Carrot Book*. Jean Galton, a Seattle-based food writer who has contributed to *Food & Wine*, *McCall's*, and *Fine Cooking* magazines, is author of *Lasagne*.

To order any of the
365 Ways Cookbooks

visit your local bookseller or call 1-800-331-3761

Our bestselling **365 Ways Cookbooks** are wire-bound to lie flat and have colorful, wipe-clean covers.

Each **365 Ways Cookbook** is $18.95 plus $3.50 per copy shipping and handling. Applicable sales tax will be billed to your account. No CODs. Please allow 4–6 weeks for delivery.

> Please have your VISA, MASTERCARD, or AMERICAN EXPRESS card at hand when calling.

• 365 •

Days of Gardening 0-06-017032-8
Delicious Low-Fat Recipes 0-06-017137-5
Easy Low-Calorie Recipes 0-06-016309-7
Easy Mexican Recipes 0-06-016963-X
Easy One-Dish Meals 0-06-016311-9
Great Barbecue & Grilling Recipes 0-06-016224-4
Great Cakes & Pies 0-06-016959-1
Great Chocolate Desserts 0-06-016537-5
Great Cookies and Brownies 0-06-016840-4
Great Soups & Stews 0-06-016960-5
Great 20-Minute Recipes 0-06-016962-1
One-Minute Golf Lessons 0-06-017087-5
Quick & Easy Microwave Recipes 0-06-016026-8
Snacks, Hors D'Oeuvres & Appetizers 0-06-016536-7
Ways to Cook Chicken 0-06-015539-6
Ways to Cook Fish and Shellfish 0-06-016841-2
Ways to Cook Hamburger & Other Ground Meats
0-06-016535-9
Ways to Cook Chinese 0-06-016961-3
Ways to Cook Pasta 0-06-015865-4
Ways to Cook Vegetarian 0-06-016958-3
Ways to Prepare for Christmas 0-06-017048-4
Ways to Wok 0-06-016643-6

FORTHCOMING TITLES

Ways to Cook Eggs 0-06-017138-3
More Ways to Cook Chicken 0-06-017139-1
All-American Favorites 0-06-017294-0
Main Dish Salads 0-06-017293-2
Jewish Recipes 0-06-017295-9
Asian Recipes 0-06-017292-4